VERONICA HALL

Veronica Sheila Hall was born in the suburbs of Manchester on 24th August 1942 the only child of Ann and Alan Barlow.

In years gone by, Veronica (known to all her friends as Sheila) worked for BBC Manchester as a Graphic Artist and then subsequently worked for a leisure company situated in the place where she has spent most of her life and where she and her husband, Jeff, now live … Delamere Forest, in the heart of the Cheshire countryside.

Veronica and Jeff were married rather late in life and so, their only 'child' is their gorgeous and deliciously bonkers Irish Setter, called Misty, who fills that post quite adequately and was, in fact, the reason and the inspiration for the trip to Ireland and this, the subsequent book.

This is Veronica's first step along the path to the world of books and, hopefully, it will be the first step of a great journey.

DEDICATION

I do so love this part of my books as it affords me the opportunity of saying 'thank-you'. Just two small words but uttered with a sincere heart...and there are so many people who merit at least some acknowledgment for all the encouragement that they have given to me over the last two years.

It goes without saying that, first and foremost, as always, I would like to dedicate this, my second book to the very special man who I am so proud to call my husband...Jeff Hall. He is and always will be my inspiration in all that my life entails. Quite simply, he is my life. Without him, nothing would be possible or even worthwhile.

In memoriam, I always like to make a special mention of my great friend, Dot Astbury. She was always my greatest advocate in all that I ever aspired to achieve in my life and so it is with a certain knowledge that I can say that any literary success that I may have with my two books would have meant so much to her.

A more recently acquired friend is Julie Hayes and, as true friendship knows nothing of the mere bounds of time, she has become very much loved and has been a source of great encouragement to me during my efforts to create a work of literary interest which will, hopefully, give some pleasure and amusement to the discerning few who may choose to open the pages of my books and, in so doing, become a part of the adventures of The Intrepid Trio.

My thanks go, also, to Laurie and Sheila Wagstaff whose friendship and genuine interest in my humble literary efforts has meant so much to me. Then, of course, I just have to mention David Buttle, my Publisher. I mean, without him, there would not have been any books. Dreams would have remained just that...dreams. As would those of all the aspiring authors whose work he has actually put into print

And last, but in no way least of all, there is Misty. Dear, dear Misty. Without our gorgeous, ever so slightly honkers, wonderful Irish Setter there would not have been any Ireland and therefore, no stories to tell. God love his honest and faithful heart.

ACKNOWLEDGEMENTS

First of all, I would like to apologise for a serious omission when I began writing my first book, back in 2008...and I am referring to the fact that although, when writing my book, I was fulsome in my praise and made particular point of extolling all of the many virtues of The Old Pub Cottage, on the Beara peninsula, in which we spent those two wonderful weeks on our first trip to Ireland, I did not mention the fact that this was but one of the range of superb cottage accommodation which is available from Welcome Cottages.

We stayed in Welcome cottages on this trip, also...The Barns, in Dunkineely, Donegal and the lovely conversion, set in the grounds of Brookfield Cottage, Tourmakeady, Co. Mayo.

Over the years, we have never been disappointed with any of the accommodation which Welcome have provided, not just in Ireland but, in Cornwall and in Scotland. These beautiful cottages have made perfect holidays even more perfect and, as I have actually made a point of mentioning in this, my second book, the customer service equally matches the quality of the accommodation. They are also dog friendly, which is one of the reasons why we first booked with them and, if you have actually read my first book, you will know all about the unexpected acquisition of our own dog, Misty.

Thanks also, to Stena Line. The crossings that we have made to Ireland could not have been made more comfortable or more enjoyable. The ship, the Stena Explorer, is very comfortable, even quite luxurious and the voyage always seems far too short (which is, of course, the reason why we have always chosen to sail on the fast Cat...our dog having to remain in the vehicle, on the car deck).The staff, both ship and shore are always quite exemplary, with nothing too much trouble. Many thanks, all round...and here's hoping that we will, in the future, be making many more journeys across the Irish Sea.

Veronica Hall 2009

ISBN: 978-1-84944-090-5

British Library Cataloguing in Publication Data.
A catalogue record for this book is available from the British Library.

Published by UKUnpublished

UKUnpublished
.CO.UK

www.ukunpublished.co.uk
info@ukunpublished.co.uk

IRELAND

THE LOVE AFFAIR

GOES ON

by

VERONICA HALL

INTRODUCTION

Having just written the word 'Introduction', perhaps it would be a good idea if I were to introduce myself. How about that for good thinking!

Little did I know just how much those few words would change my life, when they first popped into my head, en route from County Kerry to Dublin…and as those long miles fell away behind us, I, for one, was feeling just about as desolate as I had ever felt in my life.

You see, those were the actual words with which I began my first book…that first little tale of how my passionate love for Ireland was conceived, was born and, subsequently, evolved…becoming a living entity from the moment I took my very first sip from that cup of sweet nectar which goes under the name of Ireland and that one, tiny sip instantly created in that special place, somewhere deep within my soul, an all consuming passion.

This was the story of a love affair with a country and its people which, after that very first visit and, quite amazingly, in that very short space of time, inexorably cast its magical spell upon me, upon both of us. A spell of such enormous strength and power that there was no escape. Not a chance! And it was a spell under the influence of which, I knew I would forever be bound.

Just those few words but how very evocative they are to me now, as I read them once again…and what memories they arouse within me. Memories to stir the soul. Memories which make me yearn to be back, once more, in the land of dreams come true. Memories filled with a bitter-sweet nostalgia, which, for all these long months, have taken over my dreams and filled each of my days with a deep longing to return to this emerald Isle of enchantment.

So many images flood my mind, as I allow myself to be drawn back to those two glorious weeks. Yes! That's all it took. Just a mere two weeks and yet, how it changed our lives…or at least, mine…and this Technicolor kaleidoscope of images are all impatiently clamouring to attract my full attention.

Remember me! Remember me!

But then, where does one begin, when it is all so special and when each memory is still so fresh in ones mind, like photographic images which have been saved, to be treasured for all time. And what images! Glorious and unforgettable.

Images of mountains…majestic and tinged with purple in the haze of the middle distance, which offer a tantalizing promise of the splendour that they would so proudly show off to you if you would only draw a little closer, thereby giving them their own rightfully deserved inspection and admiration. They almost seem to speak to you, these Irish mountains. Towering massifs which are calling out to you to come amongst them and, in so doing, perhaps discover something inside of yourself that you didn't even know existed. That special Something which exists, deep down within all of us which seems to transcend our mere human status and raise us up, soaring, so that we feel that we can touch the sky.

Images of hills. Now there's a thing to think about. Hills covered with green sward and dotted, here and there, with the inevitable white blobs which are, in fact, the ubiquitous sheep, as they stoically graze away the peaceful day. Hills which gently sweep down to meet and greet the ever present lakes which mirror the blue sky and play host to golden reflections and rainbow sparkles as the water is kissed by the sun and then, of course, the rivers, glorious Irish rivers which, in their turn, make their own bright and silvery, serpentine way through the meadow-sweet grass, chuckling merrily to themselves as they go splashing over any rocks and boulders which may be in their path. Truly a scene to both delight and enchant.

And then last but, by no means least, the seascapes. Oh, the very thought of those white-sand beaches…an infinity of white strand…and the sea, a miracle of pure crystal. Water the colour of delicate azure or jade and so clear that one can discern every single grain of sand and each small pebble while, further out, the colour of the water changes and becomes a deep cobalt blue, with white spray, scintillating in the sunlight as the water explodes into millions of diamond chips, their fire bright and dazzling to the eye, before cascading and tumbling, playfully, over some rocky shore.

Have I at least made the back of your neck tingle and, perhaps, made you want to see some of this magic for yourself? I do hope so but, believe me, all of this is but a small insight into the magic of this country where this great love affair of mine was born. Ireland. A quite enchanting and enchanted land, that just has to be one of God's own earthly examples of paradise.

Coming down to earth again, which is just as well, before I get myself too carried away, (and there are those, and you can take my word for it, who would, quite enthusiastically and without the slightest hesitation, wish that I could be carried away…quite a long way away) I have to admit that those opening lines also leave me in something of a quandary, for, having written them, I am now sitting here like a great numpty wondering just where to go from here. You see, the first time around, there was so much to tell…all of the hows and all of the whys and the wherefores of how we happened to find ourselves on the shores of Ireland in the first place. Now, however, I really feel that I am in great danger of just repeating the same old, same old and boring the pants off all of you who have already made my acquaintance and yet, there are, hopefully, those of you who are only just tentatively testing the water, so to speak and maybe a little information about myself may make the difference between just dipping a toe into the water or, throwing discretion to the wind and jumping straight in.

On the other hand, it could all go the other way and convince you that now might be as good a time as any, to do a runner.

So, I shall just have to take a chance and ask all of those who have heard it all before to perhaps go and put the kettle on…now that really is a good idea… while I very briefly skim over a few pertinent details for the benefit of any new and all unsuspecting, prospective friends of The Intrepid Trio. I promise that I shall keep it as brief as I possibly can and then we can get on with the really important stuff.

See you later, then…and it's milk and one sugar for me, when you get back.

Ok, so, where do I begin? I suppose that the best thing that I can do is to give you a few basics and then just keep my fingers crossed that I don't bore you too much before I've even reached the bottom of page two. It seems, to me, to be the only decent thing that I can do, to at least give you sufficient information about myself so that you can then form your own opinions. The way that I see it is this…there is absolutely no point in being anything else except totally honest, at this stage in the proceedings, as you will obviously find out for yourself, soon enough, just what you have let yourself in for, or may be letting yourself in for, as the case may be…and then, well, it is entirely upon your own head whether or not you decide to come along with me and mine and stay the distance…or, as I have already suggested, leg it, while you still have the chance.

So, I can do no more than place the facts before you and then, just hope for the best.

Oh, well…here goes, then.

Without any beating about the proverbial bush, we will take first things first by saying that my name is Veronica Hall. Now, there you go! Do you see what I mean? I ask you, how obvious is that? I mean, for heaven's sake, you daft woman, (me, not you) it's in big letters, on the front cover.

Anyway, to continue. Somehow, against all the odds which may have been stacked against me over the years, I have, without any clear knowledge of where those years have actually gone, attained the ripe old age of 67 years…and that little snippet of information could just have made matters even worse. Oh boy. I can just hear you saying to yourself 'Oh no! Not a loony old pensioner. Dear God, that's all we need'! However, be that as it may, I shall do my utmost to remain undaunted and just plod on and pray that, as a result, I do not add to your already steadily rising doubts.

I do have to admit that most of my friends (and yes, I do have a few) indeed, I would probably go so far as to say that 'all' of my friends would, if they were actually pushed, quite gleefully tell you that I am, in a nice sort of way, of course, just a wee tad bonkers…and, as if that wasn't bad enough, thereby making matters infinitely worse, there is my most regrettable tendency towards acting my shoe size (4) rather than my age. I mean, for heaven's sake, where is the fun in merely acting one's age? You could, in all honesty, die of boredom, if you were to live your life by simply sticking to the proprieties. Oh no, that's no good at all! Take my word for it, you have to grab life by the scruff and give it a jolly good shaking before it turns around and bites you on the bum. (And at the age of 67 you will find very few bite marks on me. For one thing, I'm far too stubborn and over my lifetime, I have become something of an adept at blowing the proverbial raspberry in the face of this particular demon who goes under the name of Adversity).

However, for better or for worse, I am what I am and at this stage in my life, I know that I will never change. In fact, to be quite honest, I have no desire to change and, what is more, I have absolutely no intention of even trying to change. I mean, for what it's worth, it has always been my experience that being just ever so slightly bonkers (and bloody stubborn) does help enormously in the business of surviving life as most of us find it. Let's face it, very few of us ever get through life completely untouched by doom and gloom and the little nasty bits so, the ability to see a sunnier and less serious side to life's many trials and tribulations does seem to be of tremendous help in preventing you from going completely around the bend instead of, as in my case, merely being ever so slightly on the turn.

All of which is just my own humble opinion, of course.

For all my many failings, however…and I am being utterly serious here… I know that I have been truly blessed and that I just have to be the luckiest woman alive, simply because I was lucky enough to meet and am now married to a very special man, Jeffrey Hall, who was already only too aware of my inane procliverties long before we were actually married. However, to his credit, he made a considered decision that it was all in the nicest possible way and married me, anyway. Since then, I do have to admit that I have given him just cause, on many, many occasions, to feel the overwhelming desire to totally disown me, or, at least, to pretend to disown me…and I do mean only pretending. At least, I hope he was only pretending!

Now, of course, he doesn't just have me to contend with, oh no…now, it is twice as onerous as it ever was when there was just the two of us, because now, you see, he has the additional burden, thus putting his endurance to the ultimate test, of having an equally bonkers (delightfully bonkers, of course) Irish Setter, called Misty, in the same house. You would be completely accurate, of course, if you were to come to the considered conclusion that my nutty pup and I are a quite perfectly matched pair…(equally delightful, of course) and the fact that my poor Jeffy has to live with both of us under the same roof must, in all honesty, put a tremendous strain upon his natural ability to take everything in life completely in his stride. My Jeffy is always quite laid-back about pretty much everything, however, I suppose there is a limit even to his endurance. Nevertheless, when it all boils down to it, he knows that, basically, I really am quite harmless and besides, he probably just switches me off when I become a little too trying and especially tedious. Which is most of the time.

Right! That's it! I did say that I would be brief and besides, that is more than enough about me. I could go on, ad infinitum, because my transgressions are many and quite varied…I mean, there is nothing boring here, I assure you…and, it can all be verified by the fact that I have a crime sheet as long as your arm, all of it written in the very smallest of print, so that every minute detail can be documented and accounted for and then willingly undersigned and endorsed by my closest and very dearest friends. My husband being at the head of the list of signatories.

This list covers a whole multitude of misdemeanours and offences of the sort which could and probably should be held in evidence against me, however, as I do not want to run the risk of losing you before we have barely become acquainted, I shall say no more. As I have already remarked, the whole truth will, inevitably, reveal itself in the fullness of time and then you will, without a doubt, find yourself feeling extremely sympathetic towards my dear, long-suffering husband.

Seriously, please don't be put off by all my blethering. I really would hate to do that. You see, I really do, quite genuinely, want you to come along with us on our travels and experience at least some of our pleasure. Let me try to explain how I feel.

You know how it feels when something is so special to you and so absolutely wonderful that you just want to shout it from the rooftops and tell the whole world? Well, that is how I feel about this very special country, Ireland.

The activities which give my Jeffy and I such pleasure are, as I am fully aware, probably very simple and unsophisticated, at least, by most standards anyway but, maybe for that very reason, I think that you will come to derive as much enjoyment from all of these simple pleasures as we do.

So please, do come along…and I know that Misty will be overjoyed at the idea of having someone else on whom he can lavish his canine affections…and that is quite an experience, believe me. To be on the receiving end of a good dose of seeing to from our Misty is really quite something! I would even go so far as to say, quite unforgettable, in fact. God love him and his enormous paws.

Anyway, getting back to the basics once more…and talking about Misty…it was all because of Misty, who really is the most utterly gorgeous specimen of Irish Setter that you could possibly wish to meet, (so, I admit that I am just a wee tad prejudiced) that we ever set foot on the shores of Ireland, in the first place. OK, so it was, indeed, because of Misty that we had to cancel our pre-booked holiday in Sicily but, it wasn't his fault, if you see what I mean…any real blame for that has to be laid squarely at my door. I was, you see, quite typically, just too impatient. I just could not wait those few extra months until such time as we had originally planned for it all to happen which, as a consequence, completely threw everything out of sync.

The intention had been that we would have one final holiday abroad…and then, our dog, which was something that we had planned for and both wanted, so very much, and for which we were both quite prepared to make some small sacrifices. All of which was all very nice, in theory, of course, until something happened, something which had such a powerful effect on me that I knew, I just knew, with every fibre of my being, that I could not wait for, what would have amounted to, almost another year.

When I confronted him with my thoughts on the matter, Jeff, who before taking early retirement, had spent almost thirty years in the Sahara Desert and therefore, didn't care very much, one way or the other, if he never went abroad again…that was something that he only did for my sake, like so many other things that he does, just for my sake, (you see how blessed I am?)…was immediately agreeable to the idea of bringing our plans forward and, knowing him as well as I do, I would have expected no less of him. And so, that was it! No big deal. Thanks to my wonderful, amazing, understanding husband and without the slightest twinge of pain, the big decision was made. Done and dusted and with no looking back.

As a consequence, it was just before Christmas of 2007, when we actually had, to love and to cherish, our copper-coloured 'baby' of just eight weeks. He was all ours…and absolutely beautiful. In fact, I don't think that I shall ever forget that day, 4th December, when he first came into our home. I carried him into the house in my arms and when I put him down, in the middle of this large and unfamiliar room, he seemed to look around him, with those melting-chocolate brown eyes and then up at me and it was as if he was thinking to himself…'This will do for me'.

Now, of course, we had to put our money where our mouths were, so to speak. I mean, having made our decision and, in so doing, completely committed ourselves to taking on this precious little life, it was a matter of back to the drawing board, with a vengeance. Other plans had to be made, only this time, taking into account our young dog who, at the time of travelling would be eight months…so very young to be going on his first great big adventure, his first holiday…and at this point, I really do have to admit that the choice of Ireland as a venue came about for purely practical reasons as opposed to any divinely inspired flash of inspiration…(a) neither of us had ever been to Ireland before, which was plus number one and (b) we already had all our euros which had originally been earmarked for Sicily so, that was plus number two.

Anyway, whatever the reasons may or may not have been, it all seemed like a very good idea at the time…which is precisely what it turned out to be. The best idea, in fact, that we had ever had. (With one exception, of course. Deciding to get married just has to have been the best idea of them all, in fact, that was not just a good idea, that was a stroke of pure genius). And, as everyone can be clever in hindsight, little did we know, indeed, how could we have known, at that moment in time when we made our booking, for both the ferry and the cottage, for the same two weeks in June 2008 which we had previously booked for Sicily, just how much it would influence our lives ever after…mine, in particular! All of which, of course, you will already know if, that is, you have read my first book 'My Love Affair with Ireland'.

The 'Love Affair' began within only a couple of days of arriving at our destination. How I shall always remember that first evening at our 'new home'. It was so special. How could I ever forget? I mean, it was such a delightful wee cottage situated, as it was, in an equally delightful and charming village by the name of Lauragh. There was an aura, a peace and quietude that seemed to breathe new life into the two of us as we stood, side by side, our hands entwined and just taking it all in…and the whole package just seemed to nestle, so contentedly, in the quite magnificent setting of the Caha Mountains, on the Beara peninsular and, from that moment onward, well, it just became something of a snowball rolling down a steep hill, gathering speed and growing bigger and more overwhelming as each day followed another, until it became the passion that it is now.

And so, there you have it. As concisely as I could keep it, you now have something of an explanation…some of the hows and the whys and the wherefores of how we came to cross the Irish sea and fall in love…not with a person, I mean, as far as I am concerned, that position is already filled by my husband and is completely non-negotiable…but, with an entire country and the wonderful people who are what Ireland is all about. People with hearts as big as the sea that separates our two countries and who have endeared themselves to me and mine, for always.

And now, returning to the present and having disposed of those few wee formalities and got them nicely out of the way, those who were sent off to put the kettle on may return, if they would care to…and I do hope that there is some tea left. I'm just about ready to spit feathers. All this blethering is thirsty work…and, of course, now that I have everyone together again, it is my rather sneaky plan that my friends old and hopefully new, can now get their heads together and just maybe, the old, true and faithful ones will put in a good word, or three, on my behalf, with the prospective new ones who may be having some very serious doubts about my credibility at the moment, having digested the information that has just been put before them.

They took a chance on me, this faithful band of devotees and, thankfully, found that although I thoroughly lived up to the name that my dear friend Dot Astbury used to call me…Nutty Hall (it was Barmy Barlow, before my marriage. Bless her, she was of the opinion that Nutty sounded far better when prefixing the name Hall)…I really turned out to be quite nice and all that, once they were properly acquainted with me.

On a more personal level, such a lot has happened to me since I concluded my tales of our last adventures, the most life-changing event being the hip replacement surgery that I underwent at the beginning of this year, 2009. Now, as a fully paid-up member of The Intrepid Trio, I shall be able to throw myself into all our activities with both feet, so to speak and become even more Intrepid than I was before.

Unfortunately, the length of the old legs hasn't changed, so I'm still as diminutive as I ever was. Shame! It would have been nice to have acquired at least another couple of inches while he was at it, the surgeon, I mean. Hobbit I am and, obviously, Hobbit I shall remain.

Anyway, poor Jeff. I mean, now that I'm almost bionic, at least on one side, he is going to have to be a lot more on his toes from now on, if, that is, he wants to keep me out of trouble. Maybe a collar and lead would be more effective if used on me, rather than on Misty. Or, how about one of those ASBO things that are worn around the ankle? He'd certainly be able to keep tabs on me with one of those gismos. Perhaps he'd be able to sort of beam me in by remote control if it ever looked as if I was entering into a situation which could be considered to be a wee bit dodgy…like in a shop, for instance?

Flippancy aside, once again I find myself with a wee story to tell, in fact, if the truth be known, I'm practically bursting at the seams to have the opportunity of being able to relate every last moment of it. (Oh, for heaven's sake, you should know by now how excitable I can get)!

My yearning to return to Ireland has, at last, been fulfilled and, like the last time, this is a tale of our simple adventures…the adventures of The Intrepid Trio, in the land which has now become, as I have already remarked, something of a passion for me. Adventures which are all brand spanking new and which are positively demanding to be told and so, as I sit here, in front of the computer, I am just hoping that I can do justice to everything in my narrative. You see, when I think about it all now, I find that it has also become something of a passion for me to be able, ultimately, to succeed in persuading you to join us. Just for you to walk in our footsteps along the roads of Ireland, roads which will always lead into the realms of magic and beauty…a quite unsurpassable beauty. Indeed, into a land of total enchantment.

I pray that my humble efforts will achieve the outcome that I desire and that you will decide to come along with us and then…well, then you will find out for yourself just why I am so passionate about this country.

On this, our second trip to Ireland, we have actually pushed the boat out a little further than we usually do by stretching our stay to three weeks, instead of the usual two, beginning the proceedings by spending the first week in a cottage in Dunkineely, Co. Donegal. This dear little village is situated on a small peninsula which is, more or less, equidistant between the old town of Donegal and the wonderful fishing port of Killybegs. Wonderful names, are they not?…and, Killybegs…wow, absolutely perfect Seasalt Vera territory, as those of you who already know me will affirm. Just to keep my new friends in the picture, let me say that, well, the fact is, you see, that if anything can be guaranteed to make my blood start to fizz, thereby putting me in the gravest danger of prancing around like an idiot, at the same time, whooping like a Banshee and even going so far as to doing cartwheels of pure joy and excitement, it is anything that is even remotely nautical. When, like me, about 80% of the stuff that flows through your veins is sea water, then the tang of the sea, indeed, the very sight, sound and smell of the sea, is as the very essence of some exotic perfume and if only old Seasalt Vera could bottle it and, whenever she felt the need, just take out the stopper and give herself a quick blast of that blissful ozone, how amazing that would be…and going back to Killybegs, what an ideal place for Jeff to try and lose me…I mean, you can't blame him for trying, can you?

For the second and third weeks we move down to another cottage just north of Galway, at a place called Tourmakeady, which is in Co. Mayo. I mean, how about those two names. Dunkineely and Tourmakeady…not forgetting Killybegs. And again, as all of those who already know me from the last trip will remember, I do have a total fascination for all of these wonderful Irish names. Even Galway…now there is a name which immediately conjures up romantic images. Allow me, if you will, to set the scene. Picture a tranquil evening, with the sea just a gentle ripple as it kisses the shore of the bay and the sky, oh wow, the sky a blaze of glory in all the colours of a perfect sunset…am I whetting your appetite? …and now, I quote from the song…'and see the sun go down on Galway Bay'.

Maybe we will be lucky enough to actually see the sun go down on Galway Bay…who knows? Just as long as my Jeffy is with me, of course. As long as he is beside me, I'm all in favour of a bit of romance!

And that's another thing! Romance just seems to blossom in the beauty and the soft and gentle magic that is Ireland. Even the most cynical of beholders would have to admit to feeling its touch. I mean, it's nothing to be ashamed of. Romance is a wonderful thing and it can manifest itself in many and varied ways.

The truth is, you see…I mean, the fact that it is so prevalent in Ireland, is, well…it's the fairy dust and that is the absolute truth. If you are really, really fortunate and the fact is that, in order to get to be this lucky, you really do have to believe with every fibre of your being, there is just the chance that you may, and I'm only saying may, feel the presence of these playful and totally delightful, almost childlike beings.

If you just open your heart, you may just feel the soft and gentle susurration of a gossamer wing upon your cheek, as one of these precious, jewel-like creatures hovers, just there, that's it…can you not feel it?…right there, in front of your face, while at the same time, liberally lobbing tiny iridescent dust balls at you, accompanied by, if you listen very carefully, the sweet and melodic tinkle of merry, mischievous laughter.

And that little tickle on the end of your nose?…that, my friend, is the soft touch of a pair of tiny fairy feet as one of their band delicately lands there, all the better to take a good aim and make sure that their magic dust reaches all the right places, don't you know.

You think I'm joking, I expect, which is a natural reaction, I suppose but…it's true. Oh yes! It's all true! I promise you. I mean, it is all so very simple…all that you have to do is to just open your heart to them and allow them to enter your soul and reward you with their own special brand of Irish magic. Indeed, not to feel it would be to have no soul for them to enter. You cannot be anything else, except in love, if you will only allow yourself to be showered with some of this very unique fairy dust and then become completely captivated and enchanted by its overwhelming and quite spellbinding charm. (Now, referring to that lengthy crime sheet that I mentioned earlier well, one of my many faults, if you can call it a fault is, you see, the fact that I do believe in fairies…and leprechauns. Oh, and for good measure, I have also been known to talk to trees. Well, I did warn you, didn't I)?

Being serious again, I suppose that what I am doing, or rather, attempting to do, in my own simple but, honest and sincere way, is to sell a dream…the dream that is Ireland. Because, my friends, that is precisely what Ireland is…a place where you can dream your dreams and allow yourself the luxury of believing that whatsoever you may dare to dream, it will always come true.

Ireland always delivers the goods. Ireland will never disappoint a heart that is open to accept all the magic and all the beauty that she has to offer…and that comes in great abundance.

I believed. I believed with all my heart, on our first visit to this enchanted isle and I fell in love…and the love affair which was born then, now goes on and I will be so thrilled and honoured if you will come along with me and my precious loved ones and who knows, you may even fall in love yourself.

All that remains for me to do now is to keep my fingers crossed (and anything else which may conceivably be crossed). Whatever the outcome, whichever way your decision goes, I am extremely obliged to you for at least listening to my blether thus far and, well, God bless you if you should decide in my favour and stay the course. If, on the other hand, you have decided to go your own way, I thank you, also, for the time you have already given me and would like to send you on your way with one of the more humorous Irish Blessings. The sentiments, are, non-the-less genuine.

AS YOU SLIDE DOWN THE BANNISTER OF LIFE
MAY THE SPLINTERS ALWAYS BE POINTING
THE RIGHT WAY
God bless all of you, wherever you may be.

And so, my dearest friend, soon we will meet again. I always knew that we would, eventually, but that does very little to quell the feelings of excitement that fill me at this moment as I anticipate, with enormous joy, our very imminent reunion. You can have no idea how I have treasured the memories of the hours that we spent together in that wee cottage on the Beara Peninsula. I can actually feel the ambience of it all, even now, if I just close my eyes and think of it. Jeff would pile the logs on the fire, which would then send myriads of merry sparks up the chimney along with a whole package of wishes and dreams…and a feeling of warmth and love would fill up all the corners. Remember?…and now it is about to become a reality, once again, only in a different place at a different time. Two old friends, who have always shared the same pleasures and have always been of like mind, reunited.

Once again, excitement is already beginning to fizz in my veins. For heaven's sake, you know what I'm like. I mean, just the very thought of it…IRELAND. And what a world of pure magic there is in just that one word.

21

The Love Affair will go on! And on. Of that there never could have been any doubt.

Veronica Hall.
November 2009

A JOURNAL
VOL. 2 OF MY MEMORIES OF
IRELAND

Saturday 19th September 2009 until
Saturday 10th October 2009

Saturday evening, which means that a very special day is gradually drawing to a close although, as far as I am concerned, there is an equally special part of this day that is still to come…our long awaited reunion…and my conscious mind, what bit I still have of one, is floundering around like someone drowning in an extremely intoxicating cocktail made up of a combination of emotions…total euphoria and an equal amount of disbelief.

I really am trying my best to show at least a token amount of calm and lady-like decorum here but, I have to admit that all my efforts are, unfortunately, failing quite miserably. I mean, I can't even sit still for more than a few minutes at a time and then I'm on the move again…pacing up and down and looking out of the window, gazing out over Donegal Bay whilst, at the same time, keeping a lookout for you, as you come up the lane. Anyone looking on, at this precise moment, could be excused for thinking that I'm a right numpty. I mean, I couldn't be in a more agitated state of suppressed excitement if I were some sixteen year old waiting for her first date to arrive (and if anyone actually did think that, then they really do have a very serious problem with their eyesight…either that, or they have forgotten to take their dark glasses off). In all honesty, the way I'm fidgeting about, I'm going to be wearing out the carpet…and it isn't even our carpet.

Oh, for heaven's sake, this is far too much excitement for me. Am I, perhaps, just getting old? God forbid, but maybe I really am getting old. Oh, come on now, you silly old fool, do at least try to sit at peace, if it is only for just a minute, in this, our wee 'home from home'…home for the next seven days, anyway.

You, dear friend, will be here any second now and then I can, perhaps, find it possible to stop pinching myself in my, up until now, vain efforts at making all of this seem even remotely real…which is far from being easy. It all feels very surreal, in fact…the reason being, I suppose, is that I have hungered, quite literally, for this moment, ever since I last spoke to you, all those long months ago, back on the Beara peninsula and now, the long awaited moment, for which I have yearned, has actually arrived and it is, all of a sudden, a reality. Albeit, a reality that, somehow, will just not sink in. Not yet, anyway. However, the fact remains that I am actually sitting here in our cosy little cottage, in Dunkineely, waiting for you to arrive, my very much cherished friend and then, once you are actually here, maybe, just maybe, reality will finally assert itself and I can begin to behave like a normal person again, instead of some mindless idiot. (Well, maybe not. That's expecting too much, probably. Once an idiot, always an idiot).

Jeff and I have just returned from our first venture up the lane with Misty and within five minutes of setting off, the inevitable metamorphosis had taken place, as the unique stillness and quietude of an Irish evening successfully did its usual job of ironing out all the stress that might have previously been there.

All it needs, now, to make everything perfect, is to greet you and welcome you into this dear cottage, for the first time, although I know, or at least, I hope, that it will not be the last. It's just a pity that there is not an open fire. What a joy and what a difference it makes. Oh, how cosy and friendly, somehow, is the sound of the logs spitting and crackling as they send their myriads of merry, dancing sparks up the chimney in a cheery greeting towards the night sky…however, the ambience of the cottage and your welcome to it will be as warm as it ever was and, as in the past, love will fill up all the corners and light and warmth will dispel any autumnal chill from this very momentous evening.

So, I shall now do what any normal person would do, under these auspicious circumstances…I shall top up my wine glass and then, just maybe, I shall be sufficiently fortified to be able to tell you all about this very special day, without jabbering like an idiot. I mean, it couldn't get more special, could it? This day on which we have actually arrived back in Ireland. Truly, a day to remember.

Accordingly, I now declare that an appropriate celebration, something in keeping with this truly momentous moment, is most definitely called for. This celebration has to be as special as the occasion, of course…a double celebration, in fact. I mean, firstly, we have our reunion and the continuation of the special friendship which evolved and which came to mean so much to me, during our last visit to Ireland…and secondly, we have the actual fact of that much longed for return to this enchanted land.

So…Cheers! Come on in now and take warmth from the knowledge of the loving welcome that is and always will be especially for you, while I tell you of our day. This very special and memorable day.

Saturday
19th. September 2009

Thank God for small mercies, that's all I can say! Those were my sentiments at 5.45 this morning…and yes, I do emphasize the morning bit…as I was sitting there, my mind still under the duvet, with just my body behind the wheel of the car, trying to demist the windscreen, this being the time of the year when everything is soaking wet at this hour of the morning after the overnight dew has saturated everything with it's chilly, autumnal breath. However, I suppose that I can only be thankful that it wasn't quite as mind-numbingly early as it was last year when we were setting off for Holyhead.

As I am absolutely sure that I have made it abundantly clear, on more than one occasion, I will still maintain, however, that there is a sort of civilized hour before which only people with an exceptional and I do mean absolutely vital purpose…or idiots like me…would even think of forsaking their nice, cosy beds. This is, of course, only my opinion so I do most humbly apologize to all of those poor long-suffering souls to whom this early rising lark is just normal routine…adding also, my deepest sympathies and my sincere respect. As a mark of that respect and at this appropriately early hour, I would have raised my hat to you, if I could have found it, that is. I knew that it was somewhere. Oh yes, it was definitely somewhere, although I would not, at that precise moment in time have been absolutely sure where. Just one small item among many, in the unbelievable pile of bags and baggage which had already been packed into the quite amazing interior storage capacity of this vehicle...something which never ceases to amaze me, especially as most of the rear space is usually allocated, as was the case today, to the travelling comfort of our rather large canine, my own lovely 'baby', Misty, who just happens to be a particularly splendid example of the Irish Setter breed. He is two years old, well, almost...and gorgeous in every copper-coloured hair of his furry person. And doesn't he just know it! The fact that he is now about the size of a small pony is another thing entirely. Most people, when confronted with this magnificent specimen of young doggie beefcake, usually take one look at him and then, after falling madly in love with him and completely under the spell of his beguiling charm (I mean, he flashes his pearly whites at the slightest provocation, to anyone close enough to become the recipient of this special favour) at the same time remark, 'what on earth are you feeding him on? He's huge'. Or, something to that effect.

He is a wee bit on the large side, I suppose, although we don't notice it quite so much, now. He is, however, as soft as he is large, there being not so much as one aggressive bone in his entire body. There are two things, however, which more than match the size of him. Number one is his heart...I have never known a dog so full of love...and that goes for anything, or anybody and with either two legs or four. His tail is a constantly sweeping blur as it expresses, in the only way that he knows how, his total ecstasy of joyous good will to all and sundry. In fact, I don't think that it ever really stops. Even when he is sound asleep, Jeff and I so often look at each other and smile as we hear his tail thumping out it's rhythmic tattoo against the carpet. Everyone, without exception, receives the benefit of the same loving greeting and, no doubt, a big sloppy kiss for good measure, whether that someone be known or unknown. It is all one to our dear Misty and so, it really doesn't matter. God love him. Of course, the risk of being on the receiving end of one of his famous sloppy kisses is something of which all must be aware and, if necessary, take avoiding action. You just have to love him, though...which we do, in spades.

I did, of course, say that there were two things which matched his size...the second thing is his mouth...and the least said about that, the better. Let's just say that he really is...and I mean this in the nicest possible way, just a ginormous gob on legs.

I can hardly believe just how smoothly everything has gone in this, the final run up, to going to Ireland. Even this morning, there was very little to do except the usual last minute turn-offs, switch-offs and lock-ups…due entirely to the fact that we had done most of it, a bit at a time, over the last couple of days. Thursday, we did all the packing and Friday, we chucked it all into the car. (My Jeffy would be most put out by my turn of phrase, I expect, as he is very tidy and methodical and would never even think of doing anything so careless as just 'chucking').

The reason for all of this pre-planning and uncharacteristic orderliness was the unexpected, though nevertheless delightful arrival of Jeff's little sis, Gail, from Australia. And thereby hangs a tale, as they say…and it is such a truly amazing and quite extraordinary tale that I just cannot let the chance go by without telling you all about it. This is, in all truth, one of those 'life' miracles that happen so very rarely, indeed, you could say that it is a once in a lifetime miracle and, for the two of us, indeed, for the whole family, who are the chief characters in this particular miracle, it still hasn't really sunken in and the wonder of it all still seems so surreal. So please, I do hope that you will forgive me as I go off the immediate story-line, just for now. Once you have heard what I have to tell you, I feel sure that you will understand and that you will immediately exonerate me from any fault at my total digression from the present moment and, just maybe, feel a little of what we are feeling, right now, on this Saturday morning in September 2009.

So, just for now, let me take you back in time to when my darling husband, my own Jeffy, was about eight years old. At that point in time, he and his siblings…three younger brothers and his baby sister, were put into care, being split up into two different children's homes, from which establishments they were all eventually fostered out to different families and, from that time onwards, they never saw each other again for quite some time. Mum did, eventually, recover from the breakdown (I suppose you could call it that) which had rendered her temporarily incapable of looking after her little ones, and then, in the fullness of time, she happily had all of her beloved children back with her again…all except Jeff, that is. In the meantime, you see, the family who had fostered Jeff, grew to love him so much that they wanted to make him their own and so eventually applied to actually adopt him.

Imagine a mother's heart and know that when his mother eventually agreed to his adoption, it was because of her great love for him. Though it broke her heart, she felt that, as the eldest of her boys, she was helping him to, hopefully, a better life.

The fact that Jeff never saw either his mother or any of his siblings, ever again did not mean that he ever forgot them. All his life, they remained in his heart and in his thoughts. Over a span of many years, throughout his adult life, he tried many times to trace either his mum or them but, having so very little to go on, bearing in mind that this dreadfully traumatic event took place when he was only about eight years old, he never had any success. Until this year, that is, when, just out of the blue and without boring you with all the minutia, he found them...or, at least, he found his youngest brother, Austin.

From first speaking to Austin, Jeff was soon in touch with the other brothers... Dennis, Donald and, of course, his baby sister, young Gail...Gail being in Australia.

I shall just leave you to imagine our joy, especially that of my husband... although, in truth, I think I was just as overjoyed as he was. I love him, you see. It's as simple as that. His sorrow is my sorrow and his happiness is my happiness...and that is how it will always be. As this miracle...and it is nothing less than that...has unfolded, over the last few weeks, I know that I have never before seen my husband's face light up with so much unadulterated joy. And I don't know what you think but, to my mind, it is nothing less than he deserves.

Just to round off my little tale, the cherry on the top of the cake was this...over all the years, while Jeff had been trying, so many times, to discover the whereabouts of his mum and his siblings, we soon discovered, from everything that was said on that first mind-blowing meeting between the brothers, that they had also, over the years, been trying to find him. However, just as with Jeff, they also had had virtually nothing of any real substance to go on, which didn't alter the fact that they had tried and that knowledge just about made everything more or less perfect because it could, so easily, have gone the other way. This was my only concern, my only fear, in all honesty, when Jeff had said that he was going to try again. I just could not bear the thought of him being hurt...depending, of course, on what success he may have achieved this time, or lack of it, as the case may be. As you can see...and I thank God for it, all my worries were unfounded.

The only sad part of it all was that mum died just four years ago. But, do you know something?…she will be smiling now. She will know. I really do believe that. She will know! She will now know that, after all the years, fifty years in fact, all of her precious 'babies' are once again reunited and yes, she will be smiling fit to burst. And I will tell you one thing, right now, mum…this family will never be split up again. Not ever! That is a promise! We love you, all of us…Jeff, Gail, the Boys, Austin's wife, Sandra and, of course, me, your long-lost boy's wife. God bless you. God bless us all.

As for Gail, she was, in fact, due to come over to England next year, 2010 but, this miracle that had suddenly given back to her the long-lost brother whom she had never stopped loving, just about drove her demented…she was ecstatic and that just has to be the greatest understatement, ever…so much so, that there was no way that she could possibly wait that length of time. Consequently, she just took it into her head to make an unscheduled visit, two weeks being all the time that she could arrange to get off work and, that was it. No sooner had she made the decision, she booked her flight and then told us the amazing news that she was coming over on 4th September, which, as you can imagine, immediately threw the rest of the family, including Jeff and I, into a mixture of wild euphoria and total panic. Total panic momentarily taking complete control. Obviously, we wanted to spend as much time as we possibly could with Gail, as she was here for only the two weeks and actually flying back to Oz on the day that we were to be travelling to Ireland. As a result, those two wonderfully happy weeks were planned with almost military precision, in order to make the most of every single day and yet, still get our own preparations for our trip to Ireland underway. (Lesson to be learned for future occasions…you see what can be done, when you put your mind to it)? Needless to say, it was a truly memorable two weeks. I mean, fifty years is a whole cart load of catching up to do but, you'd better believe me, we gave it one hell of a shot!

And now, with many thanks for your kind interest in my additional wee story and resuming where I left off…there we were, sitting in the car and ready for immediate departure. (Bon Voyage, little sis! We love you and want you to take a whole package of it back home with you, to hold, in your heart, until we are together again).

Anyway, everything that should have been taken care of had been sorted and everybody was in the car who should have been in the car, (no visible stowaways, not unless they were lurking under some oddly shaped, blanket covered bundle which passed for a piece of luggage…possibly, wearing my hat) namely Jeff, Misty and, of course, me, behind the wheel for the immediate future. Once we actually arrive at our destination, Jeff will do the driving until such time as we are ready to make the return journey. (Now go and wash your mouth out with soapy water…this instant, woman! We will have none of that sort of talk, not just yet, thank you very much. Return journey, indeed)!

If the truth be known, I was so excited, (so what's new?) as I reversed the car out of the driveway and we were actually on the road to Holyhead. This incredibly magical moment had seemed, at least to me, as if it would never come around. I just can't begin to tell you how much I had longed for it…and for what seemed, to me at least, to be an eternity. Indeed, we should have been doing all of this three months ago, way back in June…and then my dreams were shattered when I was told that I would be unable to travel, at least such prolonged travelling, so soon after my hip replacement surgery. It goes without saying, I suppose, that I was absolutely devastated. However, there was no getting away from it…it was a matter of quite painful, though, nevertheless unavoidable fact. I could have either the surgery or the holiday but, there was no way that I could have both, not with the dates as they were.

You will, perhaps, be able to imagine how I felt. Talk about 'gutted'. However, all was not lost! Jeff said that there was nothing to discuss. I was having the operation, end of story…and not to concern myself with any worries about the holiday. He would sort out all of that. Which he did. Within a matter of days everything was very satisfactorily rearranged by our cottage people…and I cannot praise Welcome Cottages sufficiently…and new dates were arranged to suit my convalescent time span. Jeff explained the circumstances, making it quite clear that we didn't actually want to cancel but, merely postpone and they sorted everything out for us, including the ferry and, well, I just cannot thank them enough. Well done, indeed, to all at Welcome.

It seemed so strange, setting out at such an early hour of the morning that it was still dark, which is how it was this morning. I don't know why but to me, it always adds a wee touch of mystery and excitement to a journey…and, let's be honest here, I was already beginning to fizz like a well shaken bottle of pop. I mean, you know what I'm like…it doesn't take very much to get me started. For better or for worse, there really is no way of getting away from the fact that I am and always will be, quite unashamedly, a big daft kid and, to my mind, that is not such a bad thing. The spontaneous thrill of the moment just cannot be replicated…you just have to go with it and if it means that in so doing you may end up making yourself look more than just a wee bit ridiculous, then so be it. There is no fun at all in being an old fuddy-duddy… which is something that I could never be accused of. Oh, don't worry, you'll soon find out for yourself, unless, that is, you are already beginning to seriously doubt your decision to come along.

Our feathered friends still had their wee beaks tucked up under their wings, as we set forth on this new and exciting adventure. Even the most humble of sparrows had not, as yet, so much as raised his little head or opened one eye and thought to himself…'Shall I or shan't I? OK, it's cool. Rock on, man. Tweet! Tweet! Tweet! There, that's it. That's my contribution and now, if you don't mind, I'll finish off my kip'.

It was such a clear and wonderful autumn morning, with the dawn slowly breaking over the Welsh hills as the miles gradually piled up behind us and we drew ever nearer to the Port of Holyhead. After all that I have said about getting up in the morning, or rather, my regrettable inability to do just that, I would have to be forced to admit, if I were honest, that it is my loss entirely. It is, however, an unfortunate fact that I have always been particularly bad at it…getting up early, I mean. More so, many years ago…and I do mean many…than it is now. My poor mother, God love her…what a job she must have had throughout both my schooldays and the early years after I started work. Talk about 'last-minute' Charlie. These days, I can do it…oh yes, I can indeed do it, if, that is, there is some special reason for doing so but, the occasions are somewhat rare and, as I said, it is my loss. You see, I have to admit that on those infrequent occasions when I have made the effort, I have discovered the moment of the breaking of the dawn to be what is, most probably, the most startlingly beautiful hour of the day, especially on a clear morning, as was this one…and how beautiful it was as we experienced this very special moment, this particular breaking of the dawn, on this very special day, even though we were on the road.

There was very little traffic and so we had plenty of opportunity to just look around us and watch, with ever increasing pleasure, the vivid show which was being played out before our eyes, as the sun gradually ascended, rising higher and ever higher in the sky with almost every second and, as it rose, suffusing everything, hills and ocean and even the sky itself with a roseate glow of pink, gold and the pearly grey of mother of pearl. It was like driving through some enchanted land, a land where there was a quite ethereal quietude, an almost unearthly quality of silence and mysticism that was way beyond our simple, human comprehension…and it is always so transitory. Just a fleeting moment in time when God puts on one of His own spectacular productions, an extravaganza for which there is never any charge and which is staged purely for our benefit and pleasure if only we would take the trouble to look and admire. Which we very rarely do. (OK, OK, so I know that I am probably the very worst culprit of all and I am actually getting a dig in at myself, there). But really, how sad it is to miss even a second of this brief glimpse into the realms of another time, another world, especially as it is so tragically brief and then, it is gone and the harsher, more realistic light of day takes over. Even as you gaze in wonder at this daily magic lantern show, the colours fade, ever so gradually, before your eyes, second by second and then, it is all over until the whole miracle begins once again, tomorrow…and all the other tomorrows. (And I know what you are probably thinking to yourself, right now…'I bet it's a long time before she sees another one…all talk and no knickers, that one'). I mean, after all that I have previously said, it must seem to be somewhat hypocritical of me but, I do openly admit my own culpability and I do know just what I am missing when I sneak that extra hour…and let's face it, when you get to my advanced years, you really can't afford to waste too much time languishing in your nice comfy bed. The older you get the more you realize just how precious time actually is, as you never know just how much of it that you may have left…or, how little, as the case may be. (Don't worry! I have no intention of going on that particular journey, not yet…indeed, not for a long time. I have told my Jeffy that I just flatly refuse to turn my toes up until I'm at least 95. Poor lad! What a prospect).

Holyhead! Wow! Even the name makes that tingle of excitement kick in again and, oh boy! as we drove into the Stena check-in point, I was so close to acquitting myself in the usual fashion by doing a wee dance of quite ridiculous childish excitement and I wasn't even out of the car yet, for heaven's sake…and then, there we were, in line and in plenty of time to give us the added pleasure of taking in all the activities and the normal goings-on of this busy little port. And believe me, there is always a whole lot going on and a whole wealth of human-nature behavioural patterns to both interest and entertain, in such a place and in such circumstances.

Call me just plain nosey if you will but, I am and always have been, totally fascinated by the observing and studying of my fellow man (or woman, as the case may be). Ok, so I suppose that there are those who may actually be studying me just as closely at the very same time that I'm getting, perhaps, a wee bit too up-front and personal with them and, maybe, thinking to themselves…'just look at that daft woman. I mean, fancy behaving like that! You would think that she'd have more sense at her age, wouldn't you. Silly old fool'. Isn't that just priceless, though? I mean, what can I say? I really can just imagine it, can't you? The sideways glances and the quiet muttering and the nudging of each other. I'm sorry but, I just can't help it. I simply have to admit that I find the whole idea to be absolutely scrumptious and extremely amusing…and I certainly cannot deny the fact that I almost always give people every possible reason for thinking along those lines. It just seems to come quite naturally to me to act like a silly old fool. In the nicest possible way, of course. I guess I must have been born with the talent for it…and I know that I shall certainly go to my grave still practicing it.

And now, I suppose, you really are having very serious doubts as to the wisdom of your earlier decision to come along on this trek, while at the same time doing a quick calculation as to whether or not you could still have sufficient time to do a quick runner before the good ship Stena Explorer goes to sea.

Talking of which, even now, when I have, through familiarity, become accustomed, as you might say, to the sheer size of our ferry across the Irish Sea, that very familiarity has done nothing, in any way, to diminish her size. She may, however, still tower over the harbour like a multi-storey car park but, to me, she is still a vessel of the high seas and as such, she is beautiful. All ships, to me, are a thing of beauty.

I must say that I was quite surprised to see a marked difference in the amount of activity in the port, this morning. Oh, there was a goodly sized line-up of vehicles for the ferry but, somehow, everything seemed quieter than on our previous visit. No doubt, it could be down to the difference in the time of the year…the last time, it was mid-June and now, it is mid-September and the number of sailings has actually been reduced now. Not that there was any danger of becoming bored. I mean, there was still enough going on to keep me happily entertained and more than sufficient people for me to fantasize about…all of which can keep me amused for hours, just studying them and trying to imagine where they have come from and what the reason may be for their journey today. And it's amazing how quickly the time passes when you get engrossed in a bit of people scrutiny…and before you say anything, my interest is quite genuine. There is absolutely no malice in it. I assure you that it is merely observation.

Before we realized it, I mean, the time had gone by so rapidly, we were being moved on in what is the final stage before actually boarding our floating car park…which was taking up our position at the quay side and being allotted our lane number as we were passing through.

Now you may think that I'm being silly but, I always like to have at least one car in front of me at the head of our lane. Let's just say that I always feel just a tad vulnerable, stuck out there in front…and wouldn't you just know it, there I was, right at the head of lane 10. Oh well, I have two chances. When the time comes to actually embark I will either get it right and lead my merry band onto the ship, like some motorized Pied Piper…or, we will all finish up in the drink, like a bunch of suicidal lemmings. (I don't know what the correct collective term is for more than one lemming. You know?…a herd of cows, a flock of sheep…but, lemmings? Haven't got a clue, so 'bunch' will just have to do)!

Embarkation, as it turned out, was a piece of cake, as always (and we all arrived on the car deck without getting so much as a front bumper wet) and everything was very expeditiously carried out by the staff, as always…staff of both ship and shore. It really is a credit to Stena Line, the way it is made so hassle-free and then, before you have the chance to even get your sea legs stabilized, you are on the finely appointed and extremely comfortable passenger deck, where the smell of fresh coffee and bacon make the taste buds begin to water.

Now then, here's a question. What is it, I wonder, that makes the smell of certain things drive a person totally demented, even to the stage whereby you just have to have a bit of, whatever, before starting to foam at the mouth? Coffee and bacon or, maybe, some hot, fresh toast? You will, undoubtedly, know what I mean. For Jeff and I, there was no contest…it just had to be the coffee and the bacon. Quite irresistible and quite delectable (bloody gorgeous, in fact). Bacon rolls that were almost as big as bin lids. I mean, we may as well start as we intend to go on. (I shudder to think just how many extra pounds we will, no doubt, put on whilst tempted by the wonderful food that Ireland has to offer…and who cares, anyway. We will just have to walk it off, across the hills and the beaches that are to die for).

The consumption of such mouth-watering fare gave us the pleasure which the tempting aroma was intended to achieve but, it also had the effect of making us want to curl up in our comfortable leather-upholstered captain's chairs and sleep. (I for one, didn't sleep much, last night. I was far too excited). Anyway. as I am far too nosey to want to waste even a second of this exciting voyage time by sleeping, we both gave ourselves a metaphorical shake and took ourselves off to the on-board shop where we had a mooch around, eventually purchasing another of their very informative maps of Ireland…a different one from the one we bought last year, obviously…covering the new and very much more extended area of our travels this time around. Many more trips and we will have the full set! That aside, it will, I know, be of great help in planning our daily adventures at the usual early (well, reasonably early) morning meetings of The Board…namely, Jeff, myself and, of course, Misty…when, having discussed various ideas and tossed them around a wee bit, we make our decision with a show of two hands and one paw. The Intrepid Trio is, always has been and always will be, a quite fair and democratic institution. Never let it be stated otherwise.

Then, WOW…the moment that we had looked forward to for so long…the first sighting of land and the certain knowledge that this wasn't just any old land…it was IRELAND. The Stena Explorer was drawing closer and ever closer to Dun Laoghaire and do you know something…it felt like coming home. For what has felt like forever, I have longed to set foot on these shores once more and now, here we were, within about ten minutes of docking.

Needless to say, any feelings of drowsiness just disappeared to be replaced with an enormous surge of excitement and anticipation. Honestly, this was one of those moments when I came so close to embarrassing Jeff, because the urge to start doing my jumping up and down bit was almost too strong to resist. However…and I really do think that I merit just a modicum of gratitude here, I did resist and all the jigging up and down that I accomplished was purely in my head. To the relief of my aged little legs, which had stiffened up somewhat after all the driving and then, all the sitting around. Inside me, the big kid reigned supreme and I rather regretted that I hadn't just gone the whole hog, just for the sheer, unadulterated joy of it. I told you, didn't I? Silly old fool! (Me, not you). Unbelievably, it is, no longer, the pleasurable anticipation of something that is somewhere in the distant future…it is actually happening, right now, this minute and we are actually within sight of the land that I have grown to love so much.

Why is it, I wonder, that people tend to feel needlessly guilty when confronted by a member of the constabulary? I don't know if you are the same as me but, whenever I see a policeman either looking at me or sort of heading in my direction, even though I know myself to be as innocent as a day-old puppy, I immediately feel as though he's looking at me as if I were the re-incarnation of Jack the Ripper, or something. It's almost as if I still had the blood dripping from my fingers, having just shoved the dismembered body under the floorboards. It's a strange feeling…and totally daft, I know that…anyway, there we were, coming off the ferry in a very orderly fashion and there they were, the harbour police, checking every car as it passed through. God bless and save me if I ever do think of taking up smuggling or illegal immigrant transportation as a hobby because, oh boy, would I be completely useless at it. I mean, for heaven's sake, I'd look guilty before I even got started. They would only have to take one look at my face and they would arrest me on the spot, without even so much as a second thought. All it was, in the end, was that they were merely asking which country we had come from, or rather, nationality, I suppose…I mean we'd all come from the same place, when it comes down to it, namely, Holyhead. When our turn came, I just said that we were 'English'…and that was the end of it. They then smiled in a friendly fashion, waved us on our way and we were on the road…and the adventure had really begun. (Anybody got a spare pair of knickers?)

I had been praying for some nice, celestial, elderly gentleman type chappie…you know, an angel who still hasn't quite earned his wings, to walk, or maybe, hover just in front of us, with a red lamp, or something, to sort of guide us through the streets of Dun Laoghaire and put us on the right road which was, in all probability, heading in the right direction and which would, in the fullness of time, facilitate our eventual arrival in Donegal… however, it wasn't required…or rather, he wasn't required. The whole thing was accomplished so successfully that I was positive that it had all been much too easy and that surely, I must have gone wrong, somewhere along the line. I still offered up a silent prayer of gratitude, though, to the particular angel who looks over the nice men who earn a living by putting up all the signposts and for giving these lovely, lovely fellows sufficient heavenly guidance as to enable them to erect them all in all the right places. The signposts, I mean. (Let's keep things clean, now).

Talk about a piece of cake. Well, so far, so good, up to now, that is…I always make it a rule that I will never actually dismiss the possibility of getting totally and quite disastrously lost, somewhere along the way. I have always been of the opinion, you see, that it is far better to own up to a certain amount of human frailty at the very outset, for by so doing, you can save yourself from being completely and mortifyingly humiliated, later on. Still, we won't even think about that! Will we? Like I said…a piece of the proverbial cake. All will be well and we will arrive at our destination, eventually…and hopefully before it goes dark, or they feel it necessary to have to send out a search party for us.

Seriously, I don't mind admitting that it was a relief, once we were out on the open road, the correct open road, that is…and what a real gem my Jeffy is. In fact, he's an absolute star. When I am driving, particularly on strange roads, I know that I have nothing but his entire support and, if necessary, the assistance of another pair of eyes. Not that he would ever condemn me, even if I were to lose my way. Let's face it, we can all do that easily enough…if we are honest, of course.

Oh, how it feels like coming home, it really does, as we pass through the small towns which mark our route…towns like Navan, Cavan and on up to Enniskillen. Lough Erne comes right down to Enniskillen, all the long way from just outside of Belleek, through which runs the River Erne. A young man whom we had not, as yet, had the pleasure of meeting, actually told us that

Lough (pronounced like the Scottish 'Loch') Erne is the biggest in Ireland…and I can well believe it.

It wasn't too long before we were driving through a land of mountains, farmland and smaller loughs and the closer we came to Donegal, we knew that we were entering the realms of enchantment that I had, for so long dreamed of and fantasized about. At long last, my dreams were, once again, becoming a reality and everything was coming into my vision, solid and real and no longer the stuff of dreams…only the colours had changed, as the seasons had changed, from the last time my feet had walked upon Irish soil.

Our first, life-changing visit to these shores had been in early summer when Ireland presented herself in the colourful raiment of summer. She wore dresses of jewel-like colours and a green that was so vibrant it was startling and brilliant to the eye. Now the colours are of late September, early October, a fact that in no way diminishes the beauty that she is so vainly flaunting for our pleasure and approval. These autumn colours are every bit as breathtaking as were those long-gone jewels of early summer. Now we are bombarded with a vibrancy of a different kind…burnished copper, bronze and amber. Honey and gold…a jewellery box full of different shades of gold…and just as precious.

Donegal is a mountainous region, which began to become obvious as our journey progressed and the mountains, for me, will always have that 'wow' factor. As you know, by now, I may have mostly seawater in my veins but there will always be another part of me that loves and feels akin to the grandeur of the mountains. A wildness of spirit, perhaps. A feeling of oneness and belonging, when I am actually a part of the still and yet awesome and splendid isolation of these rugged peaks and feel the wind in my face as it sweeps across the barren moorland which, from what we have seen, up to now, seems to stretch as far as the eye can see, in an endless swathe of course grass and vibrant heather, slashed, here and there, with the deepest dark-brown trenches where peat has been dug out of the ground and the resultant rows of small cairns of the neatly stacked bricks of peat which have been left to dry out and harden off.

Our journey could not have been more uneventful, for which we should, of course, have been exceedingly grateful. The sun was our constant companion for every mile that fell away behind us and so, the way was truly blessed and we made good time. (I still cannot quite believe that we have travelled thus far without some kind of hiccup…I nearly said something else, then. However, there is still time).

We made just two stops along the way, for the benefit of all three of us. A sandwich, a drink and a chance for young Master Hall, in particular, to have the chance of uncrossing his legs. Dear Misty! Such a star traveller, with not so much as a peep out of him, no matter how long the journey may be. How he does love being in the car. At any given time, a quick glance rearwards will find him either contentedly gazing out of the window at the passing scenery or, flat out and probably snoring and, oh boy, can my Misty snore. Bless his enormous paws. The only time that there is any sign of agitation in his demeanour is if and when he can smell the sea…something that he appears to be capable of doing from at least a mile away…and then, the agitation is nothing other than sheer joyful excitement. (Yet another example of just what a perfect match we are to each other, my dog and I…both slightly bonkers and both seaweed and ozone addicts). My very special Jeffy has to ensure that we both receive an adequate sufficiency of said drug, on a regular basis, in order to keep us on an even keel. Preferably, at least twice a day!

From the old town of Donegal, through Mount Charles and all the way to Dunkineely, our final destination, the mountains became an almost continual presence, looming majestic and imposing. A grand and quite splendid sight in the late afternoon, well, early evening light. The Blue Stack Mountains…the very name almost calls out to the unsuspecting traveller to venture upwards into their mysterious depths and either find ones soul, or lose it, all depending on how you tend to look at things.

In the days to come, we would be getting a little more up close and personal with this massif but, for now, the distant beauty of this magnificent range of mountains had to be sufficient to the day and only served to whet the appetite a little, for all that was to come in the following week.

Dunkineely! How amazing is that name?…and such a delightful little village. What we saw of it, that is. In all honesty, we didn't see too much of it, at this point, as our main concern was finding the lovely cottage that was to be our 'home' for the next week…The Barns.

Although we had found our way thus far, without having to make too much reference to the directions that we had been given, at this point we did and, having made a turn off to the left, just at the start of the village, we were somewhat taken aback by the very narrow lane which, although neither of us said anything at the time, we both tended to think 'surely this can't be right. We must surely have gone wrong, somehow'… however, there really was no other way to go and, go it did…on and on and on until we really were convinced that we had taken the wrong turning right at the start. We had passed a mere handful of small cottages but none were the one that we were looking for.

And then, we were there. There it was. The Barns…and looking exactly as it had on the picture from the computer print-out. What we hadn't realized, you see…and we would have done if only we had bothered to have a look at the map, was that The Barns was situated on a narrow peninsula, a mere finger of land which jauntily poked its wee self out into the waters of Donegal Bay, culminating, at St John's Point, the very furthest tip of land, with a lighthouse. Oh. Wow! It's gorgeous!

Drawing the car into the allotted parking space, we scrambled out of the car, or as much of a scramble as we could manage, having been travelling for so many hours and with legs as stiff as planks of wood…and just gazed around us in the pleasurable way you do when you have just reached the destination towards which you have been travelling for hours…filled with excitement, anticipation and, if one is honest, a certain amount of relief that you have actually arrived at the place which, only those few hours before, was just a name on the map…yes, yes, I know…the one we didn't even look at. Anyway, you know what I mean.

It felt a bit weird, actually. I mean, the cottage was so exactly like the small picture, which is all that we had to go by when we made our booking…and yet, here it was, as large as life, real and solid and every bit as lovely as it had been depicted. The real thing being in no way less attractive than the picture had led us to believe.

The temptation to stand there gawking at everything around us was great but, not as great as the need to get the car unloaded and…get the kettle on. I know that I remembered to do up a flask this morning but that now feels as though it must have been at least a week ago and besides, the coffee was, by this time, well past its sell-by date. Which is just how we were beginning to feel. At least, I certainly was…but then, I suppose that I am getting to be a little past my sell-by date.

After a great deal of opening of doors and all of the various cupboards and drawers, we eventually got all our stuff stashed away, taking far longer than it should have done, of course…I mean, I do have a great tendency to get a bit carried away and more than just a little over-enthusiastic and can so very easily get side-tracked by stopping to examine this and exclaim over the other. Views from windows always have that effect on me and tend to keep me from my task, especially, like in this case, when there is some form of water at the other side of the glass. The specification for the cottage stated that it looked out over Donegal Bay and, being a mistrusting old cynic, I thought to myself…'yes, I bet it does. Probably about a couple of miles away'. I now had no option but to take off my hat (if I'd been wearing one, that is…I still hadn't come across it in the vastness of the car, but then, we were still trying to get it emptied) …and ram it into my big mouth, piece by piece and proceed to eat it. You see, Donegal Bay came almost to the front door…and was absolutely gorgeous. I can see that I will have to be surgically removed from the chair by the window. Knowing myself as well as I do, I know that I shall never want to be parted from that wonderful view.

Getting back to the unpacking, (if we didn't, we would still be at it when darkness fell)…well, we did, eventually, get it all done, with a little expert assistance from our Misty who, in times like these, always considers it to be his given duty to muck in, so to speak and give a helping paw wherever it may be needed. God bless his copper nob, he has been brilliant, a real star, throughout this long day and equally long journey.

Having relaxed for a while, at the same time making ourselves reasonably familiar with the layout of The Barns, we decided that it would be nice to do a bit of exploring outside, before we even began to think about dinner and so, with Misty running ahead of us, we set off up the lane and then it happened, just as it always does…that special kind of stillness and quietude that seems to be so unique to Ireland, settled upon us and worked its usual miracle, seeming, almost, to embrace us and, once again, it was possible to quite literally feel all the stress that we had, no doubt, been unaware was there, evaporate, leaving us feeling at peace and totally de-stressed. It really is a physical experience, almost as if you have suddenly been injected with some kind of tranquilizer. I know that I shall never forget how it felt as we stood side by side, my Jeffy and I, outside The Old Pub Cottage, last year, surrounded, as it was, by the embracing arms of the Caha Mountains. I could never forget that feeling…it was such an amazing sensation…and it was here again, now, on this small peninsula, a finger of land so narrow that, as we walked on up the lane, it was possible to actually see the sea on both sides.

The day had, by now, advanced quite a pace and it was beginning to lose the full light of day and the sun, the same one which we had been so privileged to see rise this morning, over the Welsh hills, was now going through the reverse process of going down, over this small but, oh, so lovely, part of Donegal. Yet another of God's spectacular productions and, on this very special evening, our first one spent on the shores that I have grown to love so much, it was a performance worthy of a standing ovation. A mixture of gold and silver, with just a hint of rose, seemed to replicate itself in the sea, so that the combination of the two, the sky and the ocean…and, of course, the flock of sheep which so conveniently just happened to be there and which were so perfectly positioned that they could very well have been painted onto this particular canvas, with their fleeces given the touch of Midas as the gold of the setting sun gilded them also, all came together and formed a stunning picture which seemed to etch itself into our hearts and minds and remained with us as we made our leisurely way back along the lane. Misty led the way, as always and the man who is my life walked by my side, in the twilit quietude of this small piece of Ireland, our hands entwined and our hearts as one, as we returned to our wee 'home-from-home'. For some time, before we turned our backs upon the glorious sight of sunset over Donegal Bay and the ever deepening shadows over the distant mountains, we stood, in quiet harmony, my Jeffy and I, just trying to absorb into our being as much of all of this peace and serenity, this unique and precious gift, which is presented to you at that first very wonderful moment when you set your feet upon Irish soil. The feeling of having been embraced and comforted by a pair of welcoming arms followed the two of us as we finally made our way across the forecourt and up to our own front door.

I know that I have said it before but, I have absolutely no regrets about repeating myself…a life lived in this land could only be a longer life, a happier, more contented life, a truly blessed life, with no more striving for the unattainable. Indeed, here, on this enchanted isle, all of the things that we all tend to strive so hard to acquire…thus driving ourselves into an early grave in the attempt, well, you would find that you didn't really want any of it, anyway. Here, all the beauty by which you are constantly surrounded, seems to put all else in perspective. All of which depends on just what you consider to be important to you in your life, of course. I know that for me and I also include Jeff in this, for our priorities and our pleasures in life, if somewhat simple and by that, I mean by some standards, are so very similar…the sort of thing that we have, this very evening experienced, in just the short time that we have been here, just about does it. The glow of sunset over mountains and ocean and a stillness that is like the soft kiss of an angel…that is the sort of thing that I would prefer to take to my bed (along with my husband, naturally. I mean, let's not get too carried away here…there are some things that will, hopefully, never change) rather than the mental image of some particularly violent and bloody scene from some television programme. (And before you say a single word, I shall save you the bother and say it for you…'Oh God, here we go. She's at it again. The silly old bugger has gone off in one of her pontificating moods again and you know what that means').

You see, I do know just exactly what I'm like and so I do, most humbly, make absolutely no apology whatsoever.

What a cosy, welcoming scene met us as we entered what is to be our 'home', for the next week. It went through my mind, as we entered the cottage, our minds and hearts still full of the beauty that was still out there, just on the other side of the door, to give the Irish blessing when entering any home…'May God bless all in this house'…and blessed we did appear to be, once again, as we made another tour of our abode and found it to be quite charming. The only one, tiny thing, which would have been the cherry on the top, thus making it absolutely perfect, would have been a real, open fire…however, the glow from the artificial one was homely and the modern central heating was more than sufficient to keep out the chill of the bleakest of nights.

Dinner was eventually cooked and eaten, with enormous gusto, I might add, by both humans and canine. The final arrival at our destination had completely put from our minds all thought of just how famished we had been. I mean, it really felt as if we must have been in some other time zone when we had eaten that last sandwich, somewhere along the way. It all seemed a very long time ago, anyway.

We could, of course, have gone out to eat but, the effects of the long day, no matter how exciting it may have been, were eventually taking its toll on us, all three of us and besides, what more could we have wanted, other than what we had right here.

Having been sufficienty fortified, we settled down and soon felt 'at home'…and then we did what we would be doing every night…we broke open the wine cellar and now, as I sit here, a full glass in one hand and the other caressing the soft copper-coloured, silky coat of my Misty, all I can think about is that soon, very soon, you are going to be here…actually here with me again…and how I have longed for this moment during the long, almost eternal time since that dreadful last evening, way back last June. That was a bleak moment indeed, for me, at least, when it really penetrated my false sense of 'it will never happen' and it suddenly became a stark reality…plus the added sorrow brought about by the knowledge of our final meeting. Today, my excitement has been growing by the second, knowing that this evening, all of that will forever remain, just that…a sad memory. Now, quite incredibly, you have actually been and gone. How wonderful and yet, I can still hardly believe it.

Jeff is just getting ready to go up the lane with Misty…his final exploratory outing of the evening. (Misty, I mean…not Jeff). So many new things to stick his nose into whilst leaving his own calling card for whoever, amongst the local canine fraternity, may be even remotely interested. New kid on the block, don't you know. (Again, I was referring to Misty, not Jeff). Although, you never know, of course. Now there's a whimsical wee thought. The mind boggles! (Sorry, my darling).

As always, he takes a wee piece of my heart with him, even though it is such a short parting and I shall long, with all of the remainder of my heart for his swift return.

Our first evening, spent in the welcoming bosom of this very special land, could not have been more perfect, in fact, on reflection, the entire day has been perfect and now, as I try to settle myself down to sleep, which isn't going to be easy, as I will keep going back over the day, in a sort of haphazard fashion, flashbacks to bits and pieces and in no particular order…you know how it is, when your mind just refuses to shut down…I will end the day in my usual way, indeed, in the only way possible, by thanking God for our safe and thankfully, uneventful journey, today. Uneventful in all the right ways, I mean. Our arrival being safe and sound and with no mishaps.

This is a huge room, for a bedroom, that is. I can't help looking around and enjoying the novelty of the moment. There's a big telly, over in the corner, by the door. Not that we will be needing that…and for more than one reason. Now then, behave yourself, woman!

Anyway, get to sleep, you great numpty…Ireland is out there and it will still be out there in the morning, with all the wonder and enchantment that you know so well and that only Ireland can bestow. Anyway, before I do…and you know my habits well enough…not only must I give my thanks to God for this very special day but, I must also thank my Jeffy, he who makes all my dreams come true.

My darling, you are, and always will be, my friend…my forever friend. You are my husband, my lover…my life. God bless you. I love you.

We have so much to share, you and I, now that we are back in Ireland. No one could know, more than we two, just how much magic is out there and it's just waiting for us to go out and discover it…or rather, rediscover it. Once again, we will have the opportunity to fill up yet another huge, jumbo-size album of special memories, the kind of memories that will last forever and which will serve to bond us even closer, if that is at all possible, as the years go by and the memories become more precious. To be able to share such golden moments, well, we are so fortunate…especially fortunate, just to have each other.

Sleep tight, dear Misty, my big 'baby'. Even for you, there are so many adventures just waiting for you out in that big wonderful world. Dream your doggie dreams and may they always be happy ones. God bless your true and faithful heart and you have been a good lad on this long day of travelling. Your mum loves you, too.

So, may God bless everyone and I shall look forward to seeing you tomorrow, when we will venture forth, once again, the three of us…the old team, The Intrepid Trio and we will, as always, grasp, with all our hearts, all and everything that Ireland may want to present to us. From past experience, we already know that what lies out there is special, very special…and magnificent beyond belief.

Now, get to sleep, you daft woman. It is not going to go away! And, what a comforting thought to go to sleep on…the sense of peace and tranquillity that I know is just the other side of our windows, as the waters of Donegal Bay gently lap the shore.

ⓞⓞⓞⓞⓞⓞⓞⓞⓞⓞⓞⓞⓞ

Time can be such a fickle companion…have you ever really thought about it? How easily it can lull you into such a false sense of security by allowing you to believe that you have an endless supply of it while, at the same time, its deception becomes obvious only when you finally discover that you don't actually have enough of it left to even bless yourself with.

It can give you the impression that it is actually standing still…a momentary lull, the pendulum halted in mid-swing…or, it can pass as fleetingly as the swiftest gazelle.

I can honestly say that I have experienced both of these phenomena. Over the last fifteen months, time really did feel as though it had ceased to make any further progression. A week seemed like a month and the months seemed endless. Ireland seemed to be nothing but a dream…far too much in the future to ever feel as though it would ever become a reality. But, with the usual inexorable passage of time, slow as it was, it did pass and now, here I am…only now, you see, I am experiencing being at the other end of the spectrum, the moving pendulum has begun to swing a little faster.

Dinner has been eaten and the washing up taken care of and I am actually sitting here, in what has become my favourite place, the table by the large windows in the kitchen and looking out over Donegal Bay, where the shadows of the evening and the light from the sky, although gradually fading, are now throwing bewitching highlights and shades over the water and the lights of all the wee villages, even the old town of Donegal itself, are winking and twinkling in the distance…and I'm just waiting for you to come and, by so doing, making the end of this day as special as the rest of it has been. But, it has all passed so quickly, that is the point that I am making such a long and tedious song and dance about. I mean, twenty four hours have gone by since I last spoke to you…and where did it all go?

Whatever. In the great scheme of things, I don't suppose that it really makes all that much difference…and, here you are now, so I can get started.

Today had a quite hilarious start to it, indeed, the image of that quite amazing tableau will live with me always. Anyway, first things first and you will hear all about it in due course. Oh, well…here goes.

Sunday
20th September 2009

A horse! a horse! my kingdom for a horse! Those few rather well-known words are, of course, not mine own. I have to admit to sort of borrowing them from the Master himself…namely one Mr William Shakespeare…words which were spoken so eloquently and quite earnestly by King Richard III. Borrowed though they may have been, yet they were the words which flashed through my mind for just a fleeting moment and which did seem, at the time, to be appropriate to the occasion, as I gradually dragged myself up and out of a lovely, cosy, luxuriously drowsy feeling of contentment, seemingly as the result of a lot of thumping and bumping and suppressed laughter…and it was only 7.15. in the morning. This morning, naturally.

OK, so I don't need a horse. I would certainly love to own one but, like I said, I don't actually need one…and I most definitely do not have a kingdom at my disposal to just give away willy-nilly. However, be that as it may, I would have given pretty much everything else that I possess, just to have had my camera to hand, which was, regrettably, lurking, somewhere downstairs.

You are by now, I expect, wondering just what all the excitement was about, well, picture the scenario if you will…just off to one side of the bed, about half way down the sloping ceiling, there is a skylight…ok so far?…and the picture which was being presented to my still barely focused eyes and which, I might add, as a result of this quite extraordinary scene, suddenly opened wide in both astonishment and amusement, was that of my two boys gazing at the beauty of the sunrise. Nothing out of the ordinary in that, you may be thinking, however…I shall continue. There they were, side by side, both stretched to there full height, Misty up on his hind legs, which made him the same height as his dad, their bodies arched ever so slightly backwards and in absolutely perfect symmetry with each other and then, the final ingredient which made it even more interesting and infinitely more hilarious…was the fact that, as they were both garbed only in the suit of clothes that God gave them, there was, resplendent and in all their full glory, two other parts of their individual anatomies which were pointing, again in perfect symmetry, each with the other, towards the glory of the sunrise. As God is my witness, I swear it to be true.

Well, I tell you, I nearly fell off the bed, laughing! I mean, what a sight to behold and, given the fact of actually having had a camera in my hand at that moment in time, all I can say is that, although it certainly would not have been the sort of wee snap that you could have taken to the chemist for processing, it would have been something quite unique and, extremely memorable…to say the least.

At last, having, with the greatest of difficulty, managed at least some small semblance of control and, at the same time, stopped rolling around in fits of uncontrollable laughter, I clambered up to the skylight myself. Not a very graceful sight I have to admit but then, I was rather more hampered because of my much more diminutive stature. My little legs are in no way suitable for shinning up to skylights, even at the best of times, however, not to be dismayed, nothing ventured, nothing gained and all that and by hanging on with both tooth and nail, I did, eventually, manage to get a look at what my boys had been so taken with and what turned out to be the reason for all the song and dance and all the subsequent bumping and shoving…the beauty of the day and, oh boy, what a truly magnificent sight it was.

In the meantime, Jeff had gone downstairs to retrieve my camera, eventually finding it on the coffee table in the lounge and, with this modern miracle of technology in my hands, I managed to get two or three splendid shots of the panorama which had been a miracle of quite a different nature. Mother nature herself, in fact, quite brazenly showing off and acting out before me, the celestial daily performance, the 'no charge' magic lantern show of all the heavenly colours imaginable, colours which transformed the scene into a painting by some famous artist, indeed, the greatest artist of them all…for it was a scene which, quite truthfully, could only have come from a divinely inspired brush…and which seemed to merge the sky to the waters of Donegal

Bay, blending the two and transforming them into a thing of divine glory. Colours bold and vivid. Colours soft and pastel…and then, as I watched, entranced and enchanted by it all, the colours slowly started to fade. Second by second, before my eyes, the transformation seemed to speed up and become ever more rapid, the scene softening, becoming less awesome…beautiful, of course, but less striking.

And before you say a word…I still remember what was laughingly inferred, yesterday, as the same sun was making its spectacular appearance over the Welsh hills. Something vaguely muttered about it being a long time before I ever see another one (dawn and sunrise, that is) and something about all mouth and no knickers. Well, you could have been proved correct (I'm not so sure about the 'no knickers' bit though. When you reach my rather advanced years, it's a bit too draughty to go sans knickers)…if it hadn't been for all the rumpus coming from the other side of the bed caused, of course, by my two boys pushing and shoving to gain the better position at the skylight (Misty doing most of the shoving). Quite honestly, without that, I would have almost certainly slept right through it. Until about 8 o'clock, at least and, as a consequence, would have missed the whole thing.

Tell you what, though…I'm so very glad that I didn't. It was unimaginably beautiful, as it is every time it happens, which is on a daily basis, depending, of course, upon whether the conditions allow it to be visible. However, somehow, it seemed to me to be even more beautiful than ever, this morning, because the scene was displayed, in all its glory, over water, which completely transforms everything. It gives the effect of a double image, which is double the joy.

And besides, I haven't laughed so much in ages. Apart from nearly falling off the bed I almost did myself permanent injury, merely because I was laughing so much. (Still wish that I'd had my camera, though).

Wow! What a start to any day but this, this, our special day, our first day, our first 'wakeup' in Ireland…it was pure magic. There really is nothing quite like it, is there? That inexplicable magic of that first 'wakeup' in that special place of your dreams. Quite unforgettable, in fact, especially this morning, and for more than one reason. Mental note that from now on, I never go anywhere without a camera. Maybe I should consider bringing it up with me when we come up to bed. You never know what could happen, do you?

Now, there is something to think about!

After a start like that you would imagine that it could not get much better but, as always, that turned out to be only the beginning. Half an hour or so later, we were showered and dressed (Jeff and I, I mean. Naturally, Misty was, as always, like some form of genial takeaway. Overflowing with canine joie de vivre and just ready to go) and we were all, each in our own way, more than ready to grasp the day.

The early morning routine may have been the same as always, as, perforce, it has to be, when you have a dog to consider…I mean, there really is a limit as to how long he can keep his legs crossed (I must say that our Misty does seem to have some of the characteristics of a camel however, there is a limit, even for him)…so, whilst Jeff took Misty up the lane, for their much looked forward to first morning of detailed exploration of our immediate outside environs, I got down to the task of, firstly, introducing myself to the incumbent cooker and asking it, politely, of course, (I mean you must always be careful not to rub them up the wrong way), to be kind to me and not do anything sneaky whilst I've got my back turned…like incinerating the bacon or burning the toast. I quite readily admit that I am not the most proficient cook on the planet, therefore I don't need any cookers with attitude playing any of their little dirty tricks on me, thank you very much. All cookers that I have ever become personally acquainted with, do, I have discovered, tend to have their own characteristics and, if you are really unlucky, a mind of their own that can prove to be quite daunting. It's quite unnerving at times, some of the underhand things that they can vex you with just when you least expect it. Mercifully, however, this one did seem, on the surface at least, to be quite affable and friendly and so, we shall just have to wait and see.

Breakfast was as I'd visualized it to be, in all my imaginings over the last fifteen months…happy, jolly and carefree…and just to add that extra zest, there was the ever present thrill of anticipation at the thought of all that lay ahead of us during the next seven days in this magnificent setting, in and around County Donegal. Where to start and what glories will we behold when we get there? The joy, of course, is just getting out there and finding out.

And now, if you will bear with me, I would like to just take a moment to rectify a quite serious ommission from last night. Put it down to the ravages of a long day of travelling and an overdose of ecstatic excitement…certainly on my part. Thank God that my Jeffy is so much more laid back than I am. It's a good thing that at least one of us can claim to having some sense. You will have heard this phrase used many times, I am sure but, this husband of mine, this man who is everything in life to me, really is and always will be, 'my rock'. And I'm going off on another tangent again, aren't I? In fact, what I wanted to say was this. I know that, last evening, I remarked on just how lovely the cottage was and all that but, what I should have mentioned and didn't, which was very remiss of me, was all the generous offerings which were put there for our use. In the fridge was to be found milk and butter and there was a newly baked loaf of Irish soda bread. There was, also, tea and coffee and sugar…and then we discovered that because they had been aware that there was to be a dog coming for his holidays, they had provided feeding bowls, one for water and one for food and some food, a tin of dog meat and some nice doggie treats as an extra bonus. What they had left for the benefit and comfort of us was largesse indeed and of most generous proportions. I mean, what more could you wish for…fresh soda bread spread with lashings of butter. How delicious is that? However, it matters not that we had brought with us everything that Misty was likely to need but, to consider the welfare and the comfort of a dog and in such a thoughtful way was, in my humble estimation, 'over and above'…and was very much appreciated.

We never did get to meet the actual owners of the cottage, so we never had the opportunity of thanking them, which I really would have liked to have done. Pity but, there you are. You see, when Jeff phoned a few days ago with regard to the last minute instructions for collecting the keys, we were told to just walk in, the door would be open and the keys in the wee basket on the table. Which they were. Proof, if ever proof were needed of that different way of life about which I have already made my opinions known.

That's it then! I just wanted to make some mention of it as I feel that it is most profoundly justified.

By the time Jeff returned with Misty, the breakfast was ready. Bacon, eggs and sausages had been grilled quite adequately and to my satisfaction, so obviously I must have been given the seal of approval by my unpredictable new friend, the cooker…and, having fed my two boys, we got down to the important stuff like what to do and where to go. Out came the brand spanking new map, purchased from the on-board shop on the good ship Stena Explorer and within minutes it was spread out all over the table, narrowly missing the jam pot and the resultant sticky mess (it will happen, I can assure you. In fact, by the end of our three wonderful weeks here in Ireland, split up between two cottages, it will, no doubt, have become so bedaubed with various smudges of a variety of different substances that it could prove to be of enormous interest in some scientific experiment) and routes were planned and, when it was all subsequently put to the Board, we had a unanimous show of two hands and one paw on the merits of just taking the road out of Dunkineely and seeing where it would take us. Sounded like a good idea to me, anyway, as that road, according to our excellent map, eventually brings you into the fishing port of Killybegs. That will definitely do for me…and my alter ego, Seasalt Vera!

We have become quite adept at getting ourselves organised for a days outing, now. In order to facilitate the maximum of efficiency, we simply put Misty in the car first. I, indeed, we, do appreciate the fact that he is only trying to be helpful, in his own doggie fashion, sort of lending a friendly paw, so to speak but, he does tend to get just a wee bit too enthusiastic in his efforts to put us right on one or two points and so it is better for all concerned if we deposit him first. Actually, he really quite approves of this new arrangement as he loves to be in the car and, with the tailgate left open, he will lie there in luxurious splendour, in his now greatly enlarged section of the car, surrounded by all his own personal bits and pieces, for as long as it takes. Indefinitely, in fact, should that be necessary.

At last we were sorted, with everyone belted up and ready for the adventure to begin. Without really realizing that I was actually doing it, a strange thing happened as I crossed our small courtyard and made my way to the car…I automatically glanced around, looking for O'Shaughnessy. Remember Mr O'Shaughnessy? Such a nonsensical thing for me to do, I mean, even if he is still around, (I wonder just what kind of a life-span little water voles have) he is hundreds of miles away on the Beara peninsula. I suppose that just goes to show how much I had grown to love that little fellow.

At last, we were off and following the narrow road or track, which is all it is, in all honesty, back towards the village of Dunkineely. Funny, but it didn't appear to be anywhere near as endless as it did last evening. Probably because we now knew our surroundings a little better and we were no longer actually looking for something in particular.

Dunkineely is so small that, in a car, you can be in and out of it in about thirty seconds flat and yet, it has everything that the residents could possibly need or desire. I was trying to look at everything all at once, of course, with my eyes looking every which way but, on this first brief inspection I saw a Butcher's shop, a Florist, a Hairdresser, which appeared to be unisex and one establishment which is the centre of any wee Irish village…the shop that sells everything. The small mini-market that can provide anything from a loaf of bread to a set of boot laces…plus the ever-ready friendly smile and the readiness to always spare some time to chat and listen to every one's crack. Nobody is ever rushed. You will get served, in due course but…being welcomed as if you were a long-lost friend and showing a genuine interest in you as an individual is the hallmark of any Irish village shop.

There was also a lovely little café and, and you will never believe this, six pubs. Yes, I said SIX pubs. At first, I did actually think that I'd counted seven but no, it was only six. Only six, she says! Wow. Oh boy! This is going to be quite a week.

At this point, there was a quick change of plan. The original idea had been to follow the road out of the village and carry on to Killybegs and beyond, however, we suddenly decided to about turn and head off in the opposite direction to Donegal. It seemed more appropriate, somehow, I mean, what better place to begin the proceedings than this old historic town…the named town of the County of Donegal.

As is the case with most of these Irish towns, they are small and quite intimate by comparison with the sprawling and ever expanding towns that we are used to. The yardstick by which we would measure the size of a town is of no use here. There are, of course some very large towns, cities, in fact, that would take a week to explore, but by and large, especially in these more rural or coastal areas, they are more endowed with charm than with any great stakes in square miles…the charm being in no way diminished. On the contrary. Being on the small to middling size serves only to accentuate it.

Donegal just about oozes that charm and is redolent with the vibrant sense of history that seems to exude from the very fabric of the town. The River Eske runs through Donegal as it flows down from Lough Eske and an ancient Friary stands sentinel just where the river widens before actually running into Donegal Bay. Then, across the other side of town is Donegal Castle, a very ancient pile which, even today, looks very imposing.

And so, where to begin! Everything new and alluring but, I mean, you have to start somewhere and sort of work your way around the fascinating maze of intimate little streets and the landmarks which are special to any one place. We managed to get parked up without any trouble and the very choice of that parking place more or less dictated which point of the compass we headed out on, being, as we were, actually on the side of the river and only a few hundred yards from the old Friary.

Before even reaching the Friary, however, we were accosted by one of God's earthly helpers, in the form of a quite elderly nun. She was most taken by you know who…Misty, of course…who else? We must have been talking to her for a good twenty minutes…or at least, this dear old soul was doing most of the talking. Her voice was pure magic, though…so gentle and as soft and sweet as an Irish love song but, she just never stopped. Hardly seeming to draw breath. It was as if she had just been fitted with a new set of batteries and the chatter was virtually non-stop. God love her, she was lovely! It was impossible to be rude to her and just walk away but, I do believe that we, in the space of time that we were held captive by her lyrical eloquence, must have lived through her entire life history. How many hours she had been there, at the side of the river, I had no idea. She had parked her small car very neatly, on the side of the car park nearest to the river and, with the tailgate open, she had set out her wares…small offerings which were for sale, the proceeds being, of course, for the Church. To give you a few examples. There were small items of crochet work…little table mats, that sort of thing and fancy, quite intricate bracelets made from twisted strands of wool. Knitwear, cable or bright patterns and things made out of beads. Even a wee assortment of Christmas tree decorations done in crochet work and sewn to make little snow flakes or, and these were very cleverly made, little crocheted angels. All in all, it was a quite huge variety of hand-made products and all of it very pretty. I just hope that she eventually did a decent return on the hours that she must have spent there.

Ever since I was a very small child…a good catholic child…I have always loved and revered the holy Sisters. I was taught by the nuns when I first started school at the tender age of five and it has never left me. I remember one nun in particular, from those very far off days. Her name was Sister Anthony. A huge woman, certainly by my standards and my diminutive height at that young age (and I know just exactly what you are thinking…'from what I can see, she hasn't grown much, even now') and of course, her size was emphasized even more by the great voluminous habits that they wore in those days. I tell you, Sister Anthony used to put the fear of God into me…I only had to look up at her and I would have promised to be a good girl for the rest of my life. However, if I were to meet her now, I expect that I would find her to be quite gentle and mild.

As I said, we were very loathe to hurt this dear Sister's feelings by rebuffing her, however, fate or some other form of divine intervention, eventually came to our rescue in the shape of a police patrol car (the Donegal Garda Station was, quite literally, just across the road). The young, rather dashing, police officer got out of his car and immediately started talking to her and in such a manner, both affectionate and bantering, that it was quite obvious that she was doing something that she did on a regular basis and was a familiar figure to everyone in Donegal. In all probability, I suspect that she took up this regular pitch every Sunday morning. Whatever, it was a welcome distraction and one which had the desired effect of redirecting her interest to him and away from us. We swiftly said our goodbyes and then legged it as fast as we could, in the direction of the Friary. God bless that dear soul. She was so open hearted…truly one of God's earthly angels. I know that I shall always remember her…and with real affection.

What a perfect morning. From that magnificent sunrise of a few hours ago, the day had now become one of golden splendour. We felt as if our spirits were soaring up into the sky, a sky which was the most wonderful shade of blue, wheeling and crying out joyously, in unison with the seabirds. The sun emblazoned everything with her warmth and golden light suffused the waters of the River Eske which was sparkling and reflecting the exact same blue as the sky. A very grand and imposing river launch lay in her berth, only awaiting sufficient passengers to embark on one of its regular leisurely cruises along the river and out into the bay. Knowing my mania for anything nautical, you will not be in the least surprised to learn that Jeff almost had to prise me away from the side of that beautiful boat with the intriguing gaelic name…Dun Na nGall, which actually translates into the name Donegal.

Eventually, being propelled along the riverside embankment by a firm hand (Jeff's hand) which, although kindly, meant me to go where it was intended that I should go, we came to the old Friary and my attentions were instantly refocused as I drank in the atmosphere of these ancient stones. Walls and arches and cobbled passageways, all of which were still remarkably intact and the equally ancient cemetery with headstones of all shapes and sizes, tilting over at every angle imaginable, some facing out to sea…and what a view to have for all eternity.

There was a very strong sense of the history of the place, something of which I have a quite sharply honed sensitivity and it seemed to draw my imagination like a magnet. Somehow, I felt it to be an enormous privilege just to be allowed to walk in the steps of the Friars of old who had once inhabited this ancient house of God and had lived out their holy and blessed lives behind these hallowed walls. From the elevated position of the remains of this wonderful place, the view out across Donegal Bay was stunning, with sea and sky merging into infinity. It would have been such a sweet and blissfull existence here, in this place, in those days of yesteryear. Quietude and peace. A life of prayer and holiness and a closeness to God…all of this seemed to creep into ones very soul as one walked the old pathways and maybe laid a hand upon rough, warm stone. I don't know exactly what it is but, as I have just remarked, some deeply subconscious sensitivity, something deeply entrenched within me always seems to be able to transport me back in time to the period of very real time when life went on and the people, very real people, very ordinary people, just like us, actually lived their lives in places such as this Friary. It's a strange feeling, almost as if I were walking in their very steps. I felt it very strongly once before whilst exploring the remains of Tinturn Abbey, in South Wales and yet again in and around the ancient cottage, by the waterfall, in Gleninchalquin Country Park, here in Ireland, on the Beara peninsula. This ancient religious edifice had a similar effect on me.

Only one thing spoiled this very special treat for me and that was the fact that Jeff and I had to go up separately. Dogs were not allowed amongst the remains, which was understandable, I suppose. The hallowed ground of the cemetery being the main reason, I expect, plus the fact that a lot of people do not bother their heads over much with regard to what their dog may be doing. So, we went up one at a time, the other remaining on the riverside with Misty. I missed the intimacy of having Jeff by my side, as I always do, no matter how brief the parting…and just the fact of being unable to turn to him, exchanging thoughts and well, just generally being unable to drive him completely bonkers, as I always do, by my constant chatter. Exclaiming over this and that, a sort of continuous chanting of…'Oh, Jeff come and see, come and see. Oh Jeff, look at that'. I have to admit that I'm always doing it and I suppose, if I'm honest, and the tables were reversed, even I would get fed up of my constant chattering. The eternal 'big kid' that is just me, I'm sorry to say…I am what I am and I rather suspect that, if pressed, Jeff would have admitted to being only too glad to have the opportunity to explore in peaceful, solitary splendour and, more specifically, in silence.

I had been the one to go up to the remains first and when I finally, though reluctantly, came back and it was Jeff's turn, thus leaving me in charge of Misty, he hadn't been gone more than a couple of minutes when…and it always seems to happen to me…a quite charming couple came over to me and, as you would expect, went into quite rapturous praise of a certain canine Adonis, who was, just to celebrate the fact that he was on his holidays, today wearing, along with his collar, a rather nifty and devil-may-care bandana, (which made him look like a sort of doggie Errol Flynn) who immediately went into his well practiced superstar mode, tail swishing back and to in a blur of well groomed bronze feathering while, at the same time, flashing his pearly whites for all he was worth.

You know, I sometimes can't help thinking that Misty is, in fact, a person, a real person wearing an Irish Setter suit. He just never ceases to amaze me. Maybe it is that I am just biased but he really is a quite extraordinary dog. There are times when the things that he does do actually appear to have been seriously thought out and proving, on many occasions that he also has a quite roguish sense of humour. We always know when he has done something for the sole reason of just winding us up. He will actually glance in our direction, just to make absolutely sure, don't you know, that we are in fact watching, before finally executing whatever it may be which, in his estimation would be of the most annoyance to us. I mean, you would not believe the extent of his repetoire of little Misty-isms, each one a quite trivial, though totally premeditated misdemeanour especially calculated to ensure the maximum of attention from we two hapless humans…and each has it's own 'look'. It's all in the eyes, you see. One of those 'looks' states more eloquently than any words, just what is going through that quite exceptionally wise doggie head. The one that I particularly refer to would usually be accompanied by a two finger sign…and I don't mean V for Victory. Once the said misdemeanour has been accomplished, he prances around like a canine Mr Bean. But, it all comes back to those eyes. It's the eyes that do it, every time, you see. I sometimes look into those pools of dark brown chocolate and I see a human being looking out at me. I swear to God.

These people, to get back to the story, were also on holiday in Donegal though only from some other part of Ireland. We did, however, find a link between us in the shape of a sister who just happened to live in Chester, which is only about ten miles from where we live in Delamere. Eventually, Jeff returned and the conversation carried on apace. You know, over the last couple of years, we have met up with some really lovely people, all on account of Misty. Remember those dear people from Belgium, last year? But, wherever we have had any contact with the local inhabitants we have been overwhelmed with their warmth. One of the main reasons being, of course, the innate friendliness of the Irish. It is just not in them to be anything else…and I love them dearly.

When the party eventually broke up, it was with the warmth of fond bonhomie which sent us all on our separate ways feeling blessed and just so lucky to be where we were on this glorious morning. I know that there was nowhere else that I would rather have been. I mean, I'd dreamed of nothing else for well over a year. Anyway, that feeling of well-being walked beside us as my Jeffy and I and, of course, Misty, who is always full of joie de vivre, slowly made our way back along the river, Jeff skilfully steering me past that scrumptious boat and on across town to the old and venerable Donegal Castle.

That very feeling of well-being must have glowed like some kind of an aura around us because all whom we passed seemed to smile as we walked by, indeed, the only miserable faces belonged to the unfortunate souls who were standing outside a big hotel on one side of the town square, encumbered with suitcases, some sitting on them, some leaning on them but, without exception, all looking far from happy as they awaited the inevitable taxi which would take them off to their normal life, wherever that may have been. I remember looking at them and feeling their dejection, their mind-numbing misery…and feeling sorry for them. I shall never forget how I felt when we were leaving after our first visit here…it was nothing even remotely like the normal 'end of holiday' blues, oh no! For me, at least, it was total devastation. I remember being in line at the Ferry Terminal at Dun Laoghaire and coming within an inch of turning the car around and legging it before I had the chance to change my mind. However, we will have none of that sort of talk…thoughts of departure are forbidden and anyway, who knows what could happen during the next three weeks. If we encounter enough fairy dust and believe with all our hearts, then maybe, just maybe, we won't have to leave at all.

I did, in fact, make a wish once, in a very special fairy glen. And I'm totally serious here. This is actually true. Never will I forget that very special moment, with the sun dappling on the water of the burn which was spanned by the small bridge on which I was standing, along with the wonderful man with whom I was so much in love. We were right in the heart of a secluded little glen on the Isle of Arran, off the west coast of Scotland and, with all my heart, I made my wish to the incumbent fairies of this special place…and it came true. The result is my husband, my Jeffy…my wish being, you see, that we would one day return to this very place as husband and wife. Not only did my wish come true…the fact is, we were actually married on this lovely island. And so, I shall always consider myself truly blessed by this precious gift which has since filled my life with a love and a happiness beyond anything that I have ever known.

The charm of Donegal soon made itself felt as we explored its narrow streets and peered occasionally into the window of some small shop with its tantalizing display of merchandise. Not that there was very much in the way of shops open today, it being a Sunday, which is so very different from back home where the fact of it being Sunday means nothing more than that it is just another day for raking in as much money as possible. Here, there are finer and more meaningful ways of spending a Sunday…material acquisitions are not so important that they cannot wait just one more day. Just another of the unspoken blessings of Ireland.

Walking along, content and happy in each others company and quite enchanted by our present surroundings, it occurred to me just how little we really appreciate the everyday things with which we come into contact on a daily basis or, indeed, the environs within which we exist and live our lives. Take this beautiful little historic, fortified town of Donegal. Do the residents look at it, as they go about their daily business and think 'wow', how lucky am

I to be actually living here? Maybe some do but, I bet most of them don't…and I am no different. My home town is Chester, which I mentioned very briefly, just a few minutes ago and you cannot get to be much more historic than Chester, which started out as a sprawling Roman fort and then became a town which goes back to the Middle Ages. It's origines are entirely Roman, the proof of which is to be found pretty much all over the city, for that is what it has now become, in the shape of the most amazingly intact Roman remains that, over recent years have been unearthed and lovingly preserved. There is so much more, indeed, the entire modern-day city is actually built over Roman remains, it is just that they would have to, more or less, destroy virtually everything above ground in order to reveal all these hidden wonders, this wealth of precious historical revelation of the people who once walked these roads, indeed, built these roads and brought their engineering and building skills to what would have been, in those days, just a primitive environ. I do sometimes marvel, as I walk through the streets, at what I know to be still there, just beneath the surface of this ancient city but, I don't suppose that I show sufficient awe and pride in this city that is mine own. Well, maybe just occasionally. Which is a shame.

As we approached the castle, it was possible to feel the sense of history in which this small town is steeped. The castle stands proudly in its elevated position, on a bend of the river and, standing there, on this lovely sunny morning, in the 21st century, yet it was easy to imagine how it would have been in those far off days when the castle would have dominated everything around it with, perhaps, just the few humble dwellings, outside its walls, which marked the first makings of a town. No shops, no restaurants, no posh hotels. From the ramparts of the castle, there would have been nothing to intrude upon a landscape of farmland and distant mountains, with the river making its serpentine way from Lough to Bay.

The castle still retains its dominant position, of course, but now, just across the road from it is the beautiful catholic church of Donegal, with the lovely round bell tower, or, camponile…a quite distinctive feature to this beautiful church and the two seem to vie with each other for your attention.

Seeing the congregation coming out of the church made us realize that the morning was getting on apace and that a little light refreshment would not go amiss, therefore, with our thoughts tuned in to a welcome cup of coffee, we looked for and eventually found a nice little café, which was actually open, in one of the small roads just off one of the main thoroughfares and, with a feeling of gratitude on behalf of our feet, we made ourselves comfortable at one of the outside tables. Misty was duly tethered to a conveniently situated post (tethered being a quite appropriate word to use as he has become roughly about the size of a small pony) and our tea and coffee was brought out to us by a pretty wee girl with a cheery smile and that musical Irish accent that I love so much. I mean, what more could anyone want? There we were, settled back and wonderfully relaxed, in a way which is only possible in Ireland. With the September sun bestowing its benevolence fully upon us and bringing with it that extra touch of luxury, we thought it just had to be the most perfect way in which to spend the next ten minutes or so…until, that is, that ten minutes was stretched to well over an hour by the unexpected appearance of a very charming, late sixtyish gentleman who came out of the café, saw us sitting there and immediately noticed Jeff's camera.

Well, that turned out to be only the start of it. A discussion then ensued about the virtues of said camera and that, although it was possible to own a much more expensive model (and believe me, this one was not cheap) it was possible to achieve with this very camera, everything that any photographer could ever hope to achieve. After which, he revealed to us that he was, or had been, a professional photographer. I suppose, by the so obviously knowledgeable way that he had been talking, we should have realized. He really did give the impression that he knew what he was talking about and when he took Jeff's camera into his own hands, he handled it like a professional. The obvious outcome was that, before long, the chitchat turned to a more hands-on session with the actual camera. Jeff was really put through his paces, using me as his subject (complete with a giant bottle of champagne) following the quite rapid, quick-fire instructions from our new friend, whilst getting down on one knee and snapping shot after shot, with the result that, in all honesty, I think he learnt quite a lot. (And the resultant photos were really good).

Whilst all of this was going on, I, still rather bemused by the speed with which it had all happened, kept thinking to myself…It's happening again! Here we are, back in Ireland for not even twenty four hours and once again, we two unexceptional people and our quite outstanding canine, are being given the 'full Irish', as I have come to think of it. These wonderful people are so warm and so full of genuine, open-hearted goodness that when, as has just happened, we become the recipients of their truly honest friendship, it makes me feel so very privileged. For what ever reason it may be and I shall never really comprehend it, we do seem to attract the attentions of so many lovely people. I can only assume that the initial attraction is one rather scrumptious Irish Setter, whose name shall remain unmentioned. He is already beginning to behave in a manner which denotes serious traces of a probably quite definitely merited attitude of superstar vanity.

By now, of course, our once hot refreshments were sadly cold and remained on the table, unfinished. You see, after the practical lesson in the art of making the ultimate use of the equipment that he had, Jeff and I were then invited to see this pro's portfolio, which was stored on his laptop and, after viewing these examples of his work, it became obvious that we had just had the privilege of being personally tutored by a Master. Impressive would, just about, cover it.

We could have still been there if we hadn't eventually made our polite excuses and continued on our way. My one regret being that, all through this very interesting and pleasant interlude, I had never given any thought to asking his name. Even so, we will both remember him with a great fondness. And we still have the 'special' photos with which to remember both him and the happy time that we spent with him.

Just to recap, I shall now explain, as well as I can, the giant champagne bottle. It stood, you must understand, about twenty feet high, on the gable-end wall of a wine store which was on the oposite corner of the road from where we were sitting. It was, in fact, yet another example of the very fine art of wall painting that is such a feature in Ireland. Despite the size of it, it was, in every other respect, extremely realistic...complete with popped cork and the inevitable bubbles. Later, looking at the shots of me and the bottle, I look like some demented alcoholic, with my arms wrapped, in a euphoria of delight, around this vision of alcoholic bliss. (Seriously, they really are terrific pics and the professional advice in the taking of them is more than evident).

So, having spent so much time with our new friend, we decided to get on our way, after all, this morning's visit to Donegal was only ever intended as an introductory reconnaissance...and I know that we will be back, sometime during the next week. With that in mind, we headed back and, don't think that we had completely forgotten about Killybegs…no way! We may have altered, ever so slightly, our original 'plan' for today but, I could not dismiss the chance of seeing this 'Seasalt Vera' special, for the first time. For heaven's sake, I would never have slept tonight knowing that I had been so negligent as to commit such an enormous sin of omission. The biggest fishing port in Ireland! Not a chance. Besides, I must have my daily dose of the ozone drug, the first of the day, or risk serious consequences.…at least before the saline levels in my bloodstream drop too low and a mild attack of lunacy takes over my conscious mind. If that should happen, well, anything that I may inadvertently do, I could not possibly be held responsible for. One quick snort, however, of that elixir of the ocean and all is well. Poor Jeff. Maybe, now, you are already beginning to feel some of that sympathy for him that I mentioned earlier. Indeed, no one deserves it more.

Even approaching Killybegs, I could feel that tingle which can only precede an attack of ozone deficiency. A typical addictive reaction, I suppose, to even a short delay in the inhaling or snorting, which is, I believe, to be the more accurate terminology of the imbibing of the daily fix. Once fortified, I of course went into immediate raptures over everything and, so typical of me, did my very best to look at everything at once, which is quite hard to do without actually dislocating ones neck.

I mean, how amazing can you get! Killybegs was everything that I had expected, even hoped for…and more besides. The harbour literally teems with fishing boats of all sizes, from small boats, no bigger than a dinghy to small trawlers and then, to some of the largest fishing boats that I had ever seen, the sort of boat that would leave the shelter of the harbour and be out at sea for weeks, maybe even months. One such boat bore my name, Veronica, which thrilled me hugely. Somehow, it gave me quite a feeling of kinship with her. A special bond, if you like. I shall make a point of saying a wee prayer for her safety and that of her crew, the next time that she leaves harbour.

As usual, just the sights and the blend of, to me, exotic aromas, which seem to emanate from a town which works the ocean for a living, sent me, Seasalt Vera, into the usual ecstasy of delight…and, as usual, I caused poor Jeff the utmost embarrassment with my, no doubt, overenthusiastic excitement. But then, what's new?

With a few pangs of regret, I allowed myself to be escorted away from all things nautical and we headed off, leaving Killybegs behind, just for now and within minutes, just through Largy, we came upon a narrow coastal road which we hoped would lead us into yet more in the way of picturesque landscape and we were not disappointed. But then, why was I not surprised?…you can never be disappointed in Ireland. I, of all people, should have known better than to even doubt it…and narrow it was, this new deviation, indeed, very much so, in places, yet it was so well worthwhile as it led us, climbing all the way, into the grandeur of the mountains. The views of both sea and mountains were actually becoming ever more breathtaking the higher that we climbed, which was a steady, continuous climb.

Rough moorland grass, rippling, in an ever changing pattern, as it was buffeted by the wind and then, brighter patches of autumnal purple heather making gay splashes of colour in amongst the vibrant covering of green sward and golden-brown bracken through which large outcrops of rock burst forth, thrusting themselves upwards, bold and dominating and giving a feeling of eternal endurance, a feeling that these very same outcrops of solid, living, lichen marked rock, their very shape the result of eons of being constantly exposed to the elements, had been here since time immemorial…and, of course, scenery such as this could never be complete without the ubiquitous Irish sheep.

How I love the sheep. I mean, to me, they seem to epitomize everything that I love about Ireland, as they roam the land, forever chomping away and, like today, their black faces turned in our direction with that steady gaze from eyes which seem to hold the wisdom and stoicism of the ages, looking back at us and, no doubt thinking to themselves…'here we go again, lads. Get ready to pose for more bloody tourists'. Seriously, though, have you never noticed it? Whenever you find yourself within the vicinity of a flock of sheep, as if on command, they will all turn in unison and look at you in just that way. A sort of steady, unblinking gaze whilst, at the same time, continuing their never ending mastication with jaws that don't even so much as break rhythm in their steady chomping. Of course, there is nothing at all intimidating in that look. Goodness me, no. It's just a look of patient scrutiny which always gives me an impression of the most sublime contentment… a quite happy and total resignation towards their particular lot in life. Just as long as there is some nice grass or heather to chomp at, life could not get to be much better. For a sheep, that is. In fact, if it wasn't for all these bloody tourists, intruding upon their peaceful contemplation of the more important things in life, it could be considered well nigh perfect. Like I said, for a sheep.

By this time, (and it must have had something to do with watching the continuous motion of all those masticating jaws) all of a sudden, we realized just how hungry we were and once that thought had taken a hold it began to gnaw at our subconscious like a voracious piranha until it became imperative that we find a place to stop and bring out the rations. Like NOW! The obvious place was upon us, almost before we knew it, as we rounded quite a sharp bend in the road…and there it was. The fact that it had been designated a special Viewing Point was also pretty obvious as the views were nothing if not stunning. WOW! And, there you go. I'm doing it again! I can't help it! Using that word again, I mean. Only recently, in speaking to a young newspaper reporter, I mentioned this WOW factor which, to me, is the quintessence of Ireland and I have to say that really, no matter how great may be ones command of the English language, nothing can describe the miracle that is Ireland better than that one little word. So don't be too surprised if you hear me use it quite frequently and I make no apologies for doing so.

From our elevated position, the views were, as I said, absolutely stunning, with nothing but the great Atlantic Ocean the only thing between us and America. Looking down, the cliffs and the rocky shores at the foot of the Slieve League Mountains were a riot of all the oceanic colours imaginable. From the delicate aquamarine of the clear waters close in to the shore to the deeper, cobalt blue of the middle distance. Rolling surf coming in, wave after wave, creaming and foaming around the base of the cliffs like frolicking little puppies before sending delicate, scintillating spray to fill the air with diamonds. No crashing surf today, just gentle waves, caressing and playful. A love affair between the sea and the shore.

Coming more inland, the delicate and subtle shading of green and brown, beige and gold, in all the dips and hollows of the Slieve League, blended so perfectly with the shades of such a delicate hue which came off the sea and then intermingled with the blue of the sky. A sky marred only by a few innocuous looking white clouds. A picture to stir the soul of any…and surely, there could be very few who could be so devoid of passion as to remain unmoved by the sheer magnificence of all this natural beauty. It would be impossible not to feel ones spirits soar towards the heavens at such a sight...and we were no exception.

Until we had captured everything that there was to capture, on film...or its digital equivalent...even our desperate need for sustenance momentarily took a back seat. I mean, what a situation, what a mind-numbing view to accompany our modest lunch. Modest it may have been, in the form of sandwiches and coffee, however, it was eaten with the gusto that can only be achieved when you are (a) really hungry and (b) when all the world seems to be, at that point in time, quite wonderful. When those two criteria combine, that's when it seems to crank itself up a notch or two. Strange how the appetite seems to surge or ebb in unison with the state of the human spirit. Suffice it to say that ours was in full spate and it was all washed down with great amounts of happy conversation and equal amounts of laughter. Even Misty seemed to feel the occasion merited some small imput from him as he began to systematically stick his nose into everything that we were having, with the hope that maybe, just maybe, some of it might by-pass his nose and fall into his mouth.

Duly fed and watered and with Misty being given the opportunity of stretching his long legs...amongst other things...we continued along this coast road, our eyes avidly feasting on and storing up in our own mental cameras, to be replayed again later, the ever changing vistas of this coastal beauty which remained with us, our constant companion, mile after mile. Tempting glimpses of white-gold sand denoted the presence of delightful little beaches which, unfortunately, were a long way down and seemingly inaccessible.

At a little town called Carrick, we found ourselves back on the R263 and so, with the vivid memories of the coastal road along which we had just travelled still fresh in our minds, we found new things to marvel at as we drove through mountain and moorland. Instead of the coast on our left, we now had the glory of the Slieve League and so, the predominant colours now, were the colours of the season, gold and bronze, copper and honey...and the ubiquitous green that can only be seen in this land of the green. Wherever there were swathes of grass, amongst the heather and the bracken, the green seemed even more vibrant than ever by contrast. (And that's something else that will probably instil in you the overwhelming desire, the quite inordinate temptation, to throttle me…and by that I mean my unfortunate habit of forever harping on about the 'green'. I can only beg your indulgence but can make no apology for my enthusiasm, or should I say over enthusiasm…the fact remains that it is a different green to that which you will see anywhere else. It really is. Believe me! And I know, simply because I know myself so well that, as a consequence, I will lapse, occasionally…I'm bound to. It really is, quite regrettably, inevitable. However, all that I can do is to promise that I will, at all times, do my level best to contain myself as much as I can).

From experience, we have found that you can never become complacent about Ireland. I've said it so many times, I know. It really is a precious jewel set down twixt the two bodies of water which are the Irish Sea and the Atlantic Ocean. From the northernmost part of the Republic down the the southernmost tip of the Peninsulas, it is a veritable art gallery, crammed with scenic masterpieces of such natural beauty as to stun ones credibility. That credibility has been put to the test again, today. Our first day in this wonderful County Donegal and it has managed to amaze us, in such a short space of time and without even trying…and it had, by no means, had done with us, yet.

Glencolumbkille…what a brilliant name…and Glen Bay, all of this suddenly opened out before our eyes, with the grandeur of Glen Head dominating and filling our vision in this panorama which, from our elevated position on the cliff tops could do no more than bring forth that now familiar word for which there will never be a more appropriate alternative…WOW! Remote as this scene of spectacular beauty was, there were two other cars pulled into the small space provided, just off road, for the purpose of seeing it, not through glass but, out in the open where you could feel the wind off the sea in your face and taste the salinity of the atmosphere as here, the surf did crash and explode against rock and cliffs. Cliffs that were as old as all time. Nothing gentle about this. No tender kiss of the sea against the sandy shore. This was wild! It was exhilarating! It was fantastic! This was real Seasalt Vera paradise. You know what I'm like, for heaven's sake. Even the slightest accumulation of water can send me into ecstasy…even a large puddle can do the trick…and you also know that I love the ocean in all her many changing moods but, I quite unashamedly thrill to my very bones when she is in one of her really tempestuous, sort of pissed off kind of moods.

Standing high above the surging waters of this glorious bay, on this

September afternoon, I felt as though I just wanted to fly, to glide in the teeth of the wind along with the gulls and feel their joyous exhilaration, and that feeling was given even more impetus by the fact that I was able to go with Jeff and Misty along the cliff top, covered as it was with tufts of long, wind-flattened grass…something which I would have found quite impossible to do just a few months ago. I was elated. It felt surreal to feel, once again, such an indescribable thrill, just by walking along that cliff…but then, I have learnt that the worst thing that you can do is to ever take anything, anything at all, for granted…even the most basic of things, like being able to walk.

Misty, of course, had a great time, caught up, as he was, in all the excitement. He seemed to sense the joy of the moment and immediately proceeded to create his own doggie version of joy by chasing around like the beloved idiot he is in a vain attempt to try and out-run the wind and the gulls and by just being the young, healthy Irish Setter that he is. So much energy. So much strength in those long legs…and how wonderful, just to watch and to admire, for there is much to admire in our very own canine Adonis. I know that Pride is one of the Seven Deadly Sins but my pride was obvious for all the world to see (or at least, the handful of people who just happened to be around at that moment) as I watched him having fun in his own little way, his eyes shining and his glossy coat a glory of shimmering copper.

Impressive and thrilling as was this glorious extravaganza, this miracle of coastal splendour, as the sea united with the land, its eternal lover…land with its Jurassic rocks, its towering cliffs and the surf flowing and creaming in its never ending lover's caress, all of this, quite unexpectedly, became the painted backdrop to one of Man's own miracles, a miracle of engineering, by the appearance of an Air Sea Rescue helicopter. She roared in over the top of the cliffs, large, red and very noisy. The sound of her rotors was almost deafening at such close range, which of course made it all the more exciting. I don't know if the exercise was for real or if it was merely a practice run, it didn't really matter (although I suppose it would have mattered enormously if some poor soul was in trouble out there), however, for us, who could only watch with ever growing fascination, it was the display of aerobatics and flying skills that kept us engrossed. Circling, swooping and diving and then, as if closely inspecting the rocks and the pounding surf at the base of the cliffs of Glen Head, it would stop dead, remaining almost stationary as it hovered, just yards away from us, the deep thrum of its rotors filling the air and almost seeming to make it vibrate.

After about ten minutes, it was all over. Nobody got rescued, so it was either a false alarm or just a practice. Not that it mattered…everyone had had a wonderful time…an added bonus, so to speak. Then, off it went, disappearing as suddenly as it had arrived.

The departure of the helicopter seemed to signal the disappearance of everyone else, including us. Time was now getting on but, nevertheless, we decided to carry on a bit further around this particular coastline, which eventually brought us around to the far side of Glen Head, to yet another little bay…much smaller than Glen Bay…but we stopped, in the appropriately provided car park as there was something else of great interest and only across the road from where we were parked. It seemed to be a special tourist attraction as there were already a couple of coaches parked up as we arrived. The obvious attraction was a sort of heritage museum, in the form of a collection of old-world thatched cottages, which had been arranged in such a fashion as to form what could easily have been a small village from the long-ago past. Rough tools and house-hold items lay strewn casually about, as if someone had just been using them. It was quite odd, this feeling that the past was still around in the fabric of these very humble cottages. We noticed a quite unique way of thatching in these old Irish cottages which is different to any thatching that I have ever seen before…which is what makes them so unique to Ireland. Now, how brainy do you have to be to think of that? Honestly! I've really excelled myself with that wee piece of deduction!

There was a small café within the enclosure of the museum, however, we didn't stop for, as I said, time was getting on. We gave Misty a quick run on the nice sandy beach of this small bay and then we started back, the same way that we had come and began the journey back to Dunkineely…though not before we made the discovery that our Misty had his own fleet of buses. And before you really do begin to think that I've lost some marbles, allow me to explain. Misty and buses? What on earth is she going on about, now? And I know that is what you're thinking, so there is no need to be polite. Besides, you know what I'm like! So, what happened, was this…one of the buses on the car park belonged to one of Ireland's chief carriers…Bus Eireann…and what do they have as their logo, emblazoned all down both sides of their buses? Yes, you've got it…a gorgeous Irish Setter, with it's graceful legs flexed in the attitude of a full run. I was so pleased, tickled pink, in fact, that I actually took a photograph of the side of the bus. Yes, I know! I know! That demon, Pride again. I mean, my Misty on every bus in Ireland! Wow! Which is, of course, yet something else to inflate his already expanding ego.

Our journey back was a joy, filled, as it was, with happy recollections of all that we had done and, how distant did this morning feel to us, so much had we seen and done in such a short space of time…just a few hours yet a whole world of experiences.

One thing we particularly wanted to do, before going back to the cottage was to stop off at Fintra Strand…a gorgeous, typically Irish, white-sand beach set in Fintragh Bay. Strange, the two different spellings, but that was the way of it…anyway, we had noticed the existence of this lovely beach after passing through Killybegs, what now seems like ages ago and promised ourselves that we would check it out later. To me, this was what I had dreamed of, all those long months after my surgery…dreaming of Ireland and, in particular, dreaming of being able to walk along a beach with my man and my dog. For some moments, I just stood there, taking it all in and finding it very difficult to reconcile the dream to the reality. However, after giving myself a good metaphorical shake, I just gave in to the thrill of it and almost went as daft as my dog. Just think of it…my Jeffy, my Misty and me. My two loved ones close by me and all of us behaving like adolescent idiots. Wonderful! There could not have been a more perfect way of calling it a day. I don't think I shall ever forget those very special twenty minutes, or so, that we spent on Fintra Strand on this, our first day in this very special land. Oh, we will be back, that is a certainty. It has all the makings of becoming one of our favourite places…and I don't even have to think what would be Misty's views on that…and it's not too far from 'home'.

Killybegs was a quiet haven now, with the onset of evening, but the tang of the sea and the sight of all the boats had lost none of its delight for yours truly. There is something very different about a fishing harbour, a place that actually gets its living from the sea, from an ordinary seaside resort…and that is why it has this special attraction for me. The sea must be in my blood, somewhere way back in time, for it is only when I can see it, or smell it, that I feel myself to belong.

Strange, how you soon get accustomed to things. The first time that we drove along the narrow lane leading to the cottage, which is only twenty four hours ago, it had seemed unending but now, familiarity has taken over and normality has set in.

How welcoming everything felt, as we unlocked our front door and entered our wee cottage. After such a marvellous day, it almost seemed to feel like home, which is ridiculous, seeing that we had been in residence for such a short time.

As we sat enjoying a coffee and happily going over everything that had happened on this memorable first day, the evening light was changing, ever so subtly, the lights and shades of the waters of Donegal Bay. Blue/grey was touched, here and there with a hint of peaches and roses. The sky was turning a deeper tone of the same colours with rays of purest gold shooting out from behind delicate clouds of grey and opal and mother of pearl, whilst, in the distance, the glory of the sun-washed Crownarad Mountains seemed to reach out and beckon, almost as if it were possible to walk the golden pathway across the water and step ashore in paradise.

It seemed a sacrilege to allow such a perfect evening to just slip away so, as neither of us was really hungry, we set out for a stroll across the fields, opposite the cottage, which gently slope down towards the shore. Sometimes, there are sheep in this field but, this evening, there were none and so, Misty was able to run off a bit more steam. His energy is quite boundless but what a joy it is to watch him. I never tire of that lovely sight…the graceful beauty of a lovely animal. There was evidence of rabbits all over the place and so he was ever vigilant. Even at home, across our own fields, his greatest fun is when he's chasing rabbits…not that he is very good at catching them, at least not yet. They are much too fast and canny for our boy. The fun, however, is not so much in catching one as in giving the poor wee things one almighty scare.

What a joy it was to stand, hand in hand, my Jeffy and I, looking out over the bay…the mountains of gold in one direction, Donegal and a few other little villages, dotted along the far shore and part of the Blue Stack Mountains way around to the left, in the purple, shadowy haze of distance.

We lingered for quite some time, which gave Misty a bit of extra time to play out his game of intrepid explorer and then, quite reluctantly, we made our way, slowly, back home.

Dinner was a bit of a celebration…nothing fancy but, our first proper meal…and then time to settle down for the evening. Quite suddenly, the light had gone and where we could, a couple of hours ago, see the distant villages across the far side of the bay, now, we could see the lights, twinkling like stars in the distance and where, not very long ago there was a golden pathway across the water now there was a silver highway, as the moon took up his usual nightly routine.

If I turn my head I can see Jeff as he quietly thinks ahead to tomorrow, sitting quite content, surrounded by maps and making wee notes. I know that he will have a few ideas to put before the Board, which consists of Jeff, Me and Misty, tomorrow morning and then we will discuss it and decide upon our plan of action for the day. Our famous Plan. What fun we derived from this wee bit of nonsense, last year…our morning meeting of the Board and then, our Plan. That was, of course, when we first became bitten by the special Irish bug. This tiny, wee chap has a quite harmless sting with which he injects into the ready recipient, a potion most magic…and as far as I know, there is no possible cure. Once the effects have taken a hold, they are for life.

As for me, I am sitting at the table, gazing out at the glimmer of moon-washed water and the distant twinkling lights. Jeff has just placed a glass of wine before me and now, I am all eager and excited about the prospect of your evening visit. I still can't believe that our deep and abiding friendship is about to start a new phase, another chapter. Everything is ready for you…the cottage is cosy and there is a warmth of a different kind which is just waiting for you to arrive. And here you are! Now we will move to a more comfortable place than the dining table, although, if I'm honest, I think this will be my own favourite place, from now on. The views over the water are in evidence, no matter which window you may use but, I just like it here. I can sit with my elbows on the table, my chin on my hands and just gaze out at the beauty of the scene which lies out there.

And now, if you are willing and if you will excuse my no doubt, over-enthusiastic welcome…I mean, what's new?…perhaps you will allow me to begin to tell you of our day. I shall never settle, until I do, so, as always, share it with me, please and it will help me to get it all sorted in my daft head and suitably filed away. You, of all people, know what I'm like.

Jeff and I have spent the last couple of hours just going over everything…a merging of two minds and a blending of two hearts, hearts which are so full of love, each for the other, hearts which will always beat as one…and now it is that time of the day when I like to take my own personal stock of things and give my thanks for, in truth, I have so very much to give thanks for. In saying that, it shames me to have to admit that giving thanks isn't something that I've always done. But then, I expect that we are all a wee bit guilty of that at some time in our lives. Call it part of the thoughtlessness of youth. When we are young we do tend to take everything for granted, especially in our adolescent years when we achieve the ultimate level of rebellious arrogance, even to the point of convincing ourselves that it is only what we are entitled to, after all. No. It is only when you can boast of having attained a more advanced age and have lived long enough to have experienced some of the nasty bits in life that you begin to develop the art of distinguishing the difference between what really matters and what does not and that is when you begin to realize just how fortunate you have actually been for pretty much most of your life and that the time has now come to give a word or two of thanks to the One to whom we all owe so very much.

Advancing years also makes you appreciate to the full all the little things, the simpler and much more fulfilling things. Like the love of a wonderful man or the joy of a beautiful animal or, just watching a sunset over Donegal Bay with two hands entwined and two hearts that beat as one. Does that remind you of anyone?

Anyway, before I get really carried away, allow me to return to the business in hand and carry on where I left off…as always, I thank God for all that he has given me, most of which I do not deserve. The main blessing, of course, is my Jeffy…as husbands go, I know that I have got the best…which is all the more reason why I now, in turn, give my thanks to this very special man, for his ever present love. A love that will never fail me or deceive me, or let me down.

My darling, you have made this day special for me, just as you make every day special for me, simply by being mine own. My own Jeffy. You are as the air that I breathe. You are my light in the deepest darkness, so that I am never afraid. God bless you, my husband. I love you!

And as for you, my Misty…what can I say? Once again, you have been a good lad and have made your mum and dad very proud of you. You have given us pleasure and you have brought a smile to so many other faces, along the way. May your dreams be happy, doggie dreams and may they always come true for a faithful heart such as yours. We love you.

I still can't get over just how large this room is which, as a result of what happened last night, has turned out to be something of a life-saver. Poor Misty. I did feel sorry for him and it was so out of character for him to do anything like this. I mean, ever since he was eight weeks old, he has never and I really do mean never, been any trouble during the night…not even on his very first night in his new home, a tiny wee soul, separated from mum (his real mum) and his siblings. Last night, however, for what ever reason, he just would not settle. To be honest, I didn't hear him. I mean, after the long day of driving and the subsequent excitement of our arrival, I must have zonked out very quickly and I suppose that I was more or less asleep. Eventually, however, I felt some restlessness in Jeff and when I roused myself, well, then I could hear Misty. He really sounded quite seriously distressed and as it was so unlike him, there was no way that we could just leave him like that so, Jeff went downstairs, quietened him and reassured him then lugged his bed upstairs…and up he came, lolloping up the stairs, (Misty, not Jeff) his face wearing an expression of sheepish contrition, which was so comical that it really was very difficult not to laugh and of course, that would have been quite unforgivable, because the poor lad had been quite genuinely upset. I mean, he may be a big, bold explorer when he's scouting across the fields hunting rabbits or chasing the ever elusive seagulls along the waterline on some beach…he may even be a fully paid up member of The Intrepid Trio but, when push comes to shove, God love him, he is only two years old and still very much a baby who, when scared of the dark and in a strange place, still wants his mum.

You can probably guess what happened next…yes, of course you are absolutely right…without more ado, he curled up in his bed, giving us one last apologetic look of contrition and then, almost immediately, he was snoring. And take my word for it, oh boy, can my Misty snore…and fart! Said accomplishments being performed to such a standard of excellence that he could, if it should ever be required of him, both snore and fart for England…and Ireland. Which left us to go through the whole business of trying to get settled and back to sleep again as best as we could.

Needless to say, we had no such problems tonight, in fact, he more or less took it for granted that when we came up to bed, he was coming, too. There was a fleeting look of anxiety…microseconds only…and then he was up the stairs like a streak of burnished copper, before we could change our minds and leave him to the doggie bogeyman again.

I wonder what tomorrow will bring? Whatever. You see, it really doesn't matter. It really is of no consequence because now that we are here in Ireland, every day can be guaranteed to be filled with some kind of Irish magic…the magic is always there, you see, so all you have to do is look for it and I can promise you that you will surely find it. As I told you before…it's the fairy dust.

And now I am beginning to witter, which means I need to sleep and, maybe, just maybe, dream some of the same dreams as my Misty. What do you say, funny face? Let's hope they are nice dreams tonight…dreams of mountains and beaches and surf rolling in to kiss the shore and the wind off the sea to blow away the bogeyman.

Goodnight everyone and God bless. Tomorrow will be grasped with loving hands and cherished and I hope that you will share it with us.

❀❀❀❀❀❀❀❀❀❀

As I sit here in what has now become my favourite place, (I told you that would happen, didn't I ?) just daydreaming and allowing my mind to wander, (I mean, there is plenty of empty space in there, for it to roam at will) in an effort to try and sort, into some kind of order, the events of this day, I'm gazing out, as usual, over Donegal Bay and it feels very comfortable and quite natural and yet, there is still that thrill, for me, anyway, in just looking out over, what is, this evening, smooth and placid water. Not that there is all that much to see this evening, in all honesty. Everything seems to be shrouded in a low-lying, pearly mist…that cool Irish mist which is so soft and so gentle and which I love so much. It is nothing more than a veil, as fine and delicate as gossamer and yet, it is allowing nothing more than a faint blink of light to show through from the villages across the bay. All of which is so very different from a mere twenty four hours ago when those very same lights twinkled and glittered like brilliant diamonds in the rich, dark velvet of that clear and lustrous night. Distance seemed to have a different dimension, last night, which gave the impression that those distant lights were close enough to, just maybe, reach out ones hand and grasp one of these diamonds of the night and hold it tight, like the precious thing that it was.

Notwithstanding, it has been an amazing day! In fact, it has been a wonderful day! And that, my friend, just has to be the biggest understatement, ever. Just you wait. You'll soon see and know that I am not exaggerating.

OK, so the weather has not been as good as it could have been, in fact, it has been rather wet and, all depending on how exposed we may have been at any given time, there has been a quite boisterous wind off the sea. Not a cold wind but, a wind which whipped the surface of the ocean into an ecstasy of heaving surf, thus sending spume high up the rocky shore and turning me, Seasalt Vera, into a screaming loony.

Even at this moment, as I wait for the pleasure of your company, I know that I am definitely just a wee bit the worse for wear, having suffered the effects of a quite serious overdose of the ozone drug. I mean, I feel exhilarated. I feel elated. In fact, I feel quite inordinately, as high as a kite. No wonder my darling Jeffy has taken himself off into the next room, on the pretext of planning our itinerary for tomorrow.

Seriously though, he just smiles, that gentle, loving smile, when he sees how happy I am and he has made it all so nice and cosy, indeed, all that it needs now, to add that final touch of perfection, is for you to arrive.

You will not be surprised, of course, when I tell you that I already have my customary glass of wine to hand and I promise you that it will not be the last and so, what with the warm glow in my heart from the special memories which have made today so outstanding and the bouquet emanating from a good bottle of wine, both combining to bring about a feeling of extreme contentment, I know that I could not want for anything more than all that I have right here, at this very minute, right now. I have peace. I have love. I have Jeff and I have my dear, daft pup, who is, at this moment, sitting like the devoted soul that he is, at the feet of his beloved dad. Truly, nothing could possibly improve upon a combination of blessings such as those.

I honestly can't think of any way in which today could have been improved upon, either. Of course, everyone likes to feel the sun on their face and we, my Jeffy and I, are no exception but, even if it had been a day of glorious sunshine, it could not have added any more sparkle to what has been a quite exceptional day…by my standards, anyway. Or, maybe I should perhaps amend that last statement and say…by Seasalt Vera's standards. Besides, the sun will show herself again, on another day and its beneficial warmth and cheery golden face will be appreciated all the more for a wee touch of rain. Well, quite a lot of rain, actually. I mean, let's get real here. There have been moments when it has actually come down in stair rods. Something must have well and truly pissed off whichever one of God's band of angels just happens to be in control of the weather. Not that I can complain, as it has given me the conditions which really make me feel completely alive.

Even now, just thinking back on it, I can feel a surge of total euphoria. I mean, anyone who didn't know me as well as you do, would think me to be crazy…and maybe I am but, honest to God, it has been absolutely brilliant!

I don't think there could be anywhere else quite like Ireland, where the condition of the weather matters so little. All depending on what gives you pleasure, of course…and anyway, a spot or two of sweet Irish rain never did anyone any harm. Not even when it comes down by the bucketful. At least, I don't think it ever did.

Anyway, now that you are here, I can get myself suitably cranked up and into a higher gear, which, I expect, has just made you have serious doubts and, perhaps, the rather uneasy feeling that now would be a very good time to turn around and pretend that it was all a big mistake to have come in the first place. Even so, you will soon come to see for yourself just how much fun The Intrepid Trio can derive from a wet…and I really do mean wet, day. But, of course, you will remember all my tales of our rainy-day adventures from past experience and know that nothing short of Armageddon could daunt The Intrepid Trio.

There is now a feeling of 'the calm after the storm', with the evening still and quiet and mellow and our wee home is ready, as always, to welcome you. OK, so I know that I have been blethering on, as usual but, I also know that my no doubt, typical over-enthusiasm, will, in no way, dismay you and that you will merely take it all in your stride. (Though I wouldn't blame you if you were thinking…'how on earth can I get myself out of this')?

Bless you for not saying that, even though you may have been thinking it. You know, by now, that I really am quite harmless and so please, come and make yourself at home. As always, love fills up all the corners and we are so happy to welcome you…and, well…I think you already know that.

Monday
21st September 2009

There was slightly less hilarity and rather more in the way of decorum in the bedroom department, this morning. Mind you, it is probably just as well, because I'm not exactly sure that I could have survived a repeat performance. They do say, of course, that laughter is the greatest tonic of all, but then, like everything else, they probably meant that to be in reasonable moderation. The way that I was rolling about yesterday and almost doing myself irreparable damage into the bargain, well, even Misty thought that I'd gone completely off my trolley…I mean, anybody would have thought the same, which is hardly surprising. Poor Misty, though. I'm sure he must have thought that both of us were completely raving…and no doubt despaired, totally, about the wisdom of having anything more to do with humans, especially these two rather questionable specimens, in the future. Crazy, the lot of them!

Anyway, for one thing, we had missed the glory of the sunrise, this morning, simply because there wasn't one. Oh, I know that there had been one, otherwise it would have still been dark, however, what I'm trying to say is, that it wasn't particularly noticeable.

First of all, I was rudely awakened by a cold, wet nose which had been thrust, unceremoniously and with much enthusiasm, down the back of my neck and then, when I made the big mistake of turning my head, with the vague, sort of, half asleep notion of dislodging the cold, wet fish and removing same, I realized that it was Misty. Once he was assured that he now had my total attention, he really got stuck in and proceeded to lather me with copious sloppy kisses which then had me squirming and shrieking with laughter while Misty, taking this as his cue to crank up his enthusiastic ministrations a notch or two and, quite shamefully taking undue advantage of the helpless state to which he had rendered me, then proceeded to clamp me down with one long, powerful foreleg, followed, almost immediately with the other one, all the better to finish off a good job well done. (No need for a shower, this morning. Only joking!)

I was finally rescued by Jeff, who had, by this time, made his escape and disappeared into the bathroom (coward) and then, having relieved me from the enthusiastic embrace of this large copper-coloured canine, had to don all his wet gear in preparation to take Misty up the lane. Poor Jeff. Although, to be honest, I don't think that either of them actually mind the inclemency of the weather too much…certainly not young master Hall. He loves it…the wetter the better, as far as he is concerned. I mean, rain makes muddy puddles don't you know and for our boy, mud is good. In fact, mud is absolutely the most marvellous substance, known to man…or dog. (And woe betide anyone foolhardy enough to be standing within showering distance…or should I say, splattering distance…when he decides to rid his furry person of the liquid mud that has accumulated in that once glorious, burnished, silky, copper coat).

Having been thus rescued and once again finding myself in a position to be able to breathe, (when Misty lands on top of you, it feels like a brick wall) it was lovely, just to lie for a few minutes, taking in, with enormous pleasure, my immediate surroundings and feeling that little thrill of excitement, somewhere, deep down in my stomach, as my mind (and yes, I do have one, although it may not be all that brilliant) conjured up the vista of sea and sky which I knew to be just the other side of the window (skylight).The only difference between my imagined image and the real thing was that when I did eventually get up and actually look out, the sea was veiled in a soft and gentle rain, the sort of rain that is just that little bit more than a mere mist. You know what I mean. The quintessential Irish mist which I have come to love so well. Donegal Bay was still out there…I mean, where else would it have been? It was quite unlikely to have disappeared, over night. (Stupid woman)…and, despite the ethereal iridescence of the mist and the light, showery rain, it was still every bit as beautiful as ever.

By the time my two soggy and rather bedraggled boys got back, breakfast was well on the way. My new friend, the electric cooker, seems to be one of the more obliging of their kind and so there have been no unfortunate cremations…and despite the inclemency of the weather, we ate with relish, a hearty breakfast and looked forward to the day which lay ahead of us…still untouched and just waiting to be entered into with all the gusto which is unique to The Intrepid Trio. Nobody could ever accuse us of being lacking in enthusiasm, although there are probably those who would consider us to be certifiable lunatics, who definitely need to have their heads examined by someone who knows about these things. All in the nicest possible way, of course. You see, the motto which has been adopted by The Intrepid Trio is…'make each day count'…and you do have to admit that we have given you ample proof, if proof were ever needed that, to we three, a great day is not dependant on fine weather in order to 'make each day count'.

Having demolished said hearty breakfast, out came the map, as usual, and in spreading it out all over the table, as you do, narrowly missing getting besmeared with various substances, all of which were rather sticky and gooey (I'm afraid that it will probably bear many strange smears and smudges before we've finished with it and I don't expect that we will be able to trade it in or get our money back on it when we next board the floating car park…pity) however, we did eventually come to an amicable agreement. The usual daily Plan was voted on and approved, in the usual democratic way, of course and everyone seemed more than happy with the arrangements…even Misty, who would quite happily have agreed to anything just as long as there was a chance that there may be a sausage in it for him, plus the guarantee, somewhere in his doggie contract, of at least one beach somewhere along the way.

Well, you can't be fairer than that, I suppose…and I rather think that we might be able to manage that, my gorgeous, furry beach babe, because the Plan, if we stick to it and don't go off at a tangent somewhere along the way, will eventually bring us onto that glorious west coast again only this time, somewhat higher up the coast than yesterday, having, first of all, headed north and up into the mountains. These will not be the Blue Stacks, although this grand massif will be visible in the distance, off to the right. No. The Blue Stacks are to be a special treat which we have earmarked for another day when, hopefully, they can be given our full and undivided attention.

Anyway, fortified with that full Irish, (and yes, Misty had his sausage…and more, besides) we managed to achieve a reasonably early start and, once on the road, the gentle mist which had thus blanked out the daily magic lantern show of the sunrise, seemed to open up, as if it had thought better of its earlier intentions and now wanted to clear the way for us. Which was all very much appreciated. (To whom it may concern...please note that our grateful and most humble thanks have been offered).

Just before Killybegs, we turned off and headed for a small town called Ardara. We were soon consumed with and drawn into the vastness of the miles upon miles of empty moorland (empty, except for the ubiquitous sheep, of course) which kept us company on both sides. The lower plains of the surrounding hills were an ocean of burnished gold, swaying and rippling as it was caught up in the unrestrained and joyous moorland breeze. Here and there, this golden mass of long, course grass was broken by great swathes of purple and emerald green, thereby revealing the hidden, secret treasures of September heather and sweet luscious grass. Bold, brash and quite unashamedly brazen, these vivid colours proclaimed their rightful place in this riot of glorious autumnal colour.

The road along which we were travelling wound through ever wilder and more mountainous scenic magnificence, the closer that we got to Ardara indeed, the very mountains themselves seemed to draw us towards them, beckoning us, as they reared up, on both sides, with Common Mountain on the left of us and Mulmosog Mountain on the right. They loomed up, in all their regal and stately magnificence, almost as if they were standing sentinel and so forming a natural portal through which the silvery-grey ribbon of road passed, as we drove between the two and, just beyond, at the base of Glengesh Hill, we came upon a parking place, seemingly in the middle of nowhere, positioned there, of course, for the very purpose of admiring this wild, untamed beauty which lay all around us. It was, without a doubt, the perfect place to stop and, well, just admire and try, as best one could, to absorb the quite amazing ambience of this awesome scene and cherish it.

To describe it is almost beyond my humble capabilities. The stillness and the quietude was profound and yet, at the same time, strangely exhilarating. I mean, this was truly being 'at one with nature.' Here in this wild and magnificent setting, it was possible to feel your soul soar into the very heart of the mountain wind and fly along with it, rejoicing with the almost unbearable thrill of it.

At this point, we were almost into Ardara but, just outside the town, this small town set, as it is, amongst these beautiful moors and hills, we came upon a huge lough…Sheskinmore Lough…a lough of such great length that it covered many miles before it finally flowed out into Loughros More Bay, which was way over on the west coast and from thence, into the ocean. There are loughs in great abundance in this mountainous region of County Donegal, some are small, some are large…and then there are those that are so huge that they are like inland seas. This one came under that latter heading.

Passing through Ardara, which was all that we had intended doing, we took the road which went on up to Clooney and, in so doing, discovered a hidden treasure, a gem of the utmost brilliance.

Just a few miles after by-passing Ardara, we came across one of those narrow…and I do mean narrow, coastal 'scenic routes', this one actually having a very interesting name…the Santa Anna Drive. I mean, how marvellous is that? (There I go with names again). With a name like that, we just had to follow it, regardless of what, if anything, may be at the end of it or even where it may lead us, for that matter. However, we were soon to find out…much to the unadulterated joy of Seasalt Vera and her beach bum of a dog.

Jeff eventually pulled into a place of tall sand dunes…and I mean, huge ones, topped with course beach grass and towering way above my head. (But then, with my diminutive stature, it wouldn't take much, in order to tower over my head).

Donning our wax coats, which seemed appropriate, as the wind was strong off the sea and just a wee bit chill and the rain, which, although not heavy, was quite wetting, we entered the realms of oceanic paradise. At least, Seasalt Vera's idea of oceanic paradise. Nothing could have prepared us, as we rounded the last tall sand dune, for the breathtakingly beautiful sight which suddenly opened up before us. For some seconds, to be honest, I just stood there like the numpty that I am and just gawped at this quite amazing vista of white sand, which seemed to stretch for as far as the eye could see. It was absolutely spectacular, this infinity of beach with its fringe of dunes, the long dune grasses lying flat as the wind off the sea lashed at it…and, as I have already said, these were some dunes. I kid you not, they were impressive enough to have come out of the Sahara Desert (well, almost…I mean that may be a slight exaggeration) and then, oh boy, the ocean. WOW. The ocean was a totally glorious cauldron of seething, heaving water. It was absolutely brilliant!

The wind was scouring it and sending it in, towards the beach, on massive, rolling waves. Wave after wave, after wave, crashing and thundering as they rose, curled over at the peak and then, cascaded down, in a maelstrom of flying spray, before finally running out of steam, so to speak and running up the shore.

Deep cobalt blue, tinged here and there, with a hint of green. Surf which was white and quite dazzling to the eye with spray whipping off the crests of the waves as the wind harassed it and sent it into a frenzied turmoil. Surface sand scurried along the beach on the wind as if on some urgent errand of its own and yours truly just stood there, with arms outstretched and just shrieked with the pure joy of it…something which seemed to escape from some deep and remote part of me and was accomplished with as much fervour as I could muster. I didn't even have to worry about embarrassing my Jeffy, because there was nobody else in sight. It was so brilliant and as for our daft pup, well, he did a good imitation of a whirling dervish and then, with the most comical, lopsided grin on his face, went streaking along the beach, just at the water's edge, as if his very life depended on it. Being, by that time, already covered in sand, he got into a run-about with his dad…after which, I would have been hard pressed to decide who had derived the most pleasure from it or, which of the two was covered with the most sand. Both were panting at the end of it and all three of us were behaving in a most wonderfully idiotic yet, quite ecstatic manner…I mean, it was all so unexpected. I didn't even know that we were heading for a beach, any beach…but this one. Like I said…wow. A hidden gem, indeed, the element of surprise rendering it all the more remarkable. And I must say that my Misty looked very dashing, wearing, once again, his nifty bandana…albeit a bit wet now and weighted down with the covering of wet sand. A bit like one of those knitted swimsuits that we used to wear as kids, way back in the 1950's. Do you remember? Those used to sag down around your ankles once you got them wet.

The rain came on, just as we were heading back to the car and it felt a bit like being flailed with chips of ice, being, as it was, driven by the wind but…were we in any way put out?…not a bit of it. We were, all three of us, on too much of a high to be even slightly down cast by a bit of water…well, quite a lot of water, actually. I mean, I was still laughing like a loony whilst trying my best to, with both hands, hold my hat clamped down on my head. (I told you that we were, all three of us, just on that border-line of being considered certifiable).

And so, it was a very happy Intrepid Trio who, having de-sanded you know who, the hairy one, finally continued on our way, following the same coastal road up to Portnoo and then Naran. The ocean and its paramour, that magnificent sandy beach, were our constant companion, indeed, there hardly seemed to be any break in this never ending, breathtaking infinity of white sand…it seemed to be continuous for as far as the eye could see. There were views of quite stunning splendour, of ocean and sand and even the sky, which was a constantly changing pattern of fast moving cloud, seeming to add its own theatrical, quite dramatic effect to the scene, which ever way you happened to look. There were amazing views over Dunmore Head in one direction and Inishkeel in the other and out over Gweebarra Bay, also…views which, to my mind, were as grand as any that you could find anywhere in the world.

Seasalt Vera could have stayed there forever. I mean, you know what I'm like. The slightest whiff of ozone and I'm well away. However, the morning was really getting on apace and so we reluctantly withdrew from this oceanic paradise and eventually found a nice place to pull in and break out the flask of coffee. (Please note that I always remember to bring it along with us now…full, I mean. Which must surely merit a wee bit of credit). And what a perfect spot. If we had actually been actively looking, which we weren't, not really, anyway…we could not have found anything more splendid than this and it was a place which we came upon purely by accident.

OK, so it was nothing out of the ordinary, just a few tables, situated by the bridge which spans the Gweebarra River but with such superb views down the river, towards Gweebarra Bay. Without realising it we had, in fact, driven right around the bay and were now looking out upon it from where the river flows into it. Anyway, it was totally perfect, which turned an ordinary pit stop into something a wee bit special.

By this time, the heavy rain had stopped and so, it was all so very pleasant and it would have been so very easy, just to sit there for much longer…like all day…what with the gentle ripple of the waters of the river as it flowed along its bed, sedately and without any great fuss or haste, just a mere whisper of sound, tickling the pebbles and rocks which just happened to be in its path and the birds were singing in the riverside shrubbery…such a sweet melody which was in perfect harmony with the hazy sunlight which now suffused everything with a muted glow and, as a result, filled the two of us with a wonderfully mellow feeling of well-being. It is fleeting moments in time, just such as this, which have a tendency to linger in the memory far longer than something of much greater import, have you ever noticed that?

Duly refreshed, the coffee, although from a flask, having been very welcome, we got back onto the road again and actually crossed over the bridge which, as I said, spans the Gweebarra River. Actually keeping on this same road seemed, to us, with only the map as a guide and with no real idea of what lay ahead of us, as good an idea as any other and, in the fullness of time, would, hopefully, bring us to another town, Dunglow, which then cuts through The Rosses…The Rosses being a region of moorland and loughs, which seems to form the central part of something that closely resembles an ornamental doily, with its delicately patterned, lacy border of coastline, made up, as it is, of a fantastic and intricate maze of small inlets and tiny islands with, in the distance, the larger Aran Island…or, Arranmore Island, to give it its full, Sunday-best title…and beyond all of that is, well…the vastness of the Atlantic Ocean.

Anyway…that will do for us!

The quite staggering beauty of this intricate coastline was pure Irish magic. I mean, where on earth do you start? In which ever direction the eye wandered, a seascape beyond belief, opened up to both enchant and delight the senses. So many tiny islands, each one like a precious jewel set in crystal of the deepest blue and each with its own creamy necklace as the ocean caressed each miniature shoreline.

Names like Inishkeeragh, Rutland, Termon were some of the islands, to name but a few and then, higher up the coastline there is Rosses Bay, which flows right out into the Atlantic and beyond which, are other islands with magic names…Owey, Cruit, The Stag Rocks.

Aran Island was, of course, the largest of all the islands and is, in fact, only one of three islands in the group called The Aran Islands, anyway, as luck would have it, just as we pulled into the tiny harbour, the ferry boat came in…only a small craft but one which could, quite rightfully boast of doing a regular return trip, to and from the Aran Islands, each and every day. A very important job for such a little boat and one which was carried out with great pride and enormous gusto, along with a flurry of pennants and a wee blast, or two, on the hooter. Well done, bonnie boat…and how grand you looked, in all your fine colours.

For now, the rain still held off and there was a glimmer of watery sunlight which seemed to smile down upon the wee boat as she left us, en route to the island and so, it was relaxing and such a treat to linger for a while, just sitting on some coils of rope, surrounded by lobster creels and small fishing boats, which were either floating and bobbing, at the extent of their mooring line or were pulled up onto the shale and, as the eye took in all the beauty of the scene which was being enacted before us, the other senses were satisfied in the inhaling of the intoxicating, at least, to yours truly, aromas so redolent of the ocean and the sounds of the things which make up a small harbour such as this…lapping water, the singing of rigging against masts, etc…and so, we stayed for as long as it took for the wee ferry to offload her incoming passengers and then take onboard her new, outgoing ones and then, with a final wee toot and a surge of frothy water from beneath her stern, she disappeared around the harbour wall and the lighthouse…which was then our cue to also up-anchor, so to speak and make our way further up this unimaginably beautiful coastline.

Within a fairly short distance, after leaving Burtonport, we unexpectedly discovered yet another narrow road, the sort which always ends in some quite amazingly picturesque place of scenic wonder…and this one, in no way disappointed us. Rather marvellously, this road went all the way to the very tip of Cruit Island which, on arrival, opened up even more of that scenic splendour than we had yet encountered, leaving us, momentarily, quite stunned. This narrow road had been, quite literally, so narrow, that it really had been impossible to even imagine what, if anything, could be at the end of it. The view with which we were eventually confronted, was stunning, to say the least. We were able to see the ocean, on both sides, as we progressed, especially along the latter half of the road, where it narrowed even more but, even so, it still came as a surprise when we finally reached the point at the very end, where, believe it or not, there was actually a golf club (not much chance of retrieving a lost ball in these surroundings and that's for sure) and, even more important, at least to me…the most beautiful little beach. A perfect crescent of white sand, small but as beautiful as something from the Mediterranean and with water lapping the shore that was of such unbelievable clarity that you could see every tiny shell and pebble and every little piece of the delicate, floating, frond-like weed. Indeed, it was so clear that if one put ones hand into the water, the perspective was strangely magnified…as was every single grain of sand.

But then, this is Ireland, when even the most amazing sight or experience, which can, quite simply, stun the senses, can be found just at the end of a narrow road, just such as this one and which seems, at the time, to be leading to nowhere in particular.

Needless to say, there was no doubt as to where we would stop and have our lunch. I mean, just look out there! Absolutely perfect.

And then, wouldn't you just know it? It started to rain. We had noticed, for quite some time that cloud, heavier and quite dark and forbidding, was coming in and heading our way, but had not really taken any notice of it, until now when, all of a sudden, the heavens opened and oh boy, did it rain. I mean, there was no gentle build-up to this dounpour. Oh no. Just instant stair rods. It totally hammered down!

Not to worry! The Intrepid Trio, were, yet again, not to be put off by any amount, heavy or otherwise, of precipitation…never have been, never will be…and so, it was Jeff who was the one who was immediately elected to go out to the rear of the car and retrieve the picnic bag. Poor lad. I mean, even that short exposure to this kind of rain and he came back positively dripping. Nevertheless, order was eventually achieved and, having dried him out, or rather, rung him out a wee bit, we enjoyed our humble lunch, shared as always, which goes without saying, by the furry personage in the back and, while the food was eaten, with the usual side orders of light hearted chatter, interspersed with great dollops of laughter, the rain finally ran out of steam and eventually took itself off somewhere else…after which, it started to brighten up a bit.

Sufficiently fortified, we set off up the beach, Misty charging ahead of us, as if every second counted and, after a wee scramble, even with his four legs, down the side of the dunes he went and immediately made straight for the first clump of nice, wet, soggy seaweed that he could find and proceeded to roll in it. You could almost hear him shrieking…Yippee!!

By the time that we had found a way down the dunes to beach level, I mean, we had only two legs each, as opposed to his four, he was already covered in the sticky, glutinous residue off the seaweed and, without further ado, nonchalantly flashed us one of his most devil-may-care sort of grins, before adding a layer of fine sand to this doggie-licious gunk. No one would ever have recognized him as being a gorgeous Irish Setter, however, he was in his element. Dear Misty, that dear, daft lump was just about as happy as he could be and despite the smell of him, you just had to laugh. A dunking in the sea will definitely be called for before he will be finally rubbed down and allowed back into the car.

In the meantime, we had a wonderful half an hour or so, with Jeff dashing around like a man half his age and waving great fronds of seaweed in the general direction of Misty, whilst being estatically leapt upon by this great copper-coloured canine who was wet through and even more liberally coated with seaweed gunk and sand. I mean, I really was beginning to despair at what had happened to my beautiful Irish Setter. You know…the one with the glossy, silky coat of burnished copper? What a joy, though. Moments such as these are so very precious. The two loved ones of my life were having an unbelievably happy time…and what does it matter about a bit of sand, for heaven's sake. It all comes out in the wash…or after a good dunking in the sea, as I said. (Misty, not Jeff. Although, I'm not too sure about that. Maybe both of them).

The rain started to come down again, just as we were thinking of heading off and continuing our journey but then, you see, it hadn't spoiled a truly wonderful interlude of loving companionship and enjoyment. It had gone away for the duration… for that time of special moments, spent on that glorious little beach…the kind of special moments which are the sort of which lasting memories are made. I know that I shall always carry that particular memory around with me in my own mental album of special memories. Jeff, my adored husband, dashing around and brandishing great, long lengths of slimy seaweed, like some oceanic light sabre and Misty leaping, in a blur of waterlogged, sandy feathering and grinning for all he was worth. Memories don't come much better than that. Not for me, anyway.

Getting back onto the main coastal road once more, by following the same twisting road by which we had arrived, we carried on and became ever more enchanted by the panoramic vistas of islands and ocean which were in evidence every mile of the way. So many little islands…small, medium, large…even tiny.

Eventually, we came upon a headland where there was a viewing point and even some picnic tables…I mean, what a view! The name of the headland was delicious…Bloody Foreland. Is that absolutely scrumptious, or is it not? Again, those magical names. Names which can produce the most amazing fantasies, especially if you have an imagination like mine. And I shall say no more about that, because, well, you know what I'm like.

Way out to sea there was Tory Island and then, closer in there were names like Inishbeg, Inishdooey and Inishbofin. I rather suspect that those names may be representative of small, medium and large, as that is exactly what they were. From Inishbeg, the smallest, to Inishbofin, the largest, these three islands were of increasing sizes, from small to large.

From this piece of coatline, ferries ply to and fro across to Tory Island, in fact, there are actually two routes. The longer route goes from Bunbeg and the shorter sailing leaves from Meenlaragh. Which ever route one may choose, however, it should be a very pleasant sailing across the Tory Sound, to what is quite a fair size island, with West Town and East Town to explore at ones leisure and a lighthouse on the furthest extremity, which flashes its warning beacon out over the Atlantic Ocean to guide shipping away from a coastine which could, so easily, rend a vulnerable hull. (And I shan't say a word about mermaids and sirens…or anything else, for that matter. For once, I shall keep my extravagant fancies to myself and not burden you with any of my usual fantastic imaginings. As I have just remarked…you know what I'm like).

By now, time was really getting on and so, as we had a long journey ahead of us to return to our own dear Dunkineely, we decided that we had gone far enough and that we would take the more inland and infinitely more direct N road back to Dunglow.

From there, we had the added joy of retracing our steps across the magnificent burnished moorland. The rain had, thankfully, passed away, almost as if it had never been and the early evening sunlight, although a somewhat weak and watery effort, nevertheless brightened and enhanced the rich colours of these wild and wonderful moors, making the gold even more gold and enriching the overall mellow tint of honey. In the depths of all the dips and the hollows, bronze and darkest brown revealed the whereabouts of the narrow channels from which the peat had been cut and, a pinky-mauve, delicate amongst so much vibrancy, revealed the secret places where the moorland heather had taken up residence and, of course, you cannot have moorland such as this without the usual, incumbent sheep…wet and soggy little woolly bundles, by now…poor things.

Now then, I've just thought of something! (And don't be too surprised. I can sometimes cobble together the odd thought or two). I don't know about you but, and I mean, just think about it…I do not recall ever having seen a sheep go to sleep. Am I wrong? Or what. Night or day, they always seem to be on their feet and, even if, by some chance, one of them may be actually lying down, they still don't appear to be asleep. And they certainly never seem to stop their incessant chomping. They must have extremely flexible jaws, that's all I can say. (And now, I'm really wittering again, aren't I)?

Arriving back at the cottage, we were both blissfully content with the way the day had turned out…a truly memorable day with each individual image still fresh and vivid in our minds. Especially memorable for me, for it had been a true Seasalt Vera kind of day.

Opening the door of our wee idyll was like coming home and even Misty was only too happy to flop down in a corner and have a nap until he heard the dinner gong (metaphorical, of course)…and once he does get the call to dine, you have never seen anything so fast as his sudden transition from a deep sleep to the close proximity of his well laden bowl of doggie nosh.

After such a day, it seemed to be the appropriate thing to do to make our first foray into the village of Dunkineely and make some sort of inroad into the numerous bars. I mean, six…and all together, down one side of the road. Amazing! and where do you start? At one end and work your way through, I suppose. Which idea, I fully endorse…or, just take a lucky dip and pot luck. The second alternative was the course that we chose to take and so we found ourselves in the cosy little bar named Mac's Bar.

As always, when entering any pub in Ireland, the greeting is warm and friendly and that was no different in Mac's Bar, to any other Irish pub that we had ever frequented. The cheery barmaid greeted us with a warm smile and what a joy it always is to hear the lilting accent that I have come to love so much. The few people who happened to be there, locals, of course, without exception acknowledged our presence and then they politely left us in peace to enjoy our drink. As a result, we felt a feeling of belonging. Nobody had infringed on our privacy and yet, in no way were we made to feel like strangers. That is not the Irish way, at all.

Staying at Mac's for about an hour, we bade everyone a pleasant evening and then made our way to sample what might be on offer at one of the other pubs, choosing, this time, McIntyre's Bar...and as soon as we walked in, we knew, without a doubt, that we had made the right choice.

The first thing to meet the eye was the glorious glow from a welcoming fire which came from a stone fireplace just across from the bar and the equally warm glow from the welcome of mine host, Pat McIntyre, himself. We more or less decided, there and then, that this was to be the pub for us, said decision being totally endorsed when Pat kindly told us that, instead of leaving Misty in the car, we could have brought him in with us...and very welcome he would be, too. That, of course, is absolutely taboo, back home and, regardless of the weather, all dog owners have to either leave their pet pooche in the car or, sit outside with the smoking fraternity. The main reason being, of course, is that most of our pubs are now more restaurant than pub, therefore, because of the serving of food, it has now become extremely difficult to be able to take Misty anywhere...and so, we just don't go. End of story.

Anyway, after an hour or so and with a mellow feeling of good fellowship, we eventually left our newly acquired friends at Pat's place but, with the promise of a speedy return...which was entirely and sincerely meant...after which we made our way back, along our wee peninsula, dark by now of course and, once we were settled in our cosy sitting room, we did what seemed to be the only suitable thing to do, in the circumstances...we opened a bottle of wine...with the intention of adding to the glow of warm bonhomie with which we had left Pat's Bar.

A perfect ending to a perfect day. OK, so we had had a bit of rain but, what on earth does it matter in the general scheme of things?

A great day has been had by all, both human and canine and so, now I come to the part of the day that means so much to me, when I like to sit at peace and count my many blessings, at the same time reflecting on all that I have to be thankful for, which, amongst everything else, incudes my never ending gratitude to you for, once again. patiently lending an ear to my nightly bletherings.

How often we take everything for granted...I mean, I am as guilty of doing that as anyone. However, I suppose that I have reached that stage in my life when I am beginning to appreciate things more. With age, you tend to become a little less selfish, I guess and, as I have just said, a little more appreciative of the things that are really important. I know that I have probably repeated myself on that point. Perhaps I have but, it is of no matter. Maybe it is a wee touch of guilty conscience which turns my mind towards such thoughts. Anyway, as always, I now give my thanks to God for the abundance of blessings that He constantly bestowes upon me. That very constancy in no way diminishing the enormous value of each and every one of those blessings, those special gifts which have been, quite literally showered upon me...especially since He saw fit to bring Jeffrey Hall into my life.

Oh Jeff, my own, darling husband, you are and always will be, the greatest gift of all. You see, you fill my life with joy and an unbelievable happiness and I know for a fact that, without you, my life would be a worthless thing. God bless you this night, my own dear love and thank you for making today, as every day, so special.

And as for you, Misty Hall, sleep tight. You may still have the vague odour of seaweed emanating from your furry person, but your mum and dad adore you. Just keep on dreaming those happy doggie dreams, funny face. (And keep the snoring down to a reasonable level tonight, old son. Okay)? That's a good lad.

May God bless everyone and, when we greet tomorrow's dawn, I know that this land that I have grown to love so much will give us, yet again, the splendour of her never ending beauty. Goodnight, Ireland...and God bless you too.

๑๑๑๑๑๑๑๑๑๑๑๑๑

It will come as no surprise to you when I tell you that I am spending the time, the, what seems to me, interminable time, as I await the pleasure of your company, by gazing out across Donegal Bay and before you say anything, I know what you're probably thinking. There are other chairs in this house and no, this is not the only one that will support my weight. I am, regrettably, only too aware of the fact that I now weigh-in like a baby elephant but I'm not all that bad. At least, not yet!…although I can well understand why you might be thinking what you're thinking.

It is strange, I suppose, the way that I have sort of picked out this one particular chair as my own special place. The simple reason being, you see, is that I just can't get enough of all of that. I mean, look at it, all of that, out there…it's gorgeous…and you only have to think back to last year, when I was just as besotted with my beloved Caha Mountains. Do you remember? I was forever sitting there, completely entranced and enchanted by the ever changing aspect of those beautiful mountains, mountains which I had grown to love so much and, unless it was absolutely pouring, you will recall how the top half of that stable door was always opened wide, to allow access to the sweet evening air and to give me a better view of that superb panorama. The Caha Mountains at their most beautiful, bathed, as they were most nights, in their usual wash of evening sunlight. Sometimes, it was a rosy, golden hue and then again, the aspect would be dark and sombre…but, that was only sometimes. Whatever! They were always magnificent. Now, the view over this bay has given me just as much pleasure and the aspect has been as varied and as beautiful…the mood, the colours …all dependant on the prevailing weather conditions and equally liable to change within the blink of an eye, yet never ceasing to fascinate.

This evening, with the calming aspect of the gentle waters of the bay before my eyes, there is so much to think about and while I've been sitting here I've been wallowing in the serene ambience of the room in which I am sitting and enjoying the luxury of having the time to just allow my mind to drift, gently and peacefully, just like a leaf which is floating down a peaceful Irish river, dipping and twirling, as it follows the current…and, after a day such as this, there are many and varied currents which my mind can follow and explore.

My Jeffy has really excelled himself, today, my friend. Just wait until I tell you. Really, you just won't believe it. I mean, the entire day, from start to finish, has been a miracle of sand and sea and surf…and oh boy, do I mean surf!

Allow your mind to conjure up, if you will, the image of Seasalt Vera, rather than that of just plain old Veronica Hall and then, well, you will, perhaps, have some idea of what is in store for you and, knowing me as well as you do and being equally aware of my regretful tendency to get ever so slightly carried away, especially if there is even a moderately sized accumulation of water within close proximity then, it is just possible that you may be thinking…'This could very well be the limit to that which my friendship can cope. I wonder if I have enough time to leg it, while I still have the chance.'

Seriously, I can only promise that I will do my best not to embarrass you. I can't say fairer than that, can I?…besides, my poor Jeffy was the one who had to suffer my most embarrassing exhibitions of spontaneous euphoria, as he, for his sins, got it first hand and with no possible escape route. Even Misty is beginning to, well, sort of look the other way, when his mum begins to regress in years and does her 'big daft kid' routine.

Something else which has drifted through the lazy waterways of my mind, while I've been waiting for you (and again, I shall say it before you do…that there is nothing in there with which to form a solid barrier) it seems no time at all since we arrived here last Saturday and now, here we are and it is already Tuesday evening. I know I'm daft but I can't help myself. I just want it all to last for ever. I told you it was daft.

Have you ever thought how wonderful it would be if it were possible to slow down the speed at which time passes when life is this good, this wonderful…and by that I mean as wonderful as it gets to be when one is on Irish soil? Just to be able to stop its passage, like stopping the ever swinging pendulum of a clock, even if it were only for an hour, how amazing would that be? Still, there is absolutely no point in dwelling on it. Time is the one thing that we cannot alter or manipulate just to suit ourselves, at least, not in the way that I have just been referring to so, we will just have to accept it and simply get on with enjoying each day. Not merely each day but each moment, each second… and appreciating to the full, this blessed land, this Ireland and all of the wondrous things that she has to offer. So much does she hold out, in the hand of welcome and friendship. Precious gifts, indeed. Gifts which she gives so freely, to all of those who have the inspiration to seek and, in seeking, have an honest heart with which to embrace and appreciate the treasures that are being offered. Always, always, just be ready and eager to accept the very miracle that is Ireland.

That largesse of which I have just spoken, has been showered upon us in an unbelievable abundance today and no mistake. The way that these precious gifts have been lavished upon us, I feel sure that what we have experienced this day must have constituted the equivalent of an entire week's ration of all that is Irish and beautiful, all crammed into just this one day and it has been absolutely amazing...especially for yours truly and her equally sand-happy pup. I mean, it is a proven fact that the merest whiff of the ocean can do very strange things to both the two of us.

Anyway, you are here now, for which I am extremely grateful....I can now stop fidgeting. This evening, I think I'm more eager than ever to begin my tale of the day's adventures, so, with your permission, of course, I shall waste no more time in just blethering and get on with it. Where to actually begin, though, that is the problem. It has all been so very special. Oh, for heaven's sake, just begin at the usual place...the beginning...and stop creating problems where there are none, silly old fool.

Anyway, as I make myself comfortable and ask you to do the same, I have to say that, although I love this dear cottage, I do so miss the hiss and crackle of the logs on an open fire, don't you?...that is all, the only one little thing that is missing to make everything perfect. Anyway, it is but a minor thing and of no matter, not when you contemplate the overall scheme of things and, I suppose, that is the main reason why I have gravitated to the window for the purpose of my daydreaming. Instead of finding magic castles in the flickering flames of the log fire, I now weave my dreams around the clouds and the waves and the ever fluctuating colours and patterns which drift across the distant mountains.

Now, I really will get on with it, for which you will be thinking, 'thank God for that'.

Tuesday
22nd September 2009

At least I was not awakened by the 'cold wet fish' down the back of my neck, this morning…Jeff managed a bit of perfectly timed, advance intervention and thereby rescued me from Misty's over-enthusiastic advances before he actually had the chance to get started in slathering me with that tongue of his and, in so doing…for which I was extremely grateful…saved my prone and defenceless, half asleep person, from a lethal attack of Misty-style slobbers which pass for his version of passionate kisses. God love him, (Misty, I mean) I know he means well but it does make for a somewhat soggy start to the day.

Talking about being soggy…it was unfortunate but, soggy described perfectly, the conditions with which we were greeted, this morning…in other words, it was a rather wet and dismal world into which both my boys ventured for their early-morning 'boy's only' adventures, up the lane, which consists of the two of them doing whatever comes naturally and with no real heed, on the part of either of them, as to the condition of the weather. They really are a relationship made in heaven, these two, my husband and my big, adorable, sloppy dog and I would not swap either of them for all the treasures of the universe.

Anyway, stir yourself, woman…and let's up and at it.

I was of the opinion, you see, that the very least that I could do was to make sure that there was a good breakfast for them on their return, just to show them how much I appreciate both of them, don't you know and so, having hung up dripping outer gear, it was with the usual generous helpings of happy banter and, well, just the normal camaraderie of a loving family enjoying each other's company, that we demolished generous helpings of bacon, egg and sausages, followed by toast and home-made jam. (My own 'home-made' jam, for those of you who may be even remotely interested). It was truly a breakfast fit for a prince of the realm…including my very own prince…my Jeffy. The only thing that Misty was interested in, of course, was the ever popular subject of food. The main focus of his avid interest, at this particular moment, being the sausages and, more specifically, the question of just how many of said delectable, mouth watering delicacies might eventually find their way to his regrettably, still empty bowl. I mean, every self-respecting dog worth his salt knows where his main priorities lie and that, friends, is where and when it may concern the really important things in life, the only important thing in life…food… and our Misty, young as he is, is not as daft as he may make out. No way! When it comes down to that particular and, most important subject and, especially sausages, there is no fooling our boy! He knows if and when he may have been short-changed.

In between cooking and eating, we did manage to find the time to have our usual meeting of the Board and, after a careful study of our now slightly crumpled map, our Board-level Plan for today was not, on the face of it, at all conclusive. It did not particularly single out one specific place, you see, rather, the idea was to head off in, yes, a specific direction and then, well, from that point, just see what turned up along the way. The only one 'specific' was that I wanted to stop off briefly, in Donegal. Just the one call, in order to make a quick purchase and then, I was completely at my Jeffy's disposal, to do with as he wished. (And you don't get an offer like that, every day of the week, do you? With a bit of luck, he may just remind me of that statement, later on).

Setting out in the rain was, I must admit, a little daunting, however, it was Irish rain after all and anyway, as we had the wet gear all packed up and ready to repel the worst downpour, so, what the hell. 'Who are we?… The Intrepid Trio. Are we downhearted?…The hell we are!' And besides, it didn't last too long, in fact, by the time that we had reached Donegal, the rain had stopped and the sun beamed down upon us with her cheery face wreathed in the reassuring smiles which seemed to offer a firm guarantee that her benevolent attentions would be 'rained down' upon us for the remainder of the day. Sorry about that.

Five minutes took care of my little trip to the shops, or rather, shop…and we were off in earnest and heading out towards Ballyshannon and, in the fullness of time, the town of Sligo. At least, that was the idea, anyway.

Just to digress a little…I really do believe, you know, that some of the most amazing sights and scenes that we have seen and I mean, not just seen but actually gazed at in complete rapture, places that really do have that WOW factor, of which I am constantly harping on about and which have, as a result, more often than not rendered us totally stunned, have been the ones which we have come upon completely unexpectedly. That 'something special' could have suddenly appeared just around a bend in the road or, amazingly, suddenly been there, at the end of some narrow, winding track that Jeff just happened to take a chance on and, well, our first stop this morning was just such a place and that seemed to set the trend for the rest of the day somehow, although, at that point in time, we were not aware of that.

A sign, bearing the magical symbol of the little sand castle proclaimed the location of a nice, sandy beach, somewhere in the general direction that we were heading, which was down one of those aforementioned narrow roads…not much more than a track, really…but, how to describe the scene through which we progressed, a magic grotto, almost, of the very best of nature's own treasures…and do it full justice.

On either side of us we were treated to some of the most colourful verdure imaginable. Colours of vibrant orange and red, green and purple, as all the hedgerow flowers of autumn, pushed their bold little faces up towards the sun. The deeper that we advanced into this profusion of leafy splendour the more glorious it became, only to be replaced eventually, on one side, by sweeping expanses of verdant, luscious pine forest and, on the other side, by sand dunes which rose majestically, tall and grand and completely masking, with their bulk, the breathtaking panorama of sea and sand which lay beyond.

There was no fooling our Misty, of course…he knows when there is a beach in the offing, long before we actually get there and so he was already in an ecstasy of canine joy by the time we got out of the car. Leaving us looking on, like a pair of idiots and without so much as a final look back in order to verify if we were actually coming, off he streaked, like a flash of copper-coloured lightning and by the time that we two slightly slower mortals caught up with him, he was doing his usual impression of a four-legged tornado and just about whooping in pure doggie exuberance at the total wealth of doggie-licious treasures that were just waiting for him, Misty Hall, to dive into, with all four feet…and not knowing where to start. Great lumps of seaweed or, for that matter, any other beach detritus that he could find, got tossed skywards and flung around in sheer unadulterated canine abandon. Nothing was too trivial. Everything had to be thoroughly inspected and merited at least a dig with the paw or a poke with the ever questing nose.

Now then, here's a question…and this is something which has always given me pause for thought…why is it that there is always just one shoe, particularly a trainer, lying like some poor, drowned sea slug, amongst the shingle? Never a pair. Oh no. Always, just the one…and our daft dog always finds that one, lone trainer and then we spend the next half hour trying to get it off him. Of course, Misty is in his element. All part of the game, don't you know…said game always accompanied by that gleeful look of mischievous fun, you know the one that I mean. The sort of look which would usually be accompanied by a resounding raspberry. One thing is for sure…if only my Misty were physically capable of producing such a glorious sound, you could guarantee that it would be executed with all of his usual gusto and enthusiasm.

Eventually, however, when he senses that in prolonging this particular game any longer, he might just be pushing his luck a bit too far, he will, of his own accord, drop the blessed thing and come trotting back, with a mischievous sort of grin on his face, just as if nothing untoward had happened, only to throw himself, wholeheartedly, into the next adventure that may suddenly take his fancy…that of chasing the local seagull population, being a particular favourite. Dear Misty, his youth and complete lack of experience is so very obvious. I mean, there is no stealth or cunning in the way my bold and intrepid hunter sets about this exciting caper. Oh no, God love him. He just charges in, like a bull at a gate, long legs flying and ears flapping and all that he succeeds in doing is to cause total pandemonium, as the gulls take to the air and I would hazard a guess that the raucous screeching which follows them, as they become airborne, is that of derisive laughter, at the inane antics of the large furry creature down below, gazing up at them with a daft expression on his face.

However, our immediate problem is, that we still have to persuade him to give up his current, much treasured trophy…which could take some time. Not to worry. All will be achieved, eventually. Just as long as nobody is in any particular hurry.

Following in Misty's wake, we topped the dunes and, wow. That's it! What else can I say? I mean, the sight which opened up before us was amazing. Stunning. We had discovered, purely by chance, a miracle, in the form of Murvagh/Mullinasole Strand Forest. The strand was an endless infinity, as only an Irish beach can be and, as always, of the whitest of sand, fine and soft…and then, the final perfection…the ocean. Words can barely describe this sight, which was so stunning that it was impossible not to, quite literally gasp, in sheer wonder and which could have graced the most beautiful picture postcard that you had ever seen. It was breathtaking.

Deepest cobalt blue stretched out and beyond forever and it was alive in an ecstasy of continuous movement, with row after endless row of waves curling and creaming towards the shore. Battalions of them, like advancing rows of troops, the frothy white tops of the most dazzling white, a white which was rendered all the more startling because of the immensely captivating blueness of the sea.

For what seemed like an eternity, I just stood there, motionless. Quite transfixed by the splendour of it all and then, like a demented banshee, I voiced what Misty could only show in his own doggie fashion…I let out a shriek of sheer joy at this stunningly spectacular Seasalt Vera vision which had taken all of us by surprise and then, I joined my two boys in a glorious celebration of life. A celebration of the sheer glory of just being alive on such a morning, which was now warm and golden…and in such a place…by sprinting after Jeff and Misty, or as much of a sprint as I could manage and I felt my spirits soar into the now, quite startlingly blue sky. No wonder the gulls are always voicing their own elation as loudly and as vociferously and with as much enthusiasm as they always do…I mean, just to be one with all of this, as they are. I think I shall come back as a seagull, in some other existence…if you have a choice, that is.

What a joy it was to stroll along, hand-in-hand, my Jeffy and I, along this endless stretch of paradise, our young explorer playing, in his own innocent way and becoming ever more covered in sand. Again, it was one of those special, timeless moments that you just wish could go on forever.

After finally relieving Misty of his precious 'sea monster', (the lost trainer. I mean, for heaven's sake, how does anyone lose just the one) we happily retraced our steps back to the car and after a quick coffee, a rough de-sanding job on the hairy one and a short exploratory stroll through the adjacent pine forest, we continued on our way once more…still quite incredulous of the unexpected and quite spectacular scene that we had just left behind. OK, so it was just a beach. No way! There are beaches and then, there are oceanic miracles.

The coast road followed the line of the shore for miles, with beach a continuous golden companion all the way to Rossnowlagh, a holiday 'village' which, although now deserted, was obviously very popular in the summer season and, with surf the like of which we saw today, a quite obvious surfers paradise. To ride those sort of waves would be nothing short of ecstasy. (Oh dream on, you daft woman. This is definitely one occasion when you really do have to act your age. No way is there even the remotest chance of you riding a surf board. Let's get real…you'd probably end up killing yourself)!

Indeed, the entire length of the shore, all the way down as far as Bundoran and beyond was a miracle of high, rolling waves which seemed to surge towards the land in a positive frenzy of impatience in their striving to reach the shore. These waves were monstrous, heaving and curling in upon themselves in the throws of their own ecstasy and passion as they hurled themselves towards the waiting embrace of the land. As far as the eye could see, it was a continuous oceanic moving-picture show.

Bundoran was a quite charming seaside resort, which boasted all of the usual happy, typical seaside resort amenities which I remember so well from my own childhood. As I looked around, it was so easy to allow my thoughts to slide back in time, to those now, far away days and I could imagine children with their buckets and spades and icecream cornets and kites which had minds of their own, all accompanied by the happy squeals of laughter which comes, without any effort, from carefree childish pleasure. The sort of pleasure that can only be found on a beach and by hearts that are as pure and as innocent as these babies, of whatever generation. Children will always enjoy the unsophisticated joys of sea and sand, for as long as there is sea and sand. This 'big' kid being no exception.

All of this, of course, I could only imagine, the day being a Tuesday and the only people who appeared to be in evidence were people like us who had an over-excited canine doing what comes naturally…only to a dog, of course.

By this time, we were starving and so, this seemed as good a place as any to stay for a while and have our picnic lunch whilst, at the same time, giving us the opportunity of really taking stock of our immediate surroundings…and there was so much to take in… not just the beach and the ever surging motion of the waves but, to the right of where we were now sitting, instead of just a smooth stretch of sand we found our interest taken by a most unusually shaped rock face, of almost Jurassic proportions, which met the incoming sea solidly, thus causing the most amazing explosions of spray, which, having sparkled and glittered in the refracted light as it hurled itself at these striated cliffs and the strangely contorted shapes of the rocks which formed their base, fell back and rejoined the ocean, only to repeat the process again and again.

Needless to say, having sufficiently satified our need for sustenance, we gave Misty his second thrill of the day and let him wander as his own fancy took him, while Jeff and I set out to examine these rocks at a slightly more intimate, up close and personal distance.

Yours truly was quite deservedly pleased with herself at being able to clamber over the rocks in a way that would have been impossible for me, just a few months ago. I know that it must sound so ridiculous, really, but, what a joy to be able to do, once again, something which, up until the last year, or so, I had just taken for granted.

Misty managed to render himself thoroughly soaking wet, ((nothing new, there) having jumped up and down in all and any rock pool that he could find…and there were a lot of them about…and so, a more thorough de-sanding operation had to be carried out on his wriggling, furry person before he could, once again, take up his luxurious sightseeing position in the rear of the car. Something which he does, ultimately, accept with quite dignified resignation, bless him. Not that he really has any choice in the matter…unless he was prepared to continued the journey tied to the back bumper.

As for me, today has been a miracle of quite astounding and momentous proportions…and it isn't over yet. I feel as if I'm wading though a substance like thick syrup and I know that the cause is, quite simply, a massive overdose of that special narcotic which comes from too much exposure to sea and sand…in other words, my favourite element. Sea, Sea and more Sea. From that first beach, just out of Donegal, it has been a continuous slideshow of everything that constitutes my own idea of paradise. We have explored an entire coastline of beaches…and not just any old beaches but, beaches that are just this side of heaven and which today, have been rendered even more amazingly and fantastically glorious, because of the prevailing conditions and the sheer magnificence of the incoming ocean.

With a fond farewell, we left behind this lovely little resort, our hearts filled with precious memories of all that we had seen and experienced this morning. A whole album of memories has resulted from only these few hours. Memories which will be forever and quite indelibly printed onto the backcloth of our minds.

And so, not looking out for anything in particular, we continued on our magic journey and merely enjoyed the simple pleasure brought about by the green and pleasant land through which we were travelling. It would be impossible not to think of it as stunning, all of it…and which ever way one allowed ones eyes to roam, there was something or other which would cause a gasp of pleasure or a passing remark with regard to the merits of a special view which had taken our particular attention. For instance, there were, in the distance, impressive mountains which beckoned, with an alluring grandeur, urging us towards closer inspection…which was tempting. However, although we weren't actually looking for anything specific, one name…just a name on a small signpost which could, so easily, have been missed, did, in fact, draw our attention. Strangely, it was a name that was somehow familiar, although I have no idea why it should have been so.

Mullaghmore. Even saying it, the name still sounds familiar. Mullaghmore. Familiar or not, I just love the sound of it.

This small signpost steered us away from the main road and took us along a more 'off the beaten track' kind of road, to the place which had so attracted us… Mullaghmore Bay. With a name like that, it just had to be a real gem of a place, which is exactly what it turned out to be and where there was to be found a gentle haven, a safe and gentle refuge from the heaving waters of the ocean, as the enclosing arms of the harbour walls provided shelter and protection for the many small boats and yachts, with tall masts and singing rigging, which were nestling, with their keels pulled up into the shale of the beach which held them safe and secure.

The overall first impression of this delightful wee harbour was that of vibrant colours. Colour seemed to bombard the senses, as Jeff and I stood and took stock of this small but, quite enchanting place which we had so effortlessly come upon.

As the road passed through this small village, the senses were assailed by, first of all, the usual brilliance of the quite unique emerald green, which is as Irish as only Irish can be, of the deep grass verge that covered the area between the sea wall and the road. A truly luscious green with, here and there, the jazzy and brazen colours of geraniums and other pretty late-summer flowers that flaunted, themselves quite shamelessly, from elaborate beds, which had been spaced at regular intervals, all along the front and all of it was backed by a sky of the most beautiful and totally unmarked blue. Not even the smallest puff of cloud to spoil this perfect backdrop.

Adding to this paint box of colours which were of nature's own making, colours from a more man-made source vied for ones attention, in the form of the multi-hued hulls of all the boats. There were boats of all shapes and sizes and the overall, finished picture was, quite truly, a masterpiece of vibrancy and brilliant, brazen colour. Which ever way one looked, what met the eye was a joy which seemed to tap into every one of the human senses, except, perhaps, taste. Sight. Sound. Touch and, of course, Smell…all of these were more than adequately catered for and satisfied.

For something so beautiful, it actually took no more than a few minutes to walk the full length of the main street but, believe me, every inch of it just oozed charm, from one end to the other. Charm and peace. A haven, indeed, not only for the small boats that had found a secure anchorage there but a haven, also, for the soul.

Leaving this dear place, little did we know that the oceanic extravagance with which we had been bombarded for most of the day, still had even more surprises in store for us and, unbelievably, it was something that we came upon barely a mile, or so, up the road from this peaceful and gentle harbour…just around Mullaghmore Head…and this was real 100% WOW! It was in your face. A bend in the road…and it was like another world. A world of heaving water and great explosions of surf and… there was absolutely no way that anyone, let alone someone as addicted to the ocean as yours truly, could just drive on by. This just had to be experienced to the full and which, coming to a screeching halt, we did, with my Jeffy almost leaping out of the car, grabbing his camera in sort of full leap.

We thought that we had seen surf, quite outstanding surf, only a few short hours ago but this, this was absolutely mountainous and it hit the land with all the fervour of a crazed lover. It was, in all honesty, indescribable. I can only make a very faltering effort to describe each enormous wave. Wave after crashing wave. Deep blue. Green and turquoise. The colours mixed and mingled and the spume which was generated by the sheer power and force of the water looked as if some demon laundrette had gone crazy with at least treble measures of washing detergent.

I think that Jeff actually got some of his best shots ever…and I could see that he was using techniques that had been handed down to him by our dear friend, the retired photographer, who had so enhanced and charmed our very first day in Donegal. I feel sure that the dear man would have been more than delighted that his so generously given advice had, at least, served some purpose.

As I stood at the side of the road, looking around at this stunning tableau of heaving surf and blue sky, it seemed to me that it only needed an ancient castle, keeping sentinel from the adjacent hillside, to make the picture perfect…and there it was. Whatever you may desire, Ireland will always provide…how many times have I told you that?…and there was proof indeed.

Just off to the left of where I was standing, there was the 'castle', in the shape of Lissadell House. That was its name, anyway, with emphasis on the word 'house', although it looked every inch a real castle to me. I mean, it had turrets and it had towers, so, like I said, it had to be a castle. To my mind, anyway, a fairy tale could not have produced a better one.

Oh boy! That was some kind of absolutely unbelievable experience, though. I tell you, no unsuspecting traveller could possibly have been prepared for it…and again, as I have said, so many times, it was, quite literally, just around that old bend in the road. I know that I am always harping on about that but, do you see now, what I mean?…in Ireland, it is so amazingly true… and the most spectacular and quite unforgettable Irish magic could be, quite honestly, just around that next bend! I mean, just a few minutes ago, there were we, driving along with our thoughts lingering still in the peaceful little harbour which we had just left behind us and then, there it was, full on and incredible.

Believe me, you can never, ever, take this wonderful land at just face value for she will always, in the end, show you just what her true depths are and leave you just gasping for more.

And now, well, now I really do feel completely overdosed. Oh wow! That was phenomenal! My system has been quite positively drowned in the mind blowing after effects of the narcotics of the sea…and it feels brilliant!

You know, I just cannot begin to take in the scene that we have just left behind us. It was, truly, an experience that will remain with me for always. OK, so you may be thinking 'it was just the sea' but, when this lady presents herself in such a mood, then you just have to take notice. At moments such as those by which we have just been captivated, she becomes more than just a great expanse of water, she becomes an actual living entity, a mighty and overwhelming, positively cataclysmic force of nature that has all the hallmarks of the all-powerful hand of the Almighty behind it and you can feel that power, indeed, you cannot help but feel that power, deep down in the deepest recesses of your soul, where it reverberates and stuns the senses. There is no way that you can save yourself from falling under the spell of that mighty show of strength, you just have to go with it. It will never allow you to just take it as a matter of course, to complacently shrug it off as being mundane. You just cannot help yourself or prevent yourself from being completely overwhelmed… just as we were. And in total awe of it… just as we were.

And then, tomorrow, well, tomorrow, it could be as quiet and as gentle as a village pond.

With yours truly still under the influence of that incredible, titanic show of nautical might, we decided to carry on a bit further and then, as the day was getting on a pace, maybe start thinking of heading back, as it would be quite a long run home. So, with those thoughts in mind, we said farewell to the 'castle' and followed the road across open moorland, until we hit the main road again.

All around this area, you are constantly reminded that you are in Yeats country. The memory of this famous Irish poet and dramatist, William Butler Yeats (1865-1939) is made manifest everywhere you go and he is even buried in a local churchyard. Almost everything seems to be named after him with, I might add, justly merited pride, from these lovely people, in their famous son. Even down at Rosses Point, which is where we finally made our last call, there is a grand looking hotel named after him and in Drumcliffe Bay, there is a large and colourful figure, who is standing rather jauntily on his pedestal, surrounded by the waters of the bay and which…and here I could be wrong…I assumed was probably Yeats. William, of course, also had a brother, Jack Butler Yeats (1871-1957) who was a painter and so, there is double the celebrity to cause the name of Yeats to be so openly acclaimed in this neck of the woods.

It felt so wide open, almost like being at the end of the world, at this opening into Sligo Bay. Maybe because everything was quite flat, which allowed the eye to travel, uninterrupted, across ocean and sand, towards the lighthouse or across the gentle green sward from where you could wander down onto the beach and watch, with fascination, just as we did, the young men, strong and tanned, as they gallantly tried to control the wilful ways of their colourful sand yachts.

All of this and, I think, the soft and gentle colouring, like some Turner watercolour, gave the appearance of space. The late afternoon light was so beautiful over the gentle waters of this quite sheltered bay and it all looked so fresh and clean. Gone were the crashing and thrashing mountainous waves of only a few miles back along the coast. Here, within the sheltering arms of this bay, everything was serene.

We both felt peace wash over us as we strolled along, in this, the quiet, gentle part of the day. There was no feeling of haste. Only a feeling of quiet and relaxed well being. Just a few people, that is all, strolled along the sand or across the meadow-like grass which was but slightly elevated above the beach, some, like us, with a dog, said dogs doing exactly the same as our own…dashing around like canine lunatics, as if their very lives depended upon it and, well, what can one say, except that they were all having the greatest of times in the way that is only known to dogs.

And here, we actually saw another Irish Setter, apart from our Misty, that is. It really is not the common occurance that I once thought it would be. I mean, you know what I'm like…I imagined, on our first trip to Ireland, that we would be ankle-deep in these beautiful dogs but, even then, we only saw one other in the whole of our two week stay. Remember Murphy?

We really were loathe to leave this peaceful haven but, common sense prevailed, in the end. There was no getting away from the fact that it was a long run back and really, it is no pleasure if you have to rush it, therefore, in the mellow light of this placidly serene afternoon, we headed back, passing through, as we had earlier, the quite lovely, green and pleasant farmland, with the majestic mountains such as Benbulbin, (the one which looks like a loaf shaped upsidedown cake, with its fluted sides and flat top), all quite regal and grand and decked out, as they were, in their pastel wash of gentle, evening gold.

These mountains remained our companions, at least for a few miles, anyway, until we were once more at Bundoran, which, this time, we bypassed, heading off to Ballyshannon and finally, Donegal.

Once back at Donegal, the journey was well broken and we knew that we had but a short way to go before once again reaching the now so welcome sight of Dunkineely and the wee peninsula which we had, by now, begun to think of as home, along with the now familiar and much loved view, out over Donegal Bay.

Just as it was when we first set eyes upon it, the bay and the hills and the mountains beyond, wore the same gentle mantle. Oh, we have seen it on darker evenings however, this one was just as that first and most memorable evening, the first one, which always remains solidly planted in ones mind. That softest pastel wash of rose and gold and that same, early evening sunlight streaming through the windows of the small cottage which had, for us, after such a short space of time, become, like the surroundings, to feel so familiar and loved.

Walking across our own courtyard and entering our wee cottage could not have achieved a more fitting climax to what has been a quite amazing day. No way could I have believed that a day such as yesterday, an incredible day, even by Seasalt Vera's standards, could have been surpassed but then, this is Ireland, as I am constantly stressing and, I expect, driving you potty with my constant repetition of the same old mantra. Now, well now, you will, perhaps, believe me, for truly, in this land of the most incredible beauty, it is always possible to experience something which is quite beyond belief.

How my Jeffy found all the wonderful places that we have visited today, I just do not know. He must have studied the map (our new, but no longer pristine, map) very minutely, last evening. As I was contentedly gazing out across the bay, waiting for you to arrive, all that I had to do was turn and there he was, pouring over said map, planning and doing his very best, as always, to make sure that the next day would be everything that I would enjoy. That is my Jeffy, you see. His only thought is ever and always of me and what will, ultimately, give me pleasure. Well, my darling, you have given me a day which will never be forgotten. A day, the memories of which will remain with me always and, for all the right reasons. It was special. Very special. Every second, every minute, every hour. I know that I am always saying how lucky I am to belong to this man and to be loved by him…now, perhaps, you will have some idea of what I mean and perhaps begin to understand just how lucky I really am.

After a day such as this, I do believe that anything else would have amounted to nothing short of total overload so, what could possibly have provided a more perfect ending to a perfect day, other than what we had right here…a simple meal, served up and enjoyed with large helpings of that very special love that is always there between the two of us and now, the pleasant prospect of a bottle of wine, or two…and your welcome visit. And if ever I was in danger of babbling incoherently, (so, what's new)? then I expect tonight will be one such occasion. You see, for me particularly, it has been an amazing day. Never before has my alter ego, Seasalt Vera, been so close to blowing a gasket…indeed, a whole set of gaskets. I mean, you know what I'm like when I'm even within smelling distance of the sea…so, it will not be too much of a stretch of the imagination for you to be able to visualize my present mood and condition.

Oh, I do hope that I have not put you off!

Fortunately, for all concerned, my state of previous euphoria has now settled down to a warmly contented feeling of 'mellow'. Almost a drowsy feeling, actually, just like a cat as it curls up in front of the fire and begins to purr fit to quiver its whiskers…well, that's me, right now. There is, of course, the quite reasonable notion that maybe the wine and the loving proximity of my Jeffy could have more to do with the mellow bit than anything else, although I do think that the overall ambience of my present surroundings, plus the memories of a quite magical day, have also added their own contribution.

I'm actually quite loathe to bring this special day to a close, however, in so doing, I find that, as always, I have so much in the way of humble and grateful thanks to offer…particularly so on this extra special night…for all that this day has brought, in the way of joy, for both my Jeffy and I and, of course, our much loved, darling boy, Misty.

Oh, my darling husband…you who always take over where God leaves off and always fills in any gaps…how do I thank you for oh, so much more than just today.

I always used to call you my desert prince…do you remember? Well, nothing has changed, my love. You still are and always will remain, my desert prince. If anything at all, could be said to have changed, it is simply that the love I had for you then, all those years ago, has now become even greater. God bless you, always, my own love.

And, as for you, my Misty…well, sleep tight, dear funny face. Just like your mum, you have been in a state of euphoric ecstasy all day long. Dream of all those lovely beaches, our own precious pup. Those glowing, sparkling eyes and the number of times that a complete de-sanding operation has been required, speaks so volubly of the joyous day that you have had. God bless you, too, bonnie lad.

One last look around before I settle down gives me a blissfully warm feeling of contentment. I can feel that comforting warmth emanating from the man whom I am so proud and happy to call my husband and, from the waters of Donegal Bay, just the other side of the windows, I can hear a faint whisper of gentle waves…plus, the rather more strenuous tones of my Misty as he settles into his usual symphony of orchestrated snoring…bless him…and so it is that I know that all is well with my little world and the ones whom I love so much.

God bless everyone out there…all of you dear people who are the beating heart of this wonderful land. See you tomorrow and, when that day dawns, you will find that The Intrepid Trio will be only too ready to grasp, with hands and paws, all that we know still awaits we three receptive souls.

◉◉◉◉◉◉◉◉◉◉◉◉

The hour is late…very late, in fact…and yet, dear friend, you have remained loyal and have waited up for us. That is friendship, over and above, to my mind. I mean, I'd hardly dared to hope that you would have still been here…we didn't leave the pub in the village until about twenty minutes to one. However, despite the lateness of the hour, yet, somehow, as we walked across our small courtyard, I seemed to sense that you were here…and then I knew that all was well.

My dear friend, there is so much to tell you and, for the life of me, I just don't know where to begin. OK, so it may not have been the 'off the ratings scale' type of day that yesterday was but, in its own rather more laid-back and leisurely fashion, it has been just as wonderful. Especially tonight! Tonight has been the highlight of the year, let alone just today. WOW! (and I know, I know, I know…I'm doing it again). To be honest, my feet are still hovering at least six inches above the ground and I still feel as if I'm actually dreaming the whole thing, for, in truth, tonight has been, for me, like actually living a dream…and, I do believe that it has been as profoundly memorable for Jeff, also. What ever words I may use in order to try and, I fear, quite miserably, to describe the events of the last few hours, one thing is for sure, neither one of us would have missed it, not for anything in the world. It has been one of those truly amazing experiences which happen only rarely in the average lifetime and which, because it has been so special, inevitably becomes permanently and indestructibly etched onto the very fabric of ones mind. I feel sure that nothing short of sandblasting would ever erase these particular memories…and even that may not have any effect.

Anyway, it is late. When you hear the full story, you will need no further explanation so, owing to the extreme lateness of the hour, may I suggest, first of all, a brandy?…(how about that for a good idea) and then I shall just get started.

Wednesday
23rd September 2009

What a joy to look out and see the gloriously bright and cheery outlook which greeted us this morning. There has been, of late, so much in the way of autumnal mists, especially in the early morning and the late evening however, the waters of the bay were, today, clear and sparkling in the pretty, pale glow of sunlight and almost completely unmarred by so much as a ripple, giving a virtual mirror surface which perfectly reflected a sky of the most delicate blue while, at the same time, delighting the eye as that precious early morning sun bathed everything in a lustrous rosy, golden hue…the sort of perfect morning which you just know will remain perfect for the remainder of the day.

As I looked out, the first thing to catch my eye was Misty, God love him. There he was, out and about, busy, busy, busy and hailing the morn in his usual inimitable fashion…with eyes glowing and coat shimmering as he busied himself about the urgent business of the day. All of this manic activity, would, of course, have meant nothing to a mere human but, to this dear, daft lump of a simply wonderful dog, it was very meaningful indeed. Stuff that only another dog would have appreciated, don't you know and, of course, understood the urgency of. I mean, there were flowers which needed to be poked and sniffed at. Interesting corners, in abundance, which all needed to be investigated and then, when all of that had been sorted out to his satisfaction, off he trotted, as happy as only an innocent mind and heart such as his could be, out onto the lane, just to check that all was as it should be out there. Not too far behind, of course, was my Jeffy. My two boys, once again, out on the raz and doing their special boy things…and looking forward to coming back to a loving welcome and a good breakfast.

Getting everybody and everything ready, first thing in the morning, is still a bit like a scene out of some Crazy Gang movie, (for those of you, who, like me, are of the vintage to be able to remember the Crazy Gang) although, maybe not quite so manic as it was last year. Could it actually be that we are becoming more organized? That is, of course, a possibility. And, if I wanted to lay all the blame on a poor, innocent animal, (which I won't…I mean, God forbid) and by that I mean Misty, who was only eight months on our last trip, well, he is now a quite sensible two years old. (Well, almost). We do find, however, and without laying any real blame at his quite innocent door, that it still improves the situation quite enormously, if we put him in the car, where he will lie, in regal splendour, for as long as is necessary. The car has now become Misty's special place…once ensconced, he knows that there is a whole world of canine delights just waiting for him, the young adventurer that he is, to track them down and then give them his own particular Misty-style dose of seeing to.

Maybe, it is that we have become a little more sensible ourselves and, as I said, a little more organized however, that, in no way suggests that we do not have the fun that we had last time, or the minor hilarious cock-ups. Where The Intrepid Trio are concerned, there will always be that atmosphere of fun and the joy of anticipation, the mutual love and the laughter, which is always there, ready to break through the surface and send all of us into fits of riotous mirth…and, it goes without saying, (and I use that word again) the inevitable cock-ups. That's when our dear, daft pup looks at us quite despairingly, as if it is we, the quite unpredictable humans, who are the 'big kids' and not him. And he is absolutely right, of course.

We eventually managed to get out on the road nice and early, although no clear plan of action had actually been agreed upon, except maybe a wee venture up into The Blue Stack Mountains…which is a special treat that we had been promising ourselves from day one.

However, first things first…and so we stopped off at the Post Office in the village where we were greeted with a warm and friendly smile and a gentle word or two of genial chat, by the dear lady who was the Postmistress and who, strangely enough, bore an extremely strong resemblance to The Queen. (Queen Elizabeth, naturally). I mean, she was such a dear soul. (The lady, not the Queen…although, I know that the Queen is, also). A soft and gentle face looked up at us, as I entered her small establishment, which glowed with the beauty of her smile. (Her face, not the establishment). Shiny, silver-white hair, in gentle waves, framed her pretty face and her accent was a joy, just like the aged Sister with whom we became acquainted, last Sunday, in Donegal…a soft and lyrical Irish melody.

Our feeling of well-being at just being here, in this wonderful place and on such a wonderful day was so greatly enhanced by our short meeting with this dear lady…and she gave us the impression that we had made her day special, also. Which I would like to think that we had.

Anyway, with that wee job done, we set off in search of whatever adventures may be awaiting us, The Intrepid Trio, to enter into, with the amount of enthusiasm that only we three can generate…and so, people of Ireland, be warned. We, the three, in fact, the only fully paid-up members of The Intrepid Trio, always have had a enormous capacity for getting the very utmost out of the most simple adventures and there, you see, in a nutshell, is the secret to complete happiness. To be able to derive such genuine pleasure from the most humble of sources means that you have succeeded in learning one of life's little secrets…that all you really need, to achieve true happiness is a heart which is full of love and a soul to match. Even a millionaire could not lay claim to a greater degree of happiness than we three can contrive, not even with all his money…which, to my mind, makes us particularly fortunate and abundantly blessed.

It wasn't long before we found just what we were looking for, in the shape of a narrow, single-track road, with, at the beginning of it, a sign which bore the legend 'Blue Stacks Drive'. Marvellous! Just the very thing…and, from past experience, we have discovered that these specially named 'drives' always follow the most picturesque routes, which gave us the confident knowledge, before we even got started, that we were in for a treat and, to prove my words, we hadn't been travelling along this road for more than a few minutes and we knew, immediately, that we had found the magic highway which would, eventually, lead us to the proverbial pot of gold. (And, who knows, maybe the sight of a merry face or a twinkling eye or the sound of fluting laughter. The Leprechauns are there, right enough…oh yes. You'd just better believe it).

Nothing, however, could possibly have prepared us for what lay ahead. Nothing! It was like entering a veritable wonderland.

This narrow track was suddenly ablaze with every shade of green imaginable, alternating, here and there, with deepest amber or bright orange, or even the palest shade of pure honey. Not only the hedgerows but also the ground-level verdure, were an amassed riot of brazen colours. Mountain Ash trees were much in evidence, mingling with the other hedgerow plants and with the foliage which still remained, a glowing glory of brassy gold. And berries…oh, the berries. They were a deep and unbelievable scarlet and were so prolific that the sheer weight of these large clusters of succulent fruits actually bent the more slender and tender branches with their weight, forcing them down to meet and touch the riotous and quite delectable, emerald verdure.

But, it was the wild and exotic fuchsia which showed off her finery to the most brilliant effect. These blood-red pendant droplets were like precious jewels set in the dark green velvet of their foliage. But it was the sheer quantity, that left one gasping with sheer pleasure. There were masses of them, in hedges which lined the narrow road on both sides and they were deep and dense and luxuriant, with millions of these, nature's own precious rubies, sparkling and glowing , as if with some inner fire of their own, in the sunlight…and the effect was stunning. Absolutely stunning. How could anything be so glorious and not be created by a Divine Hand?

As our way progressed, new plantations of pine forest soon replaced the hedgerows, with trees standing like a proud army of green-clad soldiers along both sides. Line upon line of the most beautiful trees, their newness still fresh and young as was obvious by the uniformity of their garb, a garment which was tailored from the brightest of emerald green needles and their number was such as to create a forest that was so cavernously deep that it was almost impossible to penetrate the black density of the interior.

The senses were immediately overwhelmed by the vibrancy of all these brilliant colours. Here, in this place, was a whole paint box of an indescribable richness, which could only have been contrived by nature and then, quite remarkably, the vivid hues of ruby and forest green were gone and we were out into the open moorland once more, which, with her own brand of beauty, regaled us with her own special blending of colours… again, there was the honey and the gold, the green, the bronze and the purple.

The mountains began to look down upon us in all their full majesty, the nearer that we came to them and, as we advanced further into them, they seemed, to us, to be almost endless. We found ourselves to be completely entranced, indeed, quite astounded by this almost boundless infinity of grand and eternal splendour, with, incredibly, peak beyond magnificent peak, soaring and reaching up towards the sky….dwarfing, into insignificance, the small and wretched creatures that were the two (correction, three) of us. We two humble mortals…and one dog. Almost as far as the eye could see, these mountains rose endlessly, into the cavernous blue sky, with only a few inconsequential clouds, hovering around their jagged tops and the only form of life that we could see, with whom we could share this wondrous miracle of nature, were the birds of prey, which wheeled and soared and played their own game of 'catch me if you can', as the playful wind caught their wings…and, the local wildlife. In this type of country, there just had to be sheep!

Our road was very narrow now, with just enough room for our passing. There was a small herd of cattle which were quietly grazing, their tails swishing, as insects hovered around them, annoyingly, in the warm morning sun…and such beautiful beasts they were who, as we approached, raised their noble heads and merely glanced our way but briefly, as we invaded their privacy. It would appear that they were roaming quite freely, these handsome animals, with no obvious sign of any form of fencing and they seemed to achieve some kind of mischievous, bovine entertainment, from blocking what little there was of the road…indeed, they showed no sign, whatsoever, of being inclined to bother themselves sufficiently to move over so, we just stopped…whereby they immediately took a great interest in these rather strange beings who were sitting in this equally rather strange metal box thing and, as if at a given signal, they all seemed to turn, en masse and peered in at us through the car windows, eyeing us with those gentle, yet wise and absolutely beautiful, brown eyes with the enviable long lashes, whilst, at the same time, chewing continuously on a mouthful of the lush, green grass which grew to both sides of our narrow highway.

Eventually, of course, they became bored with us and merely trundled off in the direction from which we had just come. No haste. Just a gentle plod. No doubt off to find some grass that may be even greener, maybe.

Still pleasantly thinking of those deep and lustrous bovine stares, we followed each twist and bend in the road and on one such bend, I suddenly exclaimed…in sheer delight, I might add…at the sight of a huge pair of those afore mentioned deep and lustrous, dark brown eyes which were staring at me from the gorgeous creamy coloured, silky, curly head which was peering at me, just like the wee child it was, from beneath the greenly foliaged bows of a wayside shrub. This darling wee calf, whose eyes were, by now, as round and as huge as saucers, watched me very closely but without any real sense of being threatened by me, as I got out of the car with my camera clutched in my hand and then, well, discretion suddenly seemed to take over as being the better part of valour, as the dear wee thing suddenly appeared to have very serious second thoughts about my integrity and made a quick dash over to its mum, who just happened to be standing close by with two other magnificent beasts with whom she was sharing the sunlit hours of this glorious morning and no doubt discussing the dubious blessings of having to keep a constant eye on what the kids were up to. This particular kid now peering at me from between his mum's back legs…and quite curious as to my intentions, now that he felt safe.

These Irish cattle really are quite gorgeous, though. I've noticed them a few times, over the last few days…the colours varying from the creamy colour of a Labrador to the deepest of rich, dark browns and a black that is as rich as ebony.

Great herds of these magnificent animals abound in this area…and they always look so clean, with never any sign of having been rolling in the mud.

Eventually, we had done, more or less, the full circuit of this Blue Stacks Drive and so we looked for and eventually found an ideal place to stop and let Misty have a stretch and ourselves a welcome cup of coffee…and, believe me, ideal was the only way to describe the small pull-in which we were lucky enough to find. It was actually quite well camouflaged by shrubbery and could so easily have been driven past, unnoticed, however, notice it we did and a gasp of sheer pleasure was the response which immediately escaped our lips, quite involuntarily, as we stepped out of the car.

We were actually at the edge of a small lough. Tall reeds and green and verdant shrubbery fringed the blue waters of this pretty lough and pine trees seemed to tumble, helter-skelter, down the shoulders of the hills which sloped down to the water's edge on the opposite side and, as a backdrop, which finished off the complete picture, there was the pale amber glow of the distant mountains, indeed, the very mountains through which we had just travelled and at which we had just marvelled. They almost seemed to preen themselves, with justifiable pride, as they displayed their magnificence against the delicate blue of the sky. Like I said, you just had to feel in awe of such a sight…and the gasp of sheer delight was a genuine reaction to this picture, which, although small and unassuming, yet, all it needed, in order to transform it into a masterpiece, was a frame. A miniature scene, indeed but, one of quite outstanding and exquisite beauty.

With everyone feeling the benefit of the short pit stop, we set off in the direction of Ballyshannon. With no offence intended, we merely bypassed this lovely town, the other day so, today we thought that it merited a more thorough inspection. I mean, just the name, Ballyshannon, was invitation enough. You know, by now, my fascination with Irish names and I do particularly love anything which happens to bear the prefix 'Bally'. To me, it is so quintessentially 'Irish', do you not think so? Anyway, it had a head start, at least, for me, purely because of its name.

One could only think of Ballyshannon (there, I just had to say it again) as being a charming little town. I mean, with a name like that, it could have been nothing less…but then, they are all charming, all these small market towns…and I do love them so much. Rather than the busy cities that we are used to, these delightful small towns are such a joy and so very pleasant, to wander around, at peace and at leisure….and that is precisely what we did, having parked up, without any difficulty, we strolled around this very picturesque little town, stopping, here and there, in order to look into a shop window or maybe take in some of the more obvious features and buildings and, of course, the most special feature of all, for obvious reasons, which was what appeared to be the main depot for our Misty's own fleet of buses…Bus Eirann.

Having seen all that we wanted to see, we stood for a few minutes, our arms resting on the sun-warmed stone of the bridge which spans the river, with that same warmth pleasant against our upturned faces and then, fully content with all that we had seen, we bade farewell to Ballyshannon. Our visit had been somewhat brief but, it was only ever intended as a passing visit…just to say that we had, in fact, been there, don't you know… and then we set off to find the place, the very special place, that I just had to see and, hopefully, be allowed to inspect on a more intimate level. For heaven's sake, we were so close and really, it would have been totally unthinkable not to and besides, I was living in hopes of maybe helping to ease the strain on Jeff's right jeans back pocket, by relieving his wallet of the odd note or three.

In explanation, let me just say that you will immediately know what I mean if I just mention the fact that we were a mere stone's throw from the Belleek factory, which is just on the edge of the small town of Belleek…and of course, in this factory, this place of dreams come true, they make the most heavenly cornucopia of all that is delicate and fragile and absolutely delectable…in fact, some of the finest china that you will ever see.

Surely my wonderful, kind and generous Jeffy could not be so hard as to see me gaze in rapturous awe, at all of this magnificence and not allow me to purchase just a tiny, tiny wee something. Be honest, now…I think you know better than that, do you not?

It certainly made for a very interesting journey, I must say, as we followed the country lanes en route to Belleek. You see, this small town is, more or less, just on the border between Northern Ireland and the Republic. Probably, just slightly over and as we progressed, well, we hardly knew where we were, from one moment to the next. One minute we would be in the Republic, with all the European road markings and signposts and then, just by going round a bend in the road, we would be driving along a road with British road markings and signposts…and that was the way of it, for quite a few miles. In and out of two different countries within the space of a mile or so.

Once we actually arrived in Belleek, little did we know just what a treat was in store for us, though. The factory, itself, was a pleasant enough brick building, quite in keeping with the surroundings, with the river running along one side and with pretty flower beds out front but, inside…wow…inside. I knew that it would be nothing short of being a mind-blowing experience but, it was magic! Just about as magic as one could imagine a real Aladdin's cave to be.

It really was the most amazing experience. I mean, just to wander around the showroom was really quite incredible. One could only look at with awe and marvel at the intricacy and fineness of some of the more expensive pieces…and when I say expensive, I really do mean, expensive. It was necessary to give just a quick glance to the content of this quite amazing collection of the most exquisite china, for it to become immediately obvious, even to someone who had absolutely no idea about the merit, or otherwise, of what they were looking at, that we were surrounded by an absolute fortune…in fact, one hardly dared to move and God forbid that anyone should sneeze, in case anything got damaged or, of all possible calamities, actually got broken.

In the end, as you would obviously have guessed, my lovely Jeffy let me buy whatever I wanted to buy and so, I chose two very lovely pieces for us, plus a couple of small, though nevertheless, pretty pieces, as presents. After which…and it had all been something of a shock to the system…in order to give ourselves time to recover, we went into their own lovely restaurant and had a coffee and a bite to eat. (Something a little stronger might have been more beneficial, especially for my poor Jeffy, bearing in mind what I had just spent, however, as someone had to remain in an appropriate condition to still drive, coffee just had to do).

Believe it or not, even the crockery in the café was Belleek china. Wow! Heavy duty stuff, it may have been but, I wouldn't like to be working in that kitchen…and that's for sure.

Clutching my precious purchases as tightly as if I were afraid that they might suddenly disappear in a puff of smoke, we returned to the car and happily allowed mere chance to dictate where we went from there. I was quite content to go anywhere now…I mean, I'd had my treat. More than sufficient for one day…more than sufficient for the rest of the week, in fact…and next week, too.

Actually, Belleek lies on the River Erne which, in due course, flows out into Lough Erne, the largest lough in Ireland and which stretches for miles, all the way down as far as Enniskillen and so, on such a beautiful day, with the sun sparkling off the blue waters of the lough, it seemed only natural that we should follow its length and explore all that nature had provided in order to produce this perfect merging of lough and woodland. There was even a castle, believe it or not. A real castle…Castle Caldwell, which was set, quite grandly, in its own deep and rambling forest.

That will do for us…and for Misty. I mean, the poor lad had been forced to stay in the car while we went around the Belleek factory, much to his disapproval and he'd only had that short break where we stopped off for coffee this morning so, a chance to charge through the forest, like the bold adventurer he is, was our way of saying 'sorry about that, old son'…and, as we set off, into the inner depths of these ancient trees, how very lovely it was, which, of course, was no surprise. This is Ireland, after all is said and done and it was an absolute dream…a perfect idyll.

Picture, if you will, a pathway, which followed the course of the lough and meandered through the deep cover of the overhead canopy of the forest trees, while the sun played a game of hide and seek, at the same time, dappling our way in an intricate pattern of lights and shade and, here and there, sending shafts of brilliant light off the ripples of the lough. It really was quite beautiful…peaceful and tranquil… the only sounds being those of nature. Water, lapping against the river bank. Birds, flitting from bough to bough and singing their own praise to the glory of the day and, the inevitable cracking sounds of small twigs and branches snapping as our intrepid explorer bounded through the trees ahead of us.

We walked for a goodly distance, although we never did reach the castle. To be honest, I think that, by then, we had walked enough, taking into account the fact that we had the same distance to cover in order to return to the car. Still, it was and had been glorious and, as we were still intent on following the lough to its full extent, which was a long way to go and would take some time, it made sense to continue on our way.

It had been a memorable moment in time, though. A memory to treasure. Mile after mile of blue water which hosted, here and there, an assortment of haphazardly arranged little islands, each one of which, in turn, played host to its own wee forest of trees. And, the castle woodland, dappled in brilliant sunlight…how lovely that was. A perfect combination, for most people but then, as if that were not enough, for me, I had the extra blessing of watching my whole life, in the shape of Jeff and Misty, some way up ahead, both so close together and both of them so intent on their own small pursuits, thus causing me to stop and take stock and offer up a wee prayer of thanks for being so lucky in having both of them to love and to cherish. Yes, indeed! Perfect memories of a perfect day.

Back on the road, once more, we eventually arrived in Enniskillen although there had been a time when we almost believed that we would never see the end of this enormous lough. Quite incredibly, it had been our constant companion for mile after mile. Endless, or so it seemed.

Having achieved our ultimate destination, it was hardly surprising that, on the journey back to Donegal, our hearts and minds were a total maelstrom of happy and joyful images, so many, in fact, which had accumulated over the course of this wonderful day. All of them such pleasant and so very happy recollections of everything that had been special and beautiful…and, well, everything that had just been another typical day in Ireland.

From the magnificence of the Blue Stack Mountains to the peace and sheer loveliness of the lough and the forest that we had just left behind…and everything in between…we had been stunned and enchanted. Is it any wonder then, that our hearts were light as we headed back towards home and, what a joy just to sit back in the loving companionship of my Jeffy and allow my thoughts to wander, knowing, full well, that he would be doing exactly the same thing, each of us with our own personal memories and savouring, both of us, each and every precious, sunny moment. A magical mosaic, made up of a combination of blue sky and soaring mountains, sun-dappled forest paths and blue and sparkling river. Not to mention all the treasures of the Belleek factory. Oh boy, will I ever forget that. Wow! I mean, you could spend a king's ransom in that place…and do it willingly…if, of course, you had that kind of money, which we haven't.

The early evening sun was quite glorious, as we pulled into our own small courtyard and just stood there, for a minute or two only, just taking in the pleasant aspect of the bay. I do so love, even after all these days, to 'stand and stare' as the poet once said. Familiarity having, in no way, lessened the deep pleasure that I derive from this lovely aspect…and it was as I was standing there gawping that I was, for once, not paying sufficient attention to what I should have been paying attention to and was taken completely off-guard, as the playful wind off the bay, although not a strong wind, got itself under the brim of my rather nifty cowboy hat and off it went, sailing up and away, more or less en route to Donegal…until, that is, a certain furry person rescued it. And I swear to God that all of this is absolutely true!

As my hat took flight, Misty did likewise, making an extraordinarily swift leap for it and then, whilst in mid-leap, grabbed the hat, quite nonchalantly, in fact…and then just stood there, with the hat clamped firmly between his pearly whites and the look of the devil in his eyes. Oh, I knew that look so well…it was the 'I dare you to get it off me' kind of look. A sort of taunting look, if you know what I mean, with his tail swishing back and forth in an attitude of 'this could be fun'. Eventually, however, he must have had second thoughts about the wisdom of pushing his luck just that wee bit too far and thereby abandoned the, what must have been, quite delectable thought of the prospective game of tug-of-war with my hat…and then, and I swear to God that this is true, he quite primly and sedately, trotted back with my hat and, in a very Irish Gentlemanly manner, just handed it back to me. Oh Misty, how could I ever have doubted you? (Quite easily, in fact). I mean, he did it in such a courteous and gallant fashion that Jeff and I, well, we just burst out laughing and I feel sure that we hurt his feelings, which, of course, was quite unforgivable but, it was impossible not to. As a result, he probably thought to himself…'thanks a lot, you pair. Just you wait 'til the next time, when I shall take great pleasure in ripping it to bits. You just see if I don't'.

At which point, having offered profuse praise for a deed well done, though I must confess with much restrained laughter, we all made our way inside. Time was of the essence now, you see. There were important things afoot and so, our meal was hastily prepared and just as hastily eaten. The reason for all this haste being, of course, that we had very special plans…and I do mean special…for the evening and we particularly wanted to get out at a reasonable time. (As things turned out, we could have stayed at home until about 10 o'clock…I mean, we weren't to know, were we? We do now, of course and I consider that, under the circumstances, we made a very creditable effort to fill in the time, in the customary way, naturally…in other words, we certainly didn't go thirsty).

Our destination was, inevitably, MacIntyre's Bar, in the village. I couldn't believe our luck as we passed the pub this morning and noticed the sign, which was standing, quite grandly, on the pavement outside the pub and declaring the gladdest of tidings that 'live' Irish music was to be held at this establishment, this very evening…and which, as the placard very plainly stated, was a regular Wednesday night occurrence. Needless to say, I was ecstatic! To say the very least, I was totally ecstatic! Indeed, that is probably the biggest understatement, ever. I think that I may, at some point or other, have indicated just how much I have always wanted to experience this particular, very special example of Irish culture. And now, wow, it was actually going to happen. I'd been in a bit of a fizz, all day, with the thought of it always hovering somewhere quite close to the surface…and now, it was actually to become a reality.

So, we arrived at the pub, in all our innocence, at about 7pm. Which may seem fairly reasonable, on the face of it, however, what we hadn't realised…and I mean, how could we have known…was that things didn't actually start to kick off until about 11pm. Dear, dear Pat. What an absolutely brilliant host he was. He was so lovely to us and in no way did he show any suggestion of what must surely have been going through his mind…that we were a right pair of numpties…and so, we had the most wonderful, the most amazing night, ever.

Pat had, very kindly, allowed Misty to come into the bar, for which we were extremely grateful and, surprise, surprise, our genial hound, having greeted everyone in his usual enthusiastic manner, immediately stretched himself out to his full length, thus taking up most of the space in front of the fire. Of course, everyone made a huge fuss of him, which he accepted with all of his usual nonchalance and aplomb and then set about greeting everyone as they entered with a quick flash of his most endearing grin and a tail which well and truly polished any ash dust from the quarry-tiled floor in front of the hearth, as it kept up its constant welcoming and rhythmic sway.

The musicians came in, one or two at a time, throughout the course of the evening and we three were made to feel so welcome. It was impossible to feel as strangers in and among the genuine warmth of the friendship which was, so openly, offered to us. Everyone, without exception, made us feel at one with them, as if we were a part of this village and a part of this, its weekly get together. Jeff made friends with one particular musician. He was such a charming young man, indeed, a very handsome young man, albeit somewhat shy, who played one of the Bodhrans (the round, Irish drum) and what a lovely sight it made, especially to my loving eyes, to see my husband and this gentle young man, with their heads together as they both gazed into the glowing embers of the fire, clearly in deep and quite earnest conversation and with my dear nutty pup pushing his way between the two, all the easier to receive the caresses of these two men. As I looked on and watched the warm glow of the fire making flickering patterns across their faces, I felt as happy as I could ever have hoped to be. I think that, in all honesty, I shall always remember that moment…as, indeed, I shall always remember the entire evening.

As I said, round about 11 o'clock, all drinks were replenished (and I won't say how many times that they had thus been topped up) and then, without any great ceremony or fuss, things started to kick off. The musicians, about twelve of them, (made up of four violins, three guitars, two bodhrans, flute, banjo and accordion) began, one by one, to drift over to one end of the room, sitting down, in no particular order and picking up their respective instruments and then, quite casually and with no great fanfare, they began to play…and it was wonderful. The mix was just right…a happy and cheerful combination of foot-tapping Irish reels and jigs and some very lovely soft and more gentle melodies. The highlight, for me, of course, was when one of them, a man who was just a little older than some of the others, sang 'The Wild Collonial Boy'. This song has always been one of my particularly favourite Irish folk songs and this man's own, personal, rendition of this rather sad song was so immensely moving. In truth, I think that quite a few were actually moved to tears, by the end of it.

Occasionally, one of their number would get up and go out for a fag..and then, he would return and another would do likewise. It was all very informal but, somehow, that was its real charm and I know that, for me, it was probably one of the most wonderful evenings of my life. I would not have missed it, not for all the world…and I know that even my Jeffy was feeling very moved by it all, by the time that we eventually left.

How long it carried on, I have no idea…I mean, it could have gone on all night, for all we knew. Anyway, we left at about a quarter to one (a.m.) and it was still in progress. By then, however, we just had to admit defeat and so, reluctantly, we bade a fond farewell to Pat and our thanks were sincere, as we shook his hand, for the great warmth of the welcome which we had received and, of course, for making Misty so welcome…which meant more to us than Pat could ever know. Apart from which, Misty's presence made the evening just that much more special…not just for Jeff and I but, I think, for everyone else, too.

Oh, dear God, our journey home was absolutely hilarious…and I feel sure that you will be able to imagine the scenario without any in-depth explanations from me. I mean, what a hoot, as we made our 'slow but sure' way, back along the peninsula, to our cottage. It was pitch dark, for a start, of course (which was probably just as well)…but we did eventually find the right place and, after a lot of laughing and tittering, in the way that you do when you are trying to keep the noise down, you know what I mean…we found the right door and the illusive, right keyhole and well, you know the rest.

What can I say?…except, 'thank you'. I did hope but, if I'm honest, I never really thought that you would have waited up for us. You really are a star!

Now, late though it is, before I bring this amazing day to a close, I must just say my usual nightly thanks.

First of all, my thanks, as always, to God, for all His blessings…and Jeffy, my own darling Jeffy. Dearest love, you have made of my life, something very special, something that is now whole and complete. Every single day and in so many ways, you show me just how much you love me and so it is that, every single day, I realize, in so many ways, just how lucky I am to be your wife…and just how very much you mean to me. God bless you, always, my husband. I love you.

And now, last but, by no means least…dear Misty…our handsome canine Adonis who can charm the pants off all whom he meets and melt the very hardest of hearts. You are very special, bonnie lad and although there may not have been much in the way of beaches today, maybe you, too, have had a special day, just as we have. I hope so. Dream your happy 'doggie' dreams, my lovely boy and know that we love you very much.

God bless us all, every one! Sleep tight and…see you tomorrow.

Ireland will give of her very best, as always and we will be ready, as always, to take her to our hearts.

ⓞⓞⓞⓞⓞⓞⓞⓞⓞⓞⓞ

A glorious evening, with a sunset of such amazing vibrancy and splendour that it has kept my eyes and my mind occupied for the last half hour with its miracle of heavenly and ever fluctuating colours, has also set the mood as this special Thursday draws to a close and, talking of moods, I should warn you that you will find me in one of those mellow moods again (it must be me, I mean, who else can I blame. It must be me just getting old, I suppose)…and yes, I've got no intention of hiding the fact that my usual glass of wine is to hand and I've been sitting here, complete with said glass of wine, flicking through the pages of that mental photograph album, the one which I always carry around with me in my heart, where all my precious memories are stored and from where they can always be retrieved, at random and savoured…and I have been positively devouring each cherished memory of the last few days. Incredibly, and in just that short space of time, we have created so many. So much indeed, too much, to really assimilate all in one go.

But, where has it all gone? That's what I want to know. Oh I know that I'm always harping on about it and I know that I am being totally childish about it all but, I can't help it. I mean, after waiting all those long and wearisome fifteen months and longing, in every fibre of my being, to return to Ireland, it just seems unbelievable that the first week is almost over. Just the one more full day, here in Donegal and then…well, at least we are only leaving one part of Ireland and moving to another.

Still, I can't complain, indeed, I mustn't even think of complaining…so, stop feeling so damned sorry for yourself, you daft woman. Silly old fool. Besides, this day is not over yet and tomorrow is still to come and will, inevitably, be another memorable day…as memorable as only The Intrepid Trio can make it.

As a matter of fact, we actually started today with a Plan but, having said that, we could have had no real idea of just what an incredible experience was in store for us. Our destination for the day was merely a name on the map, (definitely a bit worse for wear, now…the map, I mean) however, the reality was so much more than we could have imagined. Anyway, I'm beginning to blether so, if you are willing, I will just get on with it and you will be able to form your own opinions.

Thursday
24th September 2009

Needless to say, we missed the dawn chorus, this morning, which was hardly surprising, after our late arrival home, last night. I can't believe that we were out so late. I've never left a pub, at that incredible hour, in my entire life. I mean, a quarter to one in the morning and coming out of a pub! What is the world coming to! Not that I am complaining, far from it…it was absolutely brilliant! I would not have missed it for the world. Not one single, fantastic, minute of it…and neither would Jeff.

What does seem to me, to be fairly obvious, however, is that we are getting old…far too old for all this late night stuff. Our gadding days are long since gone, I fear…not that we will ever be put off by such a small detail. It gives me enormous pleasure and yes, I am very pleased and proud to say that there is still plenty of life left in these two oldies. Well, me really. I mean, Jeff is still only a youngster! He still has a way to go before he qualifies for the title of 'oldie'.

Seriously, we were not too much later than usual…I mean, with a doggie to consider you have to keep dog-friendly hours. There is little chance of a lie-in when our big lump decides that it is time to rise and shine. A wet and extremely cold nose, poked down the back of your neck, followed by the enthusiastic application of an equally wet tongue, will usually do the trick. Every time!

Looking out upon our now familiar bay, the outlook was, once again, that of a light, autumnal mist over placid water…beautiful and ethereal, a gossamer veil, a lover's caress as it gently kissed the surface of the water, whilst giving off a pretty, almost luminous and opalescent glow that proclaimed that, before too long, the sun would burn off this breath of whispery, dewy mist and eventually reveal the blue water which is always there, all the time, just waiting in the wings, ready to show off its own morning glory and emitting sparks of fire…prisms of refracted light, as the sun blinks off the gentle curl of each small ripple which flows towards the shore.

A lavish breakfast sent us on our way in fine spirits…I mean, just look out there. Who could possibly be downcast on such a glorious day? Certainly not this happy band. The Hall family are on the road and The Intrepid Trio are in fine fettle, thank you very much and that feeling of total well-being was even more enhanced by the fact that the sun was now, as we set off on our journey, beginning to win its battle with the mist and the overall prospects for the day were looking good. In fact, I would go so far as to say…positively brilliant.

Our mood was that of excited anticipation, as we settled back to enjoy the relatively long journey which lay ahead of us, in order to reach our destination, which was…Glenveagh National Park.

It was scenic splendour, quite beyond the bounds of the imagination…which is the only way that I can describe the gorgeous, quite staggering tapestry which unfolded before our eyes, as our journey progressed. This was unsurpassable beauty and enchantment which could not but delight the senses, mile after mile. This narrow, twisting lane, along which our presence seemed to be almost an intrusion, was ablaze with ruby red, in the form of millions of jewel-like droplets, vibrant and exotic, like precious rubies, the green foliage amongst which they nestled, making it appear as if they were set in a lush, green velvet. This phenomenon of the magnificent wild fuchsia seems to be everywhere and this was just another particularly vibrant display of this precious and colourful jewel of the hedgerow.. it seems to abound, along every country lane but, in certain places, it is the sheer, overpowering abundance of them which really stuns and takes ones breath away. Our present road seemed to be hemmed in, on both sides, by this wild, exotic and amazingly beautiful, fuchsia hedge and they were a truly amazing and quite glorious sight.

Barely giving one a chance to recover from that spectacle of hedgerow magnificence, the eye was once more assailed by the total splendour of the sweeping moorland. Nature once again dipped into her breathtaking resources of the gold and the copper…a copper that was, at that moment, deeply burnished by the morning sunlight and which was slashed, here and there with deep, narrow trenches, the peat trenches and an army of the small cairns of peat brickettes. They looked like a small village of little brown igloos…again, a sight that we had come across all over the county.

Needless to say, the ubiquitous moorland sheep barely glanced up at our passing, totally unimpressed by this rude interuption to their morning routine and those which might just have shown a wee spark of curiosity, simply continued their constant chomping without so much as a momentary break in rhythm.

The magnificent cattle, of which we had seen so many splendid examples, over the last few days, made a picture-postcard scene of idyllic, rustic perfection as they stood together in small herds…handsome beasts, all, in those same lustrous colours, from cream to rich tan.

And, as if that were not sufficient to delight the eyes and the senses, we eventually came into the mountains, indeed, we seemed to be surrounded by nothing but mountains. Derryveagh Mountains and Glendowan Mountains. Range after range of the most towering grandeur and majesty. Even our spirits, which were already as high as a kite, rose to a whole new level, in keeping with these heights of nature's finest and most astounding massifs. I even ventured into the realms of a little in-car entertainment, which is something that I haven't been particularly encouraged to do, after previous attempts…however, I thought that the occasion merited a bold effort and so, I struck up with the song that had been replaying, in my mind, ever since last night. 'The Wild Collonial Boy'. OK, so I only knew the words to the first verse…but at least I could complete the whole of the first verse. Surely there has to be some credit in that. Eventually, however, I knew that I was pushing my luck and that maybe, just maybe, it might be a good idea if I were to desist. I cannot help but remember one other occasion when my extremely well-meant attempts at musical entertainment was not as appreciated as it should have been and, on that occasion, I was very lucky not to find myself in orbit, somewhere out over the Irish sea. Some folk have no appreciation of my, no doubt, questionable talent. (No taste, either…which is only my own humble opinion, of course).

The mountains seemed to be our constant companions now, with inland mountain lakes, so many of them that they lay like silver mirrors, in amongst the long grasses and reeds which surrounded them. More lakes, in fact, than I had ever seen, in one small area and at one time.

And then, we somehow lost our road, or at least, eventually came to the conclusion that we must have taken a wrong turn somewhere but, in a way, it did us a favour.

In order to inspect our battered map, (you will notice that it has now progressed from being merely rumpled to being battered) we pulled in and stopped, by the side of the River Finn and, oh boy, what a picture. Quite inadvertently, we had come into what is, in fact, the very heartland of Donegal, where, in the blink of an eye or just a turn in the road, or the topping of a hill, anywhere along your chosen way, can unfold a whole new and even more stunning landscape. Around here, it is a rugged but very beautiful countryside of mountains, which we had already seen for ourselves, along with quite spectacular glens and lakes. I mean, even here, where we had now stopped, this river, the River Finn is, or so it is said, one of the finest salmon rivers in, not just Ireland but, in the whole of Europe…which will give you some idea of the very special treat that we had accidentally come across.

But, it's the views which stun the senses…views of quite incredible magnificence, especially over towards the Blue Stack Mountains which actually overshadow the banks of the River Finn…and now, not too far away, nestling in all of this scenic splendour, is our destination, Glenveagh National Park. This is truly unspoilt natural beauty of the most incredible splendour. Wild deer roam freely amongst these hills, where great outcrops of rock thrust upwards out of the living earth and the mountains, rising like mighty leviathans, soar and reach for the sky, at the same time dwarfing the lesser hills, where the golden bracken and the purple heather form a natural backcloth for the ever-present sheep which almost seem to be superglued on as they cling to their delicate, tenuous, seemingly impossible footholds.

We were not too far from the Park now and the closer that we came to it, it was becoming almost impossible to sustain a reasonable credibility of all the unimaginable splendour which just kept on and on, as if defying the mind to be able to take it all in.

This mountain range, this mighty massif, is a phenomenon that seems to go on for ever, certainly for as far as the eye can see. There actually appears to be range after range of these splendid peaks.

Precocious, cheeky little streams and rivulets trickle down the hillsides, which appear to be living entities as the sun sends sparkling highlights winking and blinking off these flowing streams of mountain water.

At this point, I just have to say that, in all honesty, never in my entire life have I seen anything quite like this. I know that I am not a particularly good example of the well travelled expert on scenery…or anything else, for that matter but, I would swear that there is very little, if anything, anywhere on this earth, which could surpass what we have had the privilege to see for ourselves, this morning. I was quite stunned by our first venture up into the mountains, the other day but, nothing…and I mean, nothing, could prepare you for all of this.

After the last few miles, where, because of the narrow roads, we were constantly brought to a temporary halt by road blocks of a rather less than run-of-the-mill variety, as a dozen or so sheep sauntered along, as if next week would do and making absolutely no effort to move over…I mean, come on girls, let's get a shift on, why don't you. In all honesty, having accepted the quite farcical humour of the whole thing, we eventually gave up and, well, just trundled along behind them until such time as they saw fit to shove up a wee bit and allow us to pass. What a lark, though! There we were, brought to a virtual standstill by a bunch of sheep…and they looked so comical as they just plodded along, taking their own time and having no intention of being rushed by anyone, with their fat little bellies swaying from side to side and their almost ridiculously thin, quite spindly, in fact, black legs appearing most inadequate to support the rest of their little woolly persons. Oh but I do love them, though. I mean, to me, the sheep seem to, somehow, be symbolic of Ireland.

Despite the traffic problems, of the woolly variety, of course, we did, eventually, arrive at Glenveagh National Park Visitor Centre and were immediately charmed by the place and eager to see all that it had to offer, which included a real castle, Glenveagh Castle. Even getting to this rather splendid castle was to be quite a novelty as we had to go on a little bus which plied back and forth, on a regular service throughout the day, from the Visitor Centre to the Castle, and visa versa.

However, by this time, we were hungry, so, the decision was that we would have our picnic lunch first…and then get the wee bus up to the castle. The picnic areas, where there were plenty of picnic tables and benches, were set in an open area just off the main car parks and were surrounded by the natural woodland that was a part of the National Park. It was all very pleasant… a peaceful place…and after the fairly long journey to get this far, it was a joy to just relax for a while and take it all in.

Poor Misty. After a quick stretch of his legs and the chance to do his necessaries, he had to suffer the huge disappointment of being put back in the car. It was unavoidable, of course, as we discovered that dogs were not allowed up at the Castle. Oh, but his dear, funny face dropped, when realization finally dawned that we were not taking him with us and we were both quite guilt-ridden as we walked away from the car. So sorry, my baby, but it cannot be helped and somehow, I promise, we will make it up to you, later.

Look after the car, babes!

Setting out on the special little bus was quite ridiculously exciting, but then, well, you know what I'm like…and, after a short trip of only 2km, there we were, pulling up outside the walls of the castle. On first impression, it had a look of 'Glenbogle' only this was a real castle, towering over the surrounding land in all its splendour, on the side of Lough Beagh.

We went all around the outside grounds, climbing up hundreds of steps as we went around different towers of all different shapes, peering out of small apertures and hanging out over the crenulated walls of keeps, and things…and then, quite out of nowhere, a fine mist dropped down over everything, damp and chill and completely enshrouding the view up Lough Beagh. The speed at which it suddenly came down was quite eerie, giving everything an almost surreal and dreamlike quality and offering to the imagination, especially one like mine, the opportunity of conjuring up even the most unlikely…and totally ridiculous! I mean, could that have possibly been some spectral apparition, a visitor from the past, who has just passed through the mist and given us a rather roguish wink? I must say that he looked very dashing and anyway, people do not go around with a sword on their hip these days…do they?

Well, for heaven's sake ! What did you expect? You know where my imagination can lead, by now. I mean, it certainly isn't beyond the realms of possibility, now…is it?

Anyway, leaving Errol Flynn to scare the living daylights out of someone else, we made our way indoors. The mist had rendered everthing quite chill and dank and so, the prospect of a visit to the small café seemed like the best idea we'd had all day.

And then, it was time to bid farewell to Glenveagh Castle. The time had passed so quickly that it came as something of a shock when we realised just how late it was getting and then of course, we became a wee bit anxious and even more guilty about our poor, abandoned baby boy and so, we made our way to the pickup point for the shuttle bus, which runs so frequently that we had a wait of only a few minutes and then we were back and on the receiving end of a quite rapturous welcome from the hairy one. His dear face was a picture of sheer canine pleasure and the casual observer could have been excused for assuming that he hadn't set eyes upon us for at least a month.

The journey back to Donegal didn't seem to take anywhere near the time that it had taken us to get up here, in the first place… probably because the way is more familiar in reverse and there were fewer woolly roadblocks. Anyway, looking back on the day, it may have been a quite splendid and remarkable day for Jeff and I but, for Misty…it was just one great, huge let-down. The very least that we could do, on the return journey, was to find the poor lad a beach. I mean, let's be fair…a chap needs to have the opportunity, at least once in the day, to let off some steam and play doggie games like chasing seagulls and digging holes in the sand…in short, all the simple pleasures that any self-respecting canine places the most store by. How is it that humans just seem totally incapable of seeing the obvious, when it is there for all dogs to see, without any trouble at all?

As luck would have it, we did manage to find one, a different one to any that we had previously been to and well, he streaked away like lightning and was soon in an ecstasy of canine delight, because, as luck would have it, the water had recently gone out, leaving the sand and, what was more important, great clumps of seaweed, all nice and wet and glistening…and altogether ideally smelly and gooey, especially perfect for our Misty's taste. You see, one of his favourite tricks is to grab hold of a nice, long length of said smelly and rather obnoxious seaweed, which he will then brandish like a jousting lance and, given the opportunity, and the close proximity of some unsuspecting stranger, poke it at that poor unfortunate, who, hopefully, will just smile, rather wanly and pass by without further comment. As luck would have it, there wasn't anyone about at this time. Anyway, it was just as glorious and just the way he likes it and all the better for rolling in.

In less than five minutes, our glorious Irish Setter, the one we usually take such pride in, the one with the burnished copper, shining, luxuriant coat was soaked through and disgustingly sticky, (just normal, in other words) with the goo from the seaweed acting as a strong adhesive which was all the better for attracting and picking up a greater coating of sand. When we got back to the car and began the usual process of trying to remove as much of this glutinous mess as we could, he just stood there, quite meekly, looking the very picture of doggie innocence while Jeff did the necessary with the towels, and I swear, he was actually laughing at us. His comical expression and the cheeky, tongue-lolling grin could not have been more eloquent. It was clearly obvious, to anyone with a reasonable knowledge of canine behaviour, that this rather smelly, sandy, furry person was telling us, in his own inimitable way that this was pay-back time…and I mean, big time…'This is for leaving me behind. So there!' There was no mistaking the expression of smug satisfaction in those melting brown eyes.

Smelly dog, or not, it was a very happy Intrepid Trio who arrived back at Dunkineely. Maybe just a tad travel-worn and somewhat unkempt but, very content with all that we had done today. As always, any aspirations we may have had when we first hit the road, this morning, have been excelled…and in spades, as always. But then, this is Ireland. That is all that I need to say. This is Ireland.

We are now a third of the way into our second trip to this quite remarkable country and I can honestly say that not once have we ever been disappointed with anything that Ireland has to offer…on the contrary, whatever our imaginings may have been, the real thing has always been so much more. Here, in this land of enchantment, you can allow your dreams and your imagination to reach the most improbable heights and, no matter how improbable those dreams may be, this country will, if you just give it the chance, fill your soul with the joy of a dream come true.

We had promised ourselves a special treat, this evening…something in keeping with the day…and so, after a clean up and spruce up, we set off, in fine style, for Donegal. What could be a better way of concluding such a special day than a special meal and, as we had been to a very fine castle whilst on our travels, we found the, what seemed to us, to be a most appropriate place…The Castle Restaurant, just across from Donegal Castle or, to give this ancient pile its other name… Red Hugh O'Donnell's Castle. I must say that he sounds like a colourful character, this Red Hugh O'Donnell. Ha! Ha!

God, it gets worse, does it not?

Sorry about that…It was a rather pathetic joke, I must admit.

Anyway, the restaurant was fantastic. As soon as we walked in, we were immediately impressed with the ambience of the place. The interior design was such that it had all the character of the old castle, even though the décor and all the fixtures and fittings, were, of necessity, only reproduction.

We were given a lovely table for two, by one of the beautiful stained-glass windows, with, at intervals along the stone walls, sconces of iron which held candles, for a more romantic atmosphere of course and, once seated and with a drink to hand, we sat back and enjoyed the luxurious surroundings, whilst anticipating with great relish, the meal which we had ordered.

You know what I'm like when confronted with a menu…big kid in a sweetie shop, that's me…so, OK…I mean, it's too late to change your mind, once the meal is on the table. I just like to be sure, that is all. Anyway, I thought that I showed, for once, on this auspicious occasion, a rare ability to be able to make a decision, a definite decision, without any prevarication whatsoever, by settling on the…wait for it…Irish Stew. That may be nothing, if not predictable but, although there were so many delectable dishes to choose from, I just had to have it…and it will not, I most sincerely hope, be the last time that I have it, over the next two weeks. (The Irish Stew, of course. OK, whatever else you may have been thinking…that, too).

Jeff had the Fish and Chips but, (and this is a huge 'but') this was no ordinary Fish and Chips. Apart from anything else, the fish was straight out of the waters off Killybegs…I mean, how fresh can you get? The poor thing was probably still swimming around, minding its own business, just a few hours ago…and now, there he was, filleted, battered and on a plate with chips.

Speaking of which, even the chips were real gourmet-type chips…and yes, I did, somewhat dishonestly, I know, sample the odd one or three. (In other words, I nicked a couple off Jeff's plate).

By the time we left the restaurant, it was dark, or almost…and how pretty this lovely old town looked, sort of all dressed up in her evening finery, with the glow of lights showing in all the shop windows and the warm halo of light which illuminated the pavement from the ornamental and very decorative street lamps…indeed, there was a definite aura of romance here, in this place and on this mellow evening. I felt quite sad, in all honesty, as we drove out of town and headed back to Dunkineely. I don't suppose we will be back…at least, not this trip. Tomorrow is our last full day before moving on…and so, well, farewell, I guess, to Donegal town. You have made us feel more than welcome and our memories of you and the people whom we have had the pleasure of meeting, will always be special ones.

The night was clear, as we followed the narrow road along the peninsula, to our now familiar little home…and how quickly the days have gone by since that very first time, when we drove down this seemingly endless track, thinking, as we went along that surely, we must have gone wrong, somewhere. It seems silly now and such a long time ago as familiarity has taken over. But, what a wealth of beauty and serenity and enchantment have we experienced in that time.

An aura of warmth and of belonging and a strong sense of the joy that we have experienced over the last week has, somehow, managed to infiltrate the very fabric of this small abode and it met us as we walked through the door, this evening. I think that maybe, that aura has emanated from us, from all the laughter and love which has filled this wee cottage, every single day for the past week and now, it is a part of the place and I hope that, when the next family come through that door, they will feel it. That joy and that love fills the entire house and, as always, even manages to penetrate to the remotest corners and that, my dear friend, is the cosy and loving atmosphere which now just awaits your arrival, in order to make the day complete.

I cannot begin to tell you of the enormous feeling of satisfaction that just being able to relive this amazing day has given to me…and the same goes for all the other nights when you have listened with such patience and fortitude to my, more often than not, over-enthusiastic blethering. It is such a great kindness that you do for me, allowing me this luxury, the luxury of being able to talk and reminisce and relive precious memories, the way you do, every night. If you ever become bored, you certainly never show it and, all that I can say is that it means everything to me. Thank you and bless you for your friendship.

What few hours still remained of this wonderful day have been spent as they can only be spent when there is a great love between two people. The loving, close companionship, the intimate, easy flow of conversation between a husband and wife and, of course, our now, slightly less smelly, much loved pup, who is now stretched out his full, quite considerable length, in front of the fire…and the aroma of a good bottle of wine. What more could anyone ask?

Everything that we have experienced this day, has been that of pure Irish magic and the fond recollections of each precious moment will certainly follow us into sleep this night but, first of all, I just have to go through my nightly routine…and, whilst we are here in this land of enchantment, where all wishes are but waiting to be granted and dreams to be fulfilled, there always seems to be so much more to give thanks for.

Today has been no exception and, with all my heart, I thank God for all that He has been good enough to give to us. Two people could not have wished for more and, for me, part of the magic that has filled this day…and this is just on a personal level… comes from the fact that everything that I have experienced, all the pleasure, all the silly and, no doubt, childish joy, has been with my Jeffy. For him to be by my side, in everything that we do, is as much a source of magic as that which is forever being showered upon us by Ireland…along with the fairy dust, of course.

It's strange but, I know that I could never even contemplate doing anything on my own…Jeff is my motivation in everything. He is as the very air that I breathe…I could not survive without either. God bless you, my darling husband…tonight and always.

OK, my Misty, I have not forgotten you. I'm afraid you have not had much in the way of excitement today but I think, by and large, that you have had a good day. In your own little way, you have made it your own. At least you are now clean and our own bonny lad, once again…although there is still a slight whiff of seaweed. Not to worry. Sleep tight, my precious pup and dream sweet and happy dreams. God bless.

God bless us all!

◎◎◎◎◎◎◎◎◎◎◎◎

This evening has been a pleasant conclusion to a great day and my thoughts are a mixture of a nostalgic sadness at the thought of leaving here and a tingle of anticipation at the prospect of all that lies ahead of us.

This may have been our last full day, here in this wonderful county of Donegal but, much as we have grown to love it, we still have our memories…wonderful memories…and, well, we are merely moving on, to yet another part of this country that I love so much.

Looking around now, at the cottage, we have got pretty much everything packed up, ready for tomorrow and I am mentally saying a fond farewell to everything that has made our stay here so joyous. At the minute, as I wait for you to arrive…surprise, surprise…I am sitting in what has become my usual place, taking the opportunity to gaze out onto Donegal Bay for the last time.

This time tomorrow, we will be in another cottage, in another place and I can only hope that you are going to be with us. I mean, it never even occurred to me that, just maybe, you might not want to. Oh please, do come…and share whatever the next two weeks will bring. The Intrepid Trio have so many more adventures to experience and wondrous things to do and places to explore. You must know that it just would not be the same if you were not with us, to follow in the steps of we three whom you have grown to know, probably better than anyone else ever has.

Anyway, while Jeff just takes Misty out and along the lane for one final farewell, come and sit with me. The tale of this, our last day in Donegal is very much in need of the telling and, although there is a certain amount of nostalgia in the air this evening, there is no real sadness. There will be no melancholy in our hearts this night, so have no fear. What was it that Shakespeare once said…something about 'parting is such sweet sorrow'…now, sitting here, I think I know what he meant.

Friday
25th September 2009

My first waking thought, this morning, was that I had been dreaming and the particular scene in my dream which seemed to be responsible for waking me up was when the brick wall fell on me. In actual fact, it wasn't a brick wall at all, merely my huge lump of an Irish Setter…about 42kilos of Irish Setter…who had, most unceremoniously, landed on top of me, or at least, the upper part of his great furry person had landed on top of me and was proceeding, as I became more alert to what was going on, to prove to me just how much he really loved me.

Jeff rescued me, for which I was grateful and then I was given the benefit of a repeat performance of the skylight spectacular, the premier of which had caused such uncontrollable hilarity, on Sunday. Once again, I was devoid of camera, which, if I have to be honest is, maybe, just as well. Little old me being done for taking pornographic photos! Well, I never did!

There was just a little touch of regret, as I pottered about the now so familiar kitchen of this dear cottage, with bacon and sausages sizzling nicely and the toast adding its own delicious aroma to that of the bacon and the coffee. This being our last full day it is also the last breakfast…a quick coffee will be all that we will be having, tomorrow. Still, it was only just a wee pang of regret…I mean, we have so much to look forward to that a quite delicious feeling of excitement is already beginning to bubble up again, just under the surface of my consciousness, as my brain (and yes, there are just a few lonely cells rattling around up there) and I, begin to anticipate this big move to yet another wonderful part of this enchanted land.

Owing to the very real fact of our imminent departure and all the subsequent packing up, in readiness for our transfer to the next cottage, we purposely left until today, what should be and, on this I feel quite sure, something very special…and that special place is our own wee peninsula. We have only covered a very small part of it…even Jeff has only walked so far along the lane with Misty, so, today we have planned to do the entire thing, all the way to the lighthouse, which is way down at the very last tip of the land.

Fortified by that good breakfast, The Intrepid Trio set out in fine style and extremely high spirits, to explore this small finger of land which has so captivated us, over the past week. There are, in fact, two narrow roads which run down the length of the peninsula…the first one is at the start of the village of Dunkineely and is, in fact, the one on which lies our little cottage and which looks out onto Donegal Bay and the other, which is at the further end of the village, eventually looks out onto McSwyne's Bay and both roads meet up, finally, about half way down, at the point where there is a pretty little beach. The last stage of the journey to the lighthouse has to be done on foot and a good, gravel pathway follows the lie of the land, across the top of the cliffs, until the lighthouse comes into view.

The morning was absolutely glorious! Indeed, it could not have been more perfect. The sun almost wore one of those smiley faces as it looked benevolently down upon us and, with no apparent effort, transformed everything into a bright and sparkling kaleidoscope of colours.

How fortunate we have been with the weather, this past week. …I mean, we have had only the one day of any considerable rain and that was last Monday…and wow…rain or no rain, what a fantastic day that was! Most mornings, there has been that gossamer veil of mist, out and over the Bay, which is only to be expected, I suppose, in September and the occasional early morning light rain but, by and large, it has been great.

Today, as if the Deity who just happens to be in charge of the weather had made an extra special effort, in view of the fact that this was, when all was said and done, our last day in this area, a heavenly canopy of blue sky was provided for us as we headed out towards the village, the intention being that we would call in at the mini-market and then, take the other, outer road down the peninsula to St. John's Point…that's the bit at the end, with the lighthouse…just as a point of interest, don't you know! Point! Get it? Oh, come on now. (Sorry! I really must stop doing this. My inane attempts at humour do leave a lot to be desired, do they not)?

I had never really thought about it but, if I had, I could not have imagined anything quite so lovely. The road hugged the sea, all the way along, right up to the point where it veers off to the beach…and even then, it is only a few hundred yards inland and small cottages and a farm or two were dotted along the coast road and up into the hills which overlook the beach. Wow…what a situation to have a cottage…I mean, it was stunning. That would do for us, for sure. (Oh, how I wish! Still, there is no point in daydreaming, you daft woman).

'Our' road joined up eventually and then, we were as far as we could go by car and, just as if conjured up by magic, there was this gorgeous little beach, small but really quite exquisite, spreading out before us in a small, yet gentle, crescent of white sand with turquoise water indolently lapping the shore…just the merest kiss…before ebbing and then repeating this gentle caress again and again and again. Three or four small boats added a splash of jaunty colour to the already idyllic scene, as they, in turn, gently bobbed up and down with each incoming swell and a couple of men, armed with fishing rods, completed the picture, turning it into a study of absolute perfection.

One very delighted Misty soon made his high spirits known, as he did his usual demonstration of just how to behave when on a beach…something that any self-respecting canine knows instinctively…and what a joy it always is, just to stand by and watch this magnificent animal enjoying himself in the way that only dogs know how. That's my boy!

After some small effort, we eventually managed to get him off the beach and, just to show that there was no ill-feeling, certainly on his part, he chased off up the pathway across the cliff-tops, towards to lighthouse, with Jeff and I following at a rather more leisurely pace. It was all so perfect! Holding hands, like a couple of young lovers, instead of two much older lovers, we strolled along, my Jeffy and I, in this idyllic place, on this idyllic day, taking in all the beauty which lay all around us, with our dear, daft, loveable dog finding his own kind of doggie happiness in the scent of rabbits and flowers and the tang of the sea which, occasionally, while stopping and raising his head, he would snuffle and sniff at, exhilarated, as always, by the smell of the ozone.

Within sight of the lighthouse, we decided to head back to the car. In all honesty, I had felt quite proud of myself having walked the distance that I had, however, I do still have my limitations and therefore, I felt that I had reached the stage where I had gone far enough…and there really was nowhere else to go, in all honesty, as the lighthouse is, after all, the end of the line.

And so, with Misty leading the way, we strolled, leisurely, back to the car, having thoroughly enjoyed our little expedition to St. John's Point and, after the exercise and the sea air, our thoughts were beginning to turn to lunch and a likely place to have it.

Killybegs! That had been the original Plan, decided upon by the Board, this morning and it still seemed like the best idea. I mean, Seasalt Vera just had to have one final fling in this small, yet quite delectable harbour. Not that either of us really needed an excuse to pay Killybegs another visit. At this stage in the proceedings, it just seemed to be the ideal place to have that extra special lunch. No butties today. Oh no! Today just had to be marked by something a bit more special than common or garden butties. Something in keeping with the mood of the day…something of a special treat…and the obvious place, or so it seemed to us, was the large hotel and restaurant which dominates the seafront of Killybegs and which can boast the most superb views overlooking the harbour.

By the time we reached Killybegs, neither Jeff nor I were quite ready to eat so, we had a stroll around the small shopping area of the town and settled for just a coffee, for the time being at least and then, with Misty in mind, we set off for Fintra Strand. It wasn't too far away and besides, the poor lad was looking just that wee bit crestfallen. I mean, he could see the sea and smell the sea but, nothing was happening in the way that was of any interest to him.

His delight was all the more profound, as a result of any slight disappointment that he may have experienced and when we eventually arrived at the beach and gave him his freedom, well, he reacted as if the entire sweep of Fintra Strand was his. All his it was…at first…and then suddenly, there appeared a small, white dog and, lo and behold, he had found himself a little friend. The owners of this little dog finally appeared also and we found out that the wee dog was named Monty. Oh boy! Our great lump, looking even more like a small pony alongside this other wee soul, was beside himself with canine delight and the two of them, friends, it would appear, for life, chased around like lunatics. Misty even ventured a little further into the sea than was his usual wont, as he chased in, without even thinking about it, in hot pursuit of Monty. In the meantime, we had become acquainted with Monty's people, who, it turned out, actually lived just up the road. Oh, my word! I mean, my jealousy knew no bounds. Imagine it…fancy being able to come out to this beach, every day. From where they lived, you could practically just roll out of bed and onto the beach. How amazing is that? Wow!

Anyway, it was a good and fortuitous meeting and we had made some new friends ourselves with this chance encounter. As for the two dogs, it was quite a job separating them…and, needless to say, they both needed a good rub down and de-sanding job, although there was a whole lot less of Monty's furry person to de-sand than our Misty.

And now, we really were hungry. Whilst the two dogs had been charging around in their ecstasy of doggie companionship, we humans had walked pretty much the full length of the beach…and back…which was a fair distance. Certainly enough to put that final edge on our appetite. So, with Misty more than content with the way his morning had turned out…from good to even better…he settled down, with quiet resignation, in the back of the car, as we retraced our steps, back to Killybegs…and that very fine and grand looking hotel.

It was quite exciting, really. I mean, it all looked very posh…and the food must be good, judging by the number of people who were already dining. We only just managed to get a table for two…and, how marvellous…positioned by the window. Brilliant!

Anyway, before you start thinking to yourself…'the length of time it takes her to decide what to have, it'll be dark'…let me just set the record straight by saying that my choice was immediate and quite definite. Seafood Chowder, with chunks of crisp, fresh bread. I mean, there really was no contest, although everything else would, no doubt, have been perfectly splendid. (You see…that's twice in two days when I have actually been able to make my mind up about something. Without taking all day to do so, if you see what I mean).

What luxury, though, having enjoyed our food, to just relax with our coffee and watch the activity of the harbour. Small boats were constantly going out or coming in but, what was most exciting was that the big one, the one bearing my name, Veronica, was heading out. She had been laying at anchor in the harbour ever since we first arrived and I don't know how long before that, however, she was on her way now, to heaven knows where and for heaven knows how long. A ship of her size could be months out at sea and my fertile imagination could, if I were to allow it free rein, conjure up quite fantastic pictures of coral seas and palm-fringed beaches. (Well, you know the sort of fantasy and intrigue that my mind could invent). Although, I expect she will not be going to anywhere quite so exotic. Much to the dismay of the crew, I expect. I'll just bet that they would have gladly traded their forthcoming expedition to, no doubt, somewhere in the Atlantic, for somewhere a little warmer and infinitely more glamorous…like the Caribbean?

As she came away from her mooring, stern first and then began the turn which would put her in the right position to leave the protection of the harbour and head out to sea, I did what I said that I would do and offered up a silent prayer for the safety of all on board whilst out on this voyage out to sea…a sea that can be so unpredictable and, for her safe and successful return to Killybegs. God speed, my beautiful boat…and a swift return. For a moment or two, I just stood and watched her go and I felt quite moved by it. Just a routine occurrence, in a place like this, where men make their living from the sea…a fishing boat setting out on a normal fishing expedition. Maybe it had something to do with the fact that I just felt something special about this particular boat. The Veronica. My boat! May God watch over you and bring you back to your safe anchorage.

Having said a nostalgic farewell to my beautiful boat we also sadly bade a very fond farewell to Killybegs. Time had passed by so quickly, with the trip to St. John's Point seeming such a long time ago…plus the fact that we had spent a lot more time down on the beach than had been our intention. The people we had been fortunate enough to share that time with, however, more than made it worthwhile. To my mind, time is never wasted when the pleasure in the time spent is as memorable as was this fleeting moment, in this special day and which was so greatly enhanced by this fortunate meeting…for us as well as our young and boisterous pup.

And there you have it, my dear friend…the day and, indeed, the week. It has been a truly memorable week…particularly special for me, in as much as it was something for which I had yearned. A yearning which had seemed to be forever just that. A yearning that was doomed to be unresolved and that felt like an eternity.

The love that became a passion, for both myself and my darling husband, after our first trip to this beautiful and very special land, goes on. Indeed, this past week has endorsed our previous infatuation and, if anything, has strengthened it. Perhaps I should amend that slightly…you see, what we feel for Ireland is so much more than mere infatuation. Yes…as the title says…The Love Affair Goes On.

Earlier, we had one final walk along the lane. The bond between this particular husband and wife seeming stronger and deeper than ever, as we shared this moment of love and happy memories. Our hearts were so full of love for each other and for the dear, daft, adorable young dog who was quite contentedly re-visiting all of his now accustomed places, where he would leave a wee message for whomsoever may, perhaps, pass along this way and be even remotely interested, later on.

Misty was here!

And, in saying that, what a wonderful time he has had, in his own innocent doggie fashion. A young head filled with his own ideas of what constitutes a good time.

There was just a slight feeling of regret at the thought of leaving Donegal…but, and here is the truth of it…the places we have visited, the sheer beauty and magnificence of all that we have seen and experienced, will remain in our hearts for always, as will the people we have met, all of whom have won special places in the hearts of my Jeffy and I. The dear Sister and our new friend, the retired photographer, from that first morning, in Donegal Town…so greatly did they influence and enhance those special, early moments of our stay here. Those early moments when everything is so new and so precious…that special 'first morning' feeling…even that was transformed and made even more special by those two fortunate meetings.

And how could we ever forget Pat. Dear Pat, from MacIntyre's Bar, in Dunkineely. He made us feel so welcome, indeed, everyone in that wee village made us feel as if we were one of them, on that quite amazing night, when Irish music came from honest Irish hearts and sent a warmth and the very spirit of this land into the souls of all who heard it. For years to come, we shall always remember that Wednesday night is Music Night, in dear Dunkineely, Co. Donegal…and, once again, we will feel the warmth of the friendship of those very special people.

Yes, only a few days yet, so many people…even those with whom our aquaintance was but casual. God bless each and every one of them…and thank you for the blessing of your friendship.

So, all has been done in readiness for our move, tomorrow. An early start will find us on the road to Galway…or rather, just a little to the north of Galway.

Anyway, everything has now been packed up, leaving us, as always, with just the last minute bits and pieces…and so, I am taking time, just a little time, before we go up to bed, to enjoy the quietude of these last, mellow moments of this somewhat momentous evening. I have, in my hand, my usual glass of wine and I'm looking out across the bay at all the twinkly lights on the far side. Donegal Bay is just as lovely, now, as it ever was. To me, it will always be lovely.

OK. That's it. No sad thoughts. Our memories are and always will be, very happy ones and tomorrow, well, tomorrow we start the whole process again. The process of making more happy memories and opening up yet another chamber in our hearts for all of the new and wonderful things which we know, without the slightest doubt, Ireland still has to offer. That is something that I have learnt, over the time that I have spent in this land…Ireland will always have the power to stun and thrill the soul of anyone who is open to accept the magic, that very special Irish magic, a magic which is totally unique and which captures the heart of all who set foot on Irish soil. This special magic is a mixture, a harmonious blend of beauty which is beyond belief and the warmth of her people… and you can actually feel the heartbeat of this nation, the heartbeat of her people and it is the people who make their country so special. It manifests itself in every warm and friendly face and every sincere and welcoming greeting.

May God bless Ireland and keep her always in the palm of His hand.

Jeff is asleep, I think. Misty, also, is well away…the snoring kind of gives it away. Just a few moments more, just to review the last few days and then I think that I will be able to settle.

Thankyou, my dear and precious husband, for all the memories and for all the love…your very precious love. You fill my days with joy and nothing in the world could ever mean more to me than you, my own love. Even though I should live to be a hundred, I shall never truly deserve, or cease to marvel at the wonder that is you. I love you, my darling.

And now, you, our own loveable, faithful and loving Misty. You may be able to snore for England…and Ireland…but you are very precious to your mum and your dad. Sleep tight, funny face. Dream sweet dreams and know that you are safe and loved.

Just one more thing, before I go to sleep…please, I need to just make sure. If I don't ask, what may seem to you to be a daft question, I know that I shall never be able to sleep…you will be coming with us, tomorrow, won't you? There is so much that will be new and wonderful and, well, it is so important that you remain a dear friend. So, please! Stay with us, to follow in our footsteps and marvel, just as we do, at whatever Ireland still has in store for us. It will make it all the more special for us. Thankyou! Deep down, I knew that you would stay true.

God bless…God bless everyone!

◎◎◎◎◎◎◎◎◎◎◎

A whole twenty four hours and so many, indeed, countless miles have intervened since we last spoke. There was, inevitably, a wee pang of nostalgic regret at leaving Donegal this morning but, it was but brief, as the ever growing fever of excitement overpowered any small feelings of melancholia.

We have now settled into our 'new' cottage and, I just know that you are going to love it. Everything about it is just perfect, including the surroundings. The fabric of the building is such that it will keep out the coldest of nights. I mean, with walls that are about three feet thick, it would withstand anything…certainly anything that the elements could possibly 'rain' down upon it. I know. I know. I keep on doing it! My somewhat pathetic attempts at whimsical humour. Sorry! Very sorry!

To continue……the cottage is, in fact, an old barn conversion, set in the quite vast and impressive grounds of the main house, where lives our lovely Host and Hostess and the conversion has been so wonderfully and skilfully crafted that it has rendered the entire ambience of the place to be comfortably rustic, in a cosy, homely sort of way and most pleasant and agreeable to the eye. But and this is a huge BUT…and you are just going to love this…there is a real fire. Yes, logs are, as I speak, sending sparks of welcome up the chimney, to offer a special greeting to a special friend.

Oh, what a treat, though. It just makes a room come alive, just to see the flames busying themselves around the glowing embers and the crackling logs.

Somehow, it satisfies all ones nostalgic feelings of what a home should be. It gives warmth and it gives a living, moving central focus around which, families have, for thousands of years, gathered. It's a mellow, cosy feeling which, no matter how one may try to emulate it, artificially, it just cannot be replicated. Only a real fire can achieve that kind of ambience…not to mention the wine. So, OK, I won't mention the wine…or the fact that I do have my first glass of the evening to hand. (And it won't be my last!)

Although we have been on the road all day, there is still quite a lot that I have to tell you. I mean, we could have journeyed from Donegal to Tourmakeady as the crow flies, so to speak, however, as there was no great rush it seemed like a good idea to make a proper day of it and, having planned our route by taking some of the more off-the-beaten-track roads, we managed to turn a mundane, cross-country trek into a jolly and very pleasant 'outing' which, in turn, led us to some quite wonderful places which would otherwise have been lost to us had we not ventured off the main roads.

Anyway, that's enough blethering, for now. You will hear about it, in full, in due course.

So that you don't lose your way, on this, your first visit to our new home, I shall just wait for you at the front door. Oh, just wait until you see all of this…it is so gorgeous! From my position, just outside the doorway, I can see the moon, riding high in the night sky and I can see the broad silver highway which travels across the huge expanse of water that is Lough Mask…a highway that seems to reach all the way up to the shining orb of the moon itself. Everything is so amazingly clear and the moon is so large and so perfectly round that the features of that dear old man-in-the-moon are clearly visible, even to the naked eye and it almost seems, to me, at least, as if that venerable, yet mischievous, lunar gentleman is actually winking at me. (Which is only to be expected, of course. I mean, any moon which hangs over this land of whimsy and good-natured humour could not help but become touched by the magic of the Leprechauns).

And now, a happy sight, indeed. You are here! Welcome to yet another 'home' in yet another part of Ireland.

Saturday
26th. September 2009

One of these days, I will learn to keep my big mouth closed, especially when I start to brag about how marvellous we are. On a number of occasions, over the last few days, you will remember how I have boasted of how efficient and organized we have become, well, I have to confess that this morning, it felt as though we had regressed fifteen months, as chaos seemed to just slip, quite naturally, into its normal, early morning slot and drive us all into fits of screaming laughter and the poor, bemused dog to retreat to a safe distance.

Why that should be, I don't know, I mean, for heaven's sake, we had done virtually everything yesterday and although we had plenty of time, panic seemed to set in, right from the start. Of course, we had a proper breakfast, which had not been our original intention…I mean, I had the wherewithal…bacon and eggs and all the etc's left over and so it did seem a shame to just throw it away…might just as well eat it. From then onwards, we were dashing around like headless chickens and Misty decided that a tactical retreat might just be a good idea, under the circumstances, until it was time to get into the car, that is.

At long last, we eventually got on the road…and it was only 9.30 so, well, I don't think that was too bad. We had even given the cottage a bit of a spring clean in that time. I don't know about you but I always like to leave anywhere that we have been occupying for any length of time, as clean, if not cleaner, than when we first arrived. I think it must be something which comes instinctively to most women…we are born, pre-programmed to immediately pick up a duster.

As always, I could not resist one final look back, to the dear wee cottage and out across Donegal Bay…what bit I could see, this morning…everything was totally enshrouded with that now familiar low, pearly mist. Maybe it was just as well, as I could not help just a small pang of sadness at leaving this small but, very special, piece of Ireland, where we had found such happiness. Still, it was not as though we were leaving the country. Behave yourself, for heaven's sake, you silly old fool…Ireland has not finished with us yet and The Intrepid Trio has not, under any circumstances, finished with Ireland.

Once we were on the road, our spirits lifted and anticipation kicked in. Quite ridiculously, we were quite overtaken by this enormous surge of excitement…or, at least, I was. I mean, you know what I'm like…I was already beginning to fidget as I sat in the passenger seat beside my Jeffy, who, thank goodness, was more able to take it all in his stride. As I have said so many times, it really is a good job that at least one of us has some sense. (And, as you know well enough, that description does not apply to me).

Donegal had gone but, it will always remain in our hearts and there was a whole wealth of Irish magic and enchantment still to come. A whole two weeks of the kind of magic that can only be found in this land of beauty, romance and…fairy dust? Yes, I did say fairy dust. One of these days you will believe me! Anyway, it was all out there, just waiting for The Intrepid Trio to find it and make it our own.

From that moment on, when it suddenly dawned on us that nothing was actually coming to an end, on the contrary, it was only just beginning, we began to feel like a couple of kids on Christmas Eve.

Our journey took us through three different Counties, as we gradually headed more and more south. From County Donegal, we then entered County Sligo and, just through the town of Sligo, we picked up the N59…and actually decided to stay on this road until we reached another, smaller town, by the name of Ballina and from there, to a place called Bangor. There was an actual plan in all of this, just in case you may be wondering. You see, we were intent on heading for the west coast where there were some interesting looking little islands and bays and inlets. With a bit of luck, we were hoping that we may come upon a nice beach…(a) we were getting hungry and, where better to break out the butty box and (b) Misty would, by then, be in need of a place to have a good run and let off some steam, amongst other things.

Our way was a wee bit off the beaten track and did, in fact, take us off our original route by quite a few miles however, it was well worth it, although we didn't know that for a fact at that precise moment when we turned off at Bangor, onto a lesser R road, the R313, to be exact and suddenly found ourselves in total oceanic paradise once again…especially beyond Belmullet where there were so many absolutely glorious bays and headlands with names like Ardmore Point and Ardelly Point. Elly Bay was a joyous curve of sweeping white-sand beach and gently lapping crystal-clear water…one of the small but, quite delightful beaches. Nothing big, or mind-blowing…although, I suppose it was quite stunning, in its own way… just a tiny crescent of Irish beach perfection. Indeed, we were actually all set to settle for this pretty little bay as our stopping off point, however, just a few yards up the road, on the opposite side to Elly Bay, Jeff spotted a quite innocuous looking sign, which could have been so easily overlooked, indicating a parking area. Well, it was worth a try, anyway.

Sure enough, there was plenty of space to park up and when we, rather stiffly, I might add, got out of the car, well, I could hear it. As soon as I actually opened the door, I could hear it…and so could my big, daft beach bum of a dog.

SEA…that was the sound which turned both myself and my daft dog into stupidly grinning loonies…and, unlike the wee bay across the road, this was no gentle lapping of gentle water, this was just the way old Seasalt Vera loves it. I mean, for heaven's sake…just listen to that!

Making our way through a tunnel-like gap in the sand dunes, all of a sudden it was like, there, great and wild and magnificent. The sand was a quite stunningly, brilliantly light sand, almost white and it stretched for miles, whichever way one looked. I just could not believe what I was looking at and it took what seemed for ever, although it was no more than seconds, in all honesty, for it to really sink in and then, well I streaked down to the water's edge (my version of a streak, of course) and just shrieked with the sheer joy of it. Meanwhile, Misty was capering around like the dear idiot he is, just as if he hadn't seen the sea for months. I mean, after all those quite unbelievable beaches that we discovered in Donegal, it was all the more amazing to find something equally as stunning, in another place and so soon and, what is more, without even trying.

Oh, but the sound of that incoming surf!

That surf was awesome, rolling in towards the shore in thunderous waves. Wave after wave, after wave. Continous rows of them and the water was so blue…truly, quite unbelievably blue and the very sound of it sent a thrill through to my very soul. I could almost feel it vibrate through my body, straight up through the soles of my feet, as it pounded against the wet sand.

Jeff, by this time, had started a run around with his already wet dog and a game of light sabres was enacted with great long lengths of seaweed...the sort that Misty would normally use to poke any unsuspecting passer-by, only today, fortunately, we had the beach all to ourselves. It really takes very little to please my two boys. The same game, always re-enacted in exactly the same way and with exactly the same amount of enthusiasm...and what a sight to fill yours truly with joy. Just to see them both so happy and full of daft, innocent fun.

To go back to something of which I have just made reference...about having the beach all to ourselves...that really is one of the quite amazing features of your average Irish beach. The main feature being, of course, is the fact that they are all, without exception, absolutely glorious but...and this is quite a substantially large 'but'...they are always, more or less, deserted. Only rarely, have we actually met up with some other dog owner...twice, maybe three times. More often than not, we have felt like the only two people to have set foot on the pristine white sand of all the many and, I do mean many, beaches that we have explored and exclaimed over, in the time that we have spent on this beautiful emerald isle.

Anyway, to continue...

Just like the two romantics that we are, we wandered along this spectacular beach for quite some time completely lost in the sheer beauty of it all. Misty was in his element, as was I...and it just felt so good. Just to be alive and taking in, with every breath, this pure air off the sea, seemed like a gift from God...which it was, I suppose and Jeff and I were as close as two people could be, with hearts as one and one hand holding tightly to that of the other. We simply wanted the moment to last forever...which, of course, was not possible...so, reluctantly, we headed back to the car. Needless to say, Misty was very much in need of his usual de-sanding job (I really don't think that he has been completely sand free, since we actually arrived) and we were, by now, quite hungry.

The luncheon formalities completed, we began the process of packing up our few bits and pieces, including our rubbish and then, before setting off once more, we gave Misty the chance of another five minutes in which to poke his ever questing nose into whatever may take his fancy (and, while he was thus poking, hopefully do his necessaries) and, I swear to God that this is true...having been mooching around for less than the stipulated five minutes, back he trots and, with an air of enormous satisfaction, sits himself down in front of Jeff and I and proffers his latest find as a token of his great love. (And of all the 'presents' that we have had the dubious pleasure of being on the receiving end, this latest one just about took the biscuit).

There, hanging from his mouth, like some intrepid hunter's trophy and topped by a pair of glowing eyes and the most self-satisfied, indeed, quite smug expression of a job well done, was a pair of sky-blue men's underpants. You may think that I just have to be making it up but, I swear it. As God is my witness, they were blue underpants…and I shudder to think wear he found them, because they looked to be quite clean. To be honest, all I can do is leave the rest to your imagination. I mean, what is he like? His dear, daft face positively glowed with the pride of this great thing that he had done. I just don't know what I can say except that we reacted in the only way possible…we both just fell about, laughing. It was the look on his face that did it, you see…he just looked so pleased with himself. God love him.

Fortunately, going back to what I said before, there wasn't another soul about to witness our embarrassment and, with the bribe of a couple of doggie treats, we did manage to get these blessed underpants off him. Jeff then threw them as far away as he possibly could and hoped that the previous owner would not be coming back to look for them.

I shudder to think what that dear, daft dog of ours will present us with, one of these days and, of course, the tide-line of a beach, any beach, is a treasure house of all kinds of interesting flotsam and jetsam which has found itself washed ashore by the latest tide and specifically, as far as Misty is concerned, for his sole benefit.

Back on the road once more, the thought of Misty and his underpants kept us amused for quite a few miles, as we had to retrace our way back to Bangor before we could continue on our main course. I mean, every time I glanced back at him, I just burst out laughing which, on top of the fact that his seating arrangements had once again been very much reduced, seemed to offend him quite deeply. Sorry, old son. Sorry for laughing and sorry for your rather less than limo-style comfort. It won't be for very long. Promise!

Bangor saw us back on the N59 again with, in the middle distance, the most superb views over Achill Sound and Achill Island over on our right hand and the majestic Nephin Beg Range of mountains way across to our left and, as you would have come to expect, by now, I was trying to look at everything at once, in my forever exuberant enthusiasm. I must say, though, that I would have given my all, just to get a bit closer to the enticingly delectable Achill Island. For some reason, the distant sight of open sea and even the name, Achill Sound, drew me there, quite inexorably. Maybe, just maybe, sometime over the next two weeks, we will be able to spend some time there…for I do believe that the distance would be perfectly manageable, if we were to make it a full days outing and get an extra early start.

The Nephin Beg mountains, well, they seemed to remain with us for mile after mile, forever there, in the middle distance, over on our left. A constantly alluring companion, with their peaks rendered all the more mysterious because of the lingering haze which, although now dissipated at ground level, by the appearance of a very pleasant warmth from the sun, still enshrouded the tops of these towering peaks, thus leaving the imagination to fill in all the gaps, so to speak.

Including the place that we had just left, indeed, all the way down this length of coastline, the scenery is that of glorious islands and bays. Very similar, in fact, to the stretch of coastline that we came upon, last week, in Donegal…across from The Rosses, if you will recall. The fancy doily. The crochet pattern of intricate design, all made up of tiny bays and miniature islands…and all with intriguing and alluring names. Remember?

Today, if we had gone just a few miles beyond where we found that beautiful beach, just now, we would have come to a small village…and a bay of the same name…that name being Blacksod. Oh, my God. That is sooooo scrumptious! I mean, Blacksod Bay. Wow. It almost oozes images of pirates and smuggling. Wonderful! That is surely the most super-delicious of all the intriguing Irish names that I have ever come across. It just has to be! Blacksod…I just had to say it again and, without a doubt, that is definitely a must for when we do manage to get this far again.

It would have been so easy to stop off at so many of these tempting places, which, although off in the middle distance, would not have taken too long to get to however, the main priority was to actually arrive at our wee cottage sometime during the same twenty four hours in which we set out, so with some small amount of common sense prevailing, we restrained ourselves and just carried on, our road now taking us down to the point of land where Mallaranny (or, Mulrany, which is another spelling of the same name) meets the Corraun Peninsula (actually within smelling distance of the alluring Achill Sound) and then follows the coast around Clew Bay and on towards Westport. Westport being the main town in this area…and from this point in our journey, we knew, with a certain amount of relief, that we had come, more or less, to within only a reasonably short distance of our final destination, Tourmakeady, on the shores of Lough Mask.

Convening a snap meeting of the Board and thereby coming to a decision as to what we still needed to do before actually arriving at the cottage, the vote was unanimously carried in favour of taking the road from Westport to Castlebar and, in said place of various mercantile establishments, where we could do a wee bit of stocking up, subsequently pay a visit to the local supermarket. Now, I have absolutely nothing against Tesco's, however, I have to say that it was with a sigh of relief that the job was finally accomplished. The wilfulness of a wayward trolley was not a whole lot of fun and the car park was absolutely heaving. We did, in fact, come to the considered conclusion that war had perhaps broken out, without our knowledge and that everyone in the immediate vicinity was stockpiling while they still had the chance.

Feeling quite light headed with the relief of leaving such an obviously busy, urban environment, we headed out on the final leg of our rather long journey by taking the road to Partry and then, at last, we were pretty much home and dry…and now, we had entered the third county of the day. County Mayo.

Lough Mask was within sight and 'home' was just a few miles along the shore of this large and quite spectacular lake. Just the sight of all that water and I was beginning to become just a wee tad excited…I mean, you know me and the fact that even the smallest accumulation of water can do very strange things to me…and this was no small accumulation of water. This was huge and seemed to stretch for miles.

Eventually, we came to the turn off where we were delighted to see, (relieved to see, as it meant that we had come to the right place), as large as life and totally gorgeous, the thatched cottage, on the corner, which we had been instructed to look out for and turn right at. So, we were 'home', or at least, more or less and, as we drew into the grounds of our new cottage, we felt, once again, that strange feeling of having been there before, purely because it was all so real after having nothing other than just a picture in our minds as to what it was like. I must say that with Welcome Cottages, what you see is what you get. Nothing has been airbrushed, so to speak, in an attempt to make things look better than they are. Every cottage that we have occupied and, that is quite a few, have, if anything, exceeded our expectations...and this one was no exception.

We were greeted, warmly, by our hostess and were immediately enchanted by this quite delightful stone-built cottage...obviously an old barn which had been converted and, very beautifully converted, at that. The outer walls were painted a quite dazzling white, said walls being at least three feet thick. I mean, nothing, not even the most inclement of climatic conditions, could ever penetrate those walls!

Leaving us to settle in, our lovely hostess, Jackie, retired to her own home... the main house, in the grounds of which lay our little cottage and I must say that we were quite surprised when we saw the extent of the grounds. I mean, even around the area of our wee cottage, we discovered that the copper-coloured Irish one actually had, for the sole benefit of his furry person, his very own small meadow to run around in. A real bonus, indeed...in fact, a vast doggie heaven of lush green (Irish Green) grass with tall, stately trees, beneath which welcome shade will be readily available to him, should the weather prove to be very hot. I mean, all we had to do was to open the back door from off the kitchen, which opened on to this glorious doggie hunting ground and he had all the space in the world in which to play out, to his hearts content, all the adventures, the imaginary exploits of the bold and intrepid explorer that he is and, what is more...safely. A stout stone wall and farm gate, kept him from getting out onto the lane. The traffic may have been very light and occasional but, well, it only takes one car.

As you might expect, the unpacking took at least twice as long as it would have done for someone else...any normal, someone else, that is...but then, I just have to allow myself to get sidetracked and, well, everything gets done in the end, so what does it matter? It's all a part of the excitement, you see, opening doors and peering into cupboards and discovering what all the said cupboards, not to mention the drawers, may or may not contain. All that aside, this humble wee cottage had something else which made it very special...a real feeling of 'home'. Let me try and explain. You know when you enter a building, any building, and immediately feel 'right'...a feeling of belonging, if you like…well, that is how I felt, as soon as I walked into this small cottage and I have to say that I don't get that feeling in every place that I may enter. Oh, it may be absolutely perfect but, not necessarily have that particular ambience, the one that I felt, instinctively, the moment that I walked through the door of this wee place.

Be that as it may. That is all just me and the way I sometimes get these strange feelings…and I know what you're thinking…'what do you expect, she is strange to begin with'. Don't worry. It's quite alright. I'm not in the least offended…and you are, of course, perfectly right.

All of this daft stuff about 'feelings' aside, there was one other very special discovery which became an extremely large, proverbial cherry, to be plonked right on top of an otherwise, almost perfect, cake…and you are going to love it and I just can't wait to see your face when you arrive here, this evening, for the very first time.

OK. OK. I'm getting on with it! What I am trying to say is that this wonderful, lovely, wee cottage has that magic something which, as you know, I consider brings a home to life…YES…a real fire! Not a big open fire but one of these black, shiny, cast iron stoves, with glassed doors…a great big one. Oh, wow! How absolutely marvellous is that? Love and warmth really will fill up all the corners, tonight, my friend.

And now, you are here…and what a joy it has been, while I've been anticipating your arrival, just enjoying the deep and velvet night, with the moon spreading its silvery mantle across the gentle waters of Lough Mask. That inevitable peace is all around us and this little cottage seems to have nestled amongst the trees and is ready to receive the night and the stars and keep everything safe until the break of dawn relieves it of its duty as protective custodian of all that dwell within its stout walls.

Now, as I go through my nightly ritual, I am filled with a feeling of extreme contentment. The sense of all that lies outside these walls, the security and the peace and the usual Irish tranquillity, is a balm for the most troubled of souls and it felt completely natural, somehow, to settle down in this dear wee cottage. Even Misty felt it I'm sure and, when we told him to go to his bed, he immediately sloped off, up the stairs and, within minutes, even from down stairs and with the television on, we could hear that sonorous, orchestrated snoring. You see, even he felt safe and settled…no doggie bogeyman, here, funny face.

Our journey, today, although purposefully longer than was absolutely necessary, has been a happy and memorable experience (particularly the lasting image of Misty with those blasted underpants) and, what is more, it has been safe. No mishaps. All OK…thank you God.

I feel that sleep will come very quickly, tonight, with the influence of the tranquillity, which is innate in any part of Ireland, slowly but surely enfolding me in its warm embrace. Oh, my Jeffy, as I lie beside you on this very special night, my heart feels so full of love for you that I know not how it will ever be able to contain it all. I never could have believed that my life could have been so transformed, but then, that was before you filled my life with wonder and made all my dreams come true.

Tomorrow, we have a second 'beginning'. A second 'first morning', when everything seems that much more special. Nothing but deep happiness and enchantment will fill the next fourteen days and every precious second will be made all the more precious because we will be together. I love you, my own darling husband…with my life. God bless you, always.

As for you, our dear and wonderful pup…and pup you will always remain to me…you give great joy to your mum and dad, even if you are a stealer of underpants (and anything else which isn't actually nailed down). Just think of all the delights which are out there, just waiting for you, Misty Hall, to embrace with the sort of enthusiasm that only an innocent heart, such as yours, can achieve. God bless you, too.

God bless everyone. God bless Ireland.

Tomorrow, The Intrepid Trio will be out in force! Which statement gives ample notice to the local population to be able to vacate the immediate area for the next two weeks. A good time to take an unscheduled holiday, perhaps.

With those two full weeks still to come, I know that we are in for a treat and that those two very special weeks will be filled with the sort of magic that can only come from this land of dreams come true.

IRELAND!

See you tomorrow!

◈◈◈◈◈◈◈◈◈◈◈◈

After a special day, just such as this one, I always love this time of peace and quietude, when, after dinner has been eaten and everything cleared away, we can enjoy the deep luxury of just being together and talking and remembering, of laughing and joking and, well, just happily wallowing in the normal loving activities which make up a small family such as mine.

On a personal level, I have loved every minute of today…and I mean ME…not Seasalt Vera. Jeff took me to a very special place which, surprisingly, was only thirty minutes, maybe, forty, from our cottage. Anyway, you will hear all about it in the fullness of time and then you will know what I'm wittering on about, because this place was particularly special to me, you see. Our friends, Denny and Julie had visited there, only last year and I had been quite envious…all the more reason why we were so delighted to find that it was so close to our new 'base'.

For now, it is sufficient to say that it's so lovely, just sitting here, in this warm and cosy cottage. Right now, at this very minute, I'm sitting at the table in the kitchen. Fairly soon, I shall have to start getting our meal but, just for now, I am enjoying a few minutes of quiet recollection of a day so full of happy hours.

The back door is wide open, allowing the sweet evening air to fill the house and also, giving Misty free access to come and go as he pleases. His attention is taken up, however, with the important chore of chasing the local rabbit population around his own private meadow…and it is such a happy picture, with the last of the evening sunlight accenting the deep coppery sheen of his glossy coat and forming long shadows across the garden.

If I glance up, I can see that my Jeffy is getting the fire going and piling on a few extra logs…again, a picture which fills my heart with love and delight and my soul with peace.

So, dear friend, your welcome will be reminiscent of the old times, on this very special night when you visit our 'new' cottage, once again.

Having just called my Jeffy to come and enjoy his first glass of wine, I know that it will not be too long before you are here and I feel, right now, that I could not wish for another, single thing. Everything is perfect…even the logs are beginning to splutter and hiss. I mean, how wonderful is that?

And now, you are here. Now there really is nothing more to add in order to achieve the ultimate perfection.

Sunday
27th September 2009

Jeff was the first to get up, as usual and what a lovely sight met my eyes indeed, a lovely sound also, as I came down the stairs and found him raking out the ashes from last night's fire. It is a chore that is somehow comforting, no doubt as a throwback to the days of childhood, when everyone had fires…and certainly no central heating. Oh, my word, no!

Oh, what a glorious morning…indeed, the morning was just about as glorious as it could possibly be, as the sun gave us of her very best and filled our little world with her golden light and the deep and quite luxurious pleasure of her September warmth. The sun was full on to our back garden, at that hour of the morning and, of course, Misty's meadow…however, at that moment he was just sitting, quite contentedly, at the back gate, happily watching the busy, chirpy morning activities of the local bird life, as they flitted back and forth on swift wings, sorting themselves out and chirruping to each other in a celebration of the day, from amongst the trees and shrubs, which themselves were so lovely, garbed as they were, in their delightful September foliage.

I went over to my big baby, just to give him a cuddle, don't you know and, as I looked over towards Lough Mask, my eyes were positively dazzled by the sheer brilliance of the sun's reflections off the water. Truly, it was, heaven! If it hadn't been for the fact that I had breakfast to sort out, I could have, quite rapturously, gazed on that beautiful lake forever.

Talking of breakfast, I had already made my first acquaintance with the incumbent electric cooker, last night, so we were no longer strangers…and, all things considered, we do seem to be getting along quite well. At least, I think that we can have a civilized relationship. I mean, the last thing that I need is an evil-minded cooker getting up to any sneaky tricks.

The feeling, for both my Jeffy and I, this morning was, in no way, a let down…on the contrary. It was, as we had hoped…just like beginning all over again. There was that same excitement, that same anticipation that you normally get on that 'first morning'…a truly special feeling which eventually, after a few days, tends to wear off. I mean, how fortunate are we to have been allowed that second chance to experience such a quite indescribable feeling.

Even sitting down to breakfast was a 'new' and wonderful occasion because we were in yet another new place. The cottage was a new novelty and the outside environs were all new and unexplored, even by our Misty.

Needless to say, having eaten our fill, the necessity of making some kind of a decision with regard to our plans for the day became the first priority and so, out came the very much 'worse for wear' map and a plan of sorts was eventually agreed upon by all the three members of The Intrepid Trio. Misty's vote was merely taken as read, of course, because he still had far more important things to attend to, like finishing off his last sausage.

And so, with everything packed into the car that we might need until our return and Misty positively gloating, now that he had all his full limo-style seating arrangements restored and with a final look around this lovely cottage, we set out, in grand style, on the continuation of this magic Irish adventure…a continuation of this great and all consuming love affair.

At this point, with your approval, of course, I would just like to tell you a wee bit about this lovely little village which is to be our home for the next two weeks. As a matter of fact, I think you will find it to be quite interesting…I know that I did.

The name Tourmakeady, or, in the gaelic Tuar Mhic Eadaigh, actually means MacEadaigh's cattle field or pasture. The local community is mainly Gaelic speaking, indeed, the Irish language does still survive, in pockets, here and there, all along the Atlantic fringe, from up in Donegal and way down to Kerry.

Here, with the lake as a barrier to the east and the mountains, the Partry Mountains, to the west, the language has managed to survive and actually binds the community together…a community with which we are to become, hopefully, fully acquainted. Over the next two weeks, we will, if we are lucky, meet at least some of the locals…and that is something which we will consider to be an enormous privilege. If our past experience is anything to go by, I know that we will be made to feel welcome in their midst…and an Irish welcome is something very special. Very special, indeed.

Getting back to the day, I found myself to be totally enchanted by the immediate environs of the cottage. Once out on the road, we found that Lough Mask really did stretch for miles…and it was so broad that well, I couldn't see the far shore. Just miles of water, which today, reflected the blue of the sky and the many small islands, tiny ones and even quite large ones, which were dotted around the lake, were all arrayed with their own miniature forest of trees and shrubs. On such a morning, it really was a sight to gladden even the heaviest of hearts…not that ours were…quite the opposite. Ours were positively soaring.

Here and there, we could see tiny beaches on to which, small fishing boats had been drawn up and families of ducks just wandered in and around the boats and the weedy, water's edge, where reeds and plants grew in abundance in the moist and mossy ground…gabbling to each other as they busied themselves about their own affairs. It was all so idyllic and splendid and I just had to remark to Jeff upon how very lucky we were to have chosen this place, however inadvertently.

So preoccupied were we with the glory of the lake that we were into the mountains before we could draw breath. Truly, just a mere couple of kilometers up the road from 'home' we were into the stunningly magnificent mountains of Joyce's Country. Yet another famous Irish writer who has given so much pride to the country that gave him birth…and this just had to be equal to some of the most splendid scenery which we have seen. There was no denying the fact that it was certainly comparable, with all the true magnificence of the mountains of Donegal. But then, Joyce Country is renowned for its great beauty and, indeed, we had been looking forward to seeing it for ourselves…we just never expected it to be so close to home…almost on our doorstep, in fact.

Once again, however, we were enchanted by the autumnal colours which we had so admired, back in Donegal. The gold and the honey. The copper and the bronze with lights and shades, patterns of a rapidly changing aspect, as the few clouds which were in evidence, chased each other across the face of the sun. Microseconds only but changing the aspect of these magnificent slopes, quite literally, by the second and creating a kaleidoscope of so many different tones of all these rich and quite wondrous September colours. Not to be outdone, here and there, great swathes of blue and silver would joyfully declare the whereabouts of a lake and, apart from Lough Mask, there were many smaller lakes which sparkled in the sunlight on this glorious day of days.

By mid-morning, I mean, we had stopped so many times, just to look and admire and, of course, take some photographs, the time had passed unbelievably quickly and we were quite surprised to find that our thoughts were turning towards the best place to stop for a cup of coffee…and the perfect place was just at the far end of Lough Mask. It was miles up the great length of the lake from that which was near to our cottage…which gives some idea as to how big it is. Anyway, it really could not have been more perfect. I mean, it was so stunning that we spent the first few minutes taking photos, before even thinking about breaking out the flask. Any self-respecting picture postcard would have been more than proud to have this breathtakingly beautiful picture on its front and, to whomsoever it may have been, to actually conceive of placing a couple of strategically positioned tables in this magnificent situation, I offer my sincere gratitude. It was a stroke of sheer brilliance. I mean, wow! And yes, I know, I'm doing it again but, you just want to be sitting where we were sitting and then you would know the reason for that statement. You would find yourself wanting to sit here for hours, just like us and allow the scene to fill your soul with the magic of all the colours and the gentle sounds of the water as it lapped against the shore or made that amazing slurping sound as it tickles an outcrop of rock and, as I was thinking along these lines and feeling the warmth of the sun on my face, around a slight bend in the line of the shore came a pair of dazzlingly white swans. Their appearance was such a perfect addition to what was, already, an idyllic scene, that they could almost have been painted on. Needless to say, that called for yet another photo…one which included the swans, this time. Honestly, when I get a camera in my hand, I just go bananas…and usually end up deleting at least half of my pictures, having taken so many of the same scene. Jeff has always said that I'm a menace when armed with a camera but, I never take offence…or, any notice, for that matter and a raspberry usually does the trick and I then just carry on as normal and Jeff just grins and gives up.

I must confess that we remained at this beauty spot for much longer than we would normally have done, for a quick pit stop, anyway. The moment was so sublime, that we could so easily have stayed there forever however we did, eventually, get on our way again and immediately carried on to the place which had been such a cause of great excitement and in saying that, I mean for yours truly. An anticipation which had kept me bubbling over ever since the perusal of our veteran map, earlier this morning and the subsequent decision to visit Cong. That was the place that I was so eager to see. The small village of Cong.

In explanation, for any who do not make any connection with the name, let me just say that, one of my all time favourite films is The Quiet Man. Quite an old film but, nevertheless, as wonderful now, as it was when it was first filmed and…what I'm actually leading up to is that a large part of the film, indeed all of it, was actually filmed either in the village of Cong itself, or, somewhere in the hills around and about. Even Cong Church and Cong Castle are very much recognizable if one should happen to watch the film. Indeed, very little has changed, if anything…and the entire village is redolent with the persona and history of the making of the film and, of course, its stars, John Wayne, Maureen O'Hara, Barry Fitzgerald etc.

I was totally fascinated by the whole thing…and it is no real exaggeration when I say that it is possible to actually feel the presence of John Wayne, wherever you go. Even in Cong woods, where we eventually walked for a while, in order to let Misty have a much needed (and appreciated) runabout, it was immediately plain to see and recognize, places along the river where scenes from the film had been enacted.

How long we stayed in the village, I don't really know. There was so much to see and, even if John Wayne and the film crew had never set foot in the place, it was still a lovely little village and it had a sort of inbuilt magnetism which made it almost impossible not to be so attracted to it, in its own right.

I wondered how long it would be before a certain furry person would attract some attention and, it was here, in Cong, on our very first day, that it actually happened. We were just walking through the village, completely absorbed by the many things of interest which were all around us, when, out of the blue, in the narrow streets of Cong, it happened…and that was when there came upon the scene, this huge American…I mean, he must have been at least six feet four…and he went into total, ecstatic raptures over you know who.

Oh, we had all the fuss and the extolling of the supreme magnificence of this great, daft dog of ours and he, Misty, I mean, just about grinned his pearly whites right out of his mouth, in his fervent efforts to show just how marvellous he really was. The big showoff was actually enjoying every single moment of it and accepted all the praise and admiration with all the usual aplomb that we have become accustomed to.

Before we actually parted company with our tall Texan, and that's just the name that I gave him, we had heard so much about him and the fact that he, also, had owned Irish Setters, that it felt as if we were old buddies, instead of new acquaintances. Seriously, though…he was a lovely guy and yet another example of the way we meet and have met, on other occasions, so many lovely people, all on account of our glorious specimen of doggie youth who, I might add, is beginning to get feelings of grandeur well above his own self. In other words, he is becoming unbearably big headed! Only joking…I mean, are we proud, or are we not?

I was so wrapped up in everything about John Wayne (the real John Wayne, this time. Remember me and my jaunting cart driver, last year, in Killarney National Country Park? Oh, but he was sublime. Be still, my beating heart. I mean, to be so infatuated, at my age, honestly. Silly old fool)! that I didn't even notice the time or the fact that I was hungry…until my Jeffy reminded me and so, with a degree of reluctance, we made our way back to the other side of the village, where we had left the car and although I know that we will be back, I hated to go.

As we drew away from Cong, we began to keep an eye open (the other eye was taken up with the beauty of the passing scenery) for a suitable place to stop and break out the butties. In fact, we had not travelled all that far out of Cong when we found the perfect place…a lovely little bay…Cushlough Bay. At first, we weren't too sure if we may have been trespassing, as it gave the impression of being perhaps, a private boating club but, no, it was open to anyone who wanted to just spend some time, like us, in a pretty wee place…and pretty it was, with lots of brightly painted boats either drawn up onto the shore or bobbing about at their moorings. It made for a pleasant interlude and the enjoyment of our simple lunch was enhanced by the gentle waters of this wee bay and, of course, the whole thing was so perfect for both myself and my alter ego, Seasalt Vera. I mean, boats. That'll do for me, any time. (No doubt when I actually do turn my toes up, Jeff will have me cremated, Viking fashion and left to float out to sea).

Before heading back to Tourmakeady, we decided to pay a visit to

Westport...I mean, it was our main big town after all and it wasn't actually out of our way. I don't know why we by-passed it, yesterday, calling instead at Castlebar. Anyway, it seemed like a good idea...a nice way in which to round off the day's activities and, as things turned out, we found it to be a lovely town. Certainly, a very picturesque town.

The town centre was particularly lovely. OK, so there were streets of shops and commercial buildings but, it had all been made to look so attractive. Every corner of the town, every lamp post, in fact, seemed to be a mass of flowers. There is a river which runs right through the centre of town and all along its length, every bridge which spanned it...and there were many...were absolutely ablaze with flowers, indeed, everywhere one looked, festoons of flowers and baskets of flowers turned an ordinary town into a veritable Garden of Eden. Even the Garda Station was an absolute picture postcard. Never, in my life, have I seen a Police Station that looked less like a Police Station. I mean, it looked more like some pretty little villa from somewhere around the Med. You see, even this small building was absolutely ablaze with flowers.

We were just remarking on the fact that it was the prettiest cop shop that we had ever seen when our train of thought was well and truly shattered by the friendly, American-accented hail, from way across the other side of the street...'Hey there! Is that Misty?' On looking in the direction from which this jovial greeting had come, we saw, much to our surprise...yes, you've got it...our friendly American (my tall Texan) whom we had first met, a few hours ago, in Cong. He was lovely though and so sincere...I mean, he came across that street in such a state of pure joy that you would have been excused for thinking that we were some long-lost relatives whom he had mistakenly considered to have departed this earth, years ago. He then went into further raptures over you know who and was thrilled to bits when old sloppy chops gave him a demonstration of just how to show friendship to a dog lover, even though said dog lover was a comparative stranger. He went on his way, eventually...and I think that he was almost sad to part company with us. The pleasure had been mutual, though. Once again, we had enjoyed an extra ration of pleasure from that chance meeting with a complete stranger...my 'tall Texan'...and I think I would be right in thinking that, when he gets back to the US of A, he will be recounting his meeting with us and our gorgeous pet pooch, to all who may be prepared to listen.

By now, time was getting on but, nevertheless, we had a good wander, with Misty behaving like a perfect gentleman as he sedately walked at his dad's side…and we even stopped at a nice little café, with outside tables which were set on this very quaint but quite narrow, cobbled street and enjoyed a coffee which had not come out of a flask. The flask is all very well, when one happens to be in the middle of nowhere, however, there comes a time in the day when what remains of the contents of said flask are well and truly past the old sell-by date. Anyway, thank you, Westport, for something a wee bit up market and a jolly sight more enjoyable.

As all good things have to eventually, come to an end, we did the sensible thing and made our way back to Tourmakeady. However, there was yet one more delight in store for us, before we actually arrived back at the cottage and that came in the shape of Tourmakeady Woodland Nature Trail…with the added bonus of its own waterfall. I suppose that we must have passed it, last evening however, we were so busy looking out for particular things that we obviously missed it.

Late as it was getting and, of course, by now, we were feeling a little tired nevertheless, we pulled into the wee car park and, for Misty's sake, more than anything, we walked the meandering trail through this very beautiful forest, with the gentle gurgling of the river a constant reminder of what was awaiting us at the end…the waterfall…and once we got into our stride, we forgot that, only a few minutes ago we were feeling somewhat jaded. Our pathway was only narrow and twisted and turned as it made its own way beneath the spreading canopy of gold and bronze foliage formed by the pressing mass of trees which grew quite densely, off to both sides. We didn't particularly time it but, it was a fair size walk and then, well, you could hear it. The sound was that of a large amount of crashing, thundering water and when we rounded the last bend, there it was. The waterfall towards which we had been walking for what seemed like quite a long time.

Knowing me, you will not be at all surprised when I said to Jeff that it looked like a fairy glen. It was just the way it was all set out, you see and I swear, I came so close to seeing living proof, honestly and wow…you see, my nose just tickled…that just had to be one of those precious jewel-like creatures. Just making themselves known, don't you know.

The waterfall was a goodish drop from a cliff top that was a gorgeous blaze of autumnal colours which radiated from the variegated shrubbery which either adorned the top or trailed down the rock face and the full spectrum of colours which were formed by a myriad of miniature rainbows, which constantly came and went as the low, evening sun caught in the happy, splashing water. The greatest joy, to us, though, was the reaction of Misty to what could only have been a complete and indescribable delight in his doggie eyes…the pool…a huge pool, into which the cascading water from the falls was a constant thing with the sound of it a thrill, as is anything in nature which is one of such beauty and force. Needless to say, he was in said pool within seconds and splashing around with all the gusto and the innocent joy of a child, which is all he is, really…just a big kid in an Irish Setter suit. There was a wee bench just off to one side of the pool and we sat there, my Jeffy and I, at peace and quite content just to watch our dear, daft lump have his fun.

Even I was quite loathe to leave this mellow and peaceful place, however, we really had no choice, I mean, we couldn't stay there all night and so, with a great deal of coaxing and eventually, resorting to bribery, we managed to get Misty out of the water and headed off, back along the autumn splendid trail and to the car.

Within minutes, that is all, we were home…and how beautiful it all looked. The evening sun was golden across the lake and our own wee garden and Misty's Meadow were bathed, also, in this mellow, golden light. It really was quite indescribably lovely…and the peace…that unique quietude…unique to Ireland, anyway, fell upon us like a blessing and just made a perfect day all the more perfect.

On the way back, we actually discovered the location of yet another 'local' pub…The Lough Mask Inn. We had found the other one as we set out, this morning…Paddy's Thatched Bar…an absolutely scrumptious, as the name obviously suggests, thatched building, no bigger than the average cottage. Anyway, with two pubs in a quite close proximity to home, we will do very well, thank you very much.

Dinner was depatched accordingly and, what do you think?…off we went to sample the wares at Paddy's Bar. On closer inspection it was even more lovely than we had thought, as we just passed by, this morning. Certainly the outside aspect and especially around the back, where sweeping lawns run right down to the gently rippling edge of Lough Mask and, after dark, the floodlit scene is every bit as beautiful as that same scene bathed in sunlight…in fact, it is far more romantic…which, of course, set the mood for the latter half of the evening. After our pleasant interlude at Paddy's place, we returned home and, with the fire spluttering merrily, we tossed caution to the wind and broke open the wine cellar and well, you could not have timed it better! Welcome.

What a perfect end to a perfect day and such a lot to try and assimilate and get sorted, especially for me…but then, that is where you come in, you see…you help my daft head get around this mosaic of small, individual images which have made today so special and enable me to file them all away in the right order.

Anyway, it is that time again and I thank you God, for a wonderful day and as I spend the final hour gazing into the magical pictures in the glowing embers of the fire and wallow in the comfortable security of the loving proximity of my darling husband (the hairy one as already taken himself off to his bed of doggie dreams…we can hear him!) I feel ashamed, almost, to be so lucky. Thank you my Jeffy…I know that I am always going on about John Wayne but, you are my star, my very own shining star and my love for you is forever. God bless you.

Sleep tight, my Misty. You have charmed so many people today…your big fan, the tall Texan…and all who received the benefit of your Irish charm as you walked, as good as gold and like a true Irish gentleman, through the streets of Westport. You always make your mum and dad very proud. Happy dreams and God bless your dear and faithful heart.

God bless Ireland…and we will be out, in full force, tomorrow and ready to enjoy all the special magic that is just out there waiting and, as I think back to those stunning mountains which proclaimed that we were in Joyce Country…could that really have been just this morning?…we need go no further than just up the road. As if!

See you, tomorrow…and thanks for listening.

◎◎◎◎◎◎◎◎◎◎◎

Such a glorious evening and, what an appropriate way to bring this quite memorable day to a close…memorable for me that is and on a very personal level. Anyway, you will hear all about it in due course and, when you have, well, then you will know what I mean. Let me just say that I am, at this moment, as I enjoy this mellow part of the day and lose myself in the peaceful aspect of the gentle waters of Lough Mask, feeling just a tad smug and self-satisfied. With just cause, I might add. It is not in my usual nature to be smug about anything but, I do think that today, you may be able to find it in your heart to excuse me. You will see eventually and then you can either castigate me for my feelings of enlarged self-importance or, give me a small round of applause.

Jeff has just gone for a stroll along the lane, with Misty…I mean, the evening just cries out for it really, as it is, quite truthfully, absolutely beautiful and, as the lane follows alongside the shores of the lough, there is that indescribable tranquillity, that quite uniquely special peace and quietude…an Irish quietude. This picture of complete and utter tranquillity, as one also takes in the colours, all the pastel, gentle, colours of early evening, comes together and combines to perfection, with the gentle sounds of the water. Not to mention the quite endearing sound of squabbling ducks, as they fuss about and do their own things…in the way of ducks, of course.

Before he went out, he had already set a light to the fire and now it is beginning to hiss and splutter a wee bit and, by the time that my Jeffy returns and you arrive, it will be cosy and inviting, as darkness will, by then, have fallen and, in so doing, have changed the aspect of the lake to a silvery, shining mirror and everything will have closed down to await another bright and glorious morn.

And now, at last, you are here and I can begin my tale. As you will no doubt imagine and I know that you will not be in the least surprised, I have been so eager to get started. (I know. I know. I can hear you saying…'So what's new!')

Here goes then.

Monday

28th September 2009

There was so much laughter this morning…I mean, we were all
rendered quite helpless and stupid by it all…that you could have been excused
for thinking 'It will all end in tears, before bedtime'. It didn't, of course, but
even so, I do believe that I would have taken the chance.

The cause of all this mirth…the culprit, the guilty party, the felon which,
under the circumstances, seems to be a much more appropriate word, of all
this hilarity… and I will give you three guesses, not that you will actually need
all three was, it goes without saying, the copper-coloured furry person who
goes by the name of Misty. And, throughout the entire hilarious episode he
maintained this attitude of total innocence…in fact, he actually seemed quite
inordinately pleased with himself and obviously could not understand what
had caused these four lunatic humans to behave in such an unseemly fashion.

Making himself thoroughly at home, my dear, daft dog had made
himself a den amongst the wonderful long meadow-grass and the shrubbery
which made up his play area and, as with his den in the garden back home, he
had decorated said den with all kinds of intriguing odds and ends…trouble
was, you see, that all these particular odds and ends, bits and pieces,
whatever…well, they did not belong to us. They were, in fact, stolen. Every last
thing had been, systematically, nicked, from somewhere around the back of Pat
and Jackie's house, sometime over the last few days. Oh, there was nothing of
any value, (except to Misty, of course. I mean, to him, it was treasure trove of
the highest order) for which we were extremely grateful. Things like a plastic T
piece, the sort of thing that you would find amongst your under-sink water
works. An old paint brush also seemed to take pride of place in his collection.
Oh, there were so many little, worthless, oddments, God love him and the only
reason that we discovered his latent tendencies toward kleptomania was the
white sock which was his trophy for today and which he had stolen from a pair
of wellies…Jackie's, I think, that had been standing, minding their own
business, outside the front door of the main house. With all the innocence in
the world, he sort of waved this sock at me, taunting me, if you will, when he
spotted me through the open kitchen door as I was preparing breakfast and,

naturally, getting it off him seemed to be the most important thing at the time which, of course, was entirely the wrong thing to do. In Misty's mind, it all suddenly became a great game.

During all of this palaver, Pat and Jackie came by and when we showed them Misty's collection of stolen booty, well, that was it, we all just broke up. The very idea of the whole thing suddenly seemed so ludicrous that we just burst out laughing, which made his nibs look even more self-important.

There is, in fact, a final, rather amusing moral to all of this and that is the fact that both Pat and Jackie are working Police Officers. Yes! Gards...both of them...and no doubt working out of that same pretty little Police Station, in Westport, that I mentioned only yesterday. Thank God for their good natured sense of humour, that's all I can say, as they both saw the funny side to these nefarious goings on by our four-legged tealeaf...I mean, we could, so easily, have finished up banged up and cooling our heels in one of the pretty little cells, in said pretty little Police Station, as three totally undesirable bad lots awaiting deportation on the next ferry back to England. Only joking, of course.

Having re-established some form of self-control, we all eventually went our separate ways with a joking suggestion that we just give everything back, all in one go, before we leave. What a lark, though...and our adorable kleptomaniac still couldn't quite get into his daft head, just what all the fuss and been about. Oh, to be so loveable and so innocent and with a heart as pure and blameless as his.

Anyway, that was only the start of what turned out to be a wonderful day...and we hadn't even had breakfast yet. Needless to say, the happy and joyous frame of mind continued and went with us and stayed with us, as we finally set out for what was the second place of importance which had been way up there, at the top of our metaphorical list of priorities. Certainly my own list of priorities, anyway. Cong had been one, which we visited yesterday and today, well, today we headed out towards the second one...the Connemara Mountains...and I was in my usual state of 'why don't you grow up' excitement. So, nothing new there. Once an idiot, always an idiot. You must admit, though, that just the name sends the imagination into overdrive. OK. OK...so, mine, anyway. Connemara...There, you see. I just had to say it again. I mean, that is pure Irish magic. It is, though...isn't it?

Specifically, as we convened our usual Board meeting, this morning, Jeff had suggested the Connemara National Park, which sounded pretty good to me, I mean, we have been to some quite spectacular National Parks in this wonderful country. Do you remember Killarney National Country Park and Gleninchalquin, last year? What a wealth of splendour and quite unimaginable magnificence we found in those two places (not to mention John Wayne)… and only last week, the wonderful Donegal National Park. Again, incredible scenic beauty. Some of the best that we had ever seen. So, without any doubt as to what we were about to find in yet another of these Irish natural treasures, we agreed with a unanimous show of two hands and one quite large paw, that Connemara National Country Park was our ultimate destination, although in this country, well, I mean, the possibilities are endless as to what delights may just be around that old bend in the road, (there, I've said it again) as one makes ones way to that one specific destination.

Setting out via Westport (and keeping well away from the Police Station, just to be on the safe side, don't you know) and, just to prove what I have just said…only a short distance out of Westport, we came upon a lovely beach. We weren't especially on the lookout for a beach but, when we saw the wee brown sign with the sandcastle legend we thought it would be a good idea to stop…for the benefit of the hairy one, of course and, well, OK, me too. I mean, last week's excesses of ozone and seaweed, which had almost caused old Seasalt Vera to blow a few tubes, was now beginning to wear off and the time had come when a rather critical top-up was becoming something of an urgency. I mean, from past experience, you will know by now, that a prolonged shortage can bring about quite serious changes, to both me and my nutty pup…a bit like werewolves and full moons, if you get my drift.

It doesn't get any better, does it?

Bertra Strand was the name of the beach…or so proclaimed that little brown sign, which sent us off down a road off to our right and gave promise of a beach at the end of it. Of course, whenever you follow one of these signs, you can always guarantee that the promise of enormous joy and the most beautiful of oceanic delights will always be fulfilled…and this lovely Bertra Strand was no exception.

Again, it was a very narrow lane, which seemed to taper even more, the closer we came to within sight of the sea. (Misty already had his nose sticking out through the gap at the top of the rear window and was chuffing in the scents of all the delectable sea smells, the closer that this lane brought us to what can only be his own idea of doggie paradise).

Eventually, we arrived at the end of the road and it opened out into a properly paved car park and then…here I go again…wow! Wow, again and again. I mean, which ever beach you may happen to discover in Ireland, they are all, in a greater or a lesser degree, absolutely amazing…and all worthy of the use of that word.

There wasn't a prize for the one who managed to get out of the car and down onto the sand the first, although, with four legs, it is obviously possible to cover the distance in half the time of just two. However, Jeff and I were not too far behind our quite overjoyed canine and a fine old time was had by all.

Bertra was quite a long beach with, up above the level of the shoreline, a high ridge of sand dunes which ran parallel with the beach and which, at the far end, formed a barrier between two bodies of water…on the left was the sea, rolling in on large breakers and then, on the right, there was a sort of huge lake, as large as an inland sea and this double vista, a merging of the sea and the sky and the dunes really was quite extraordinarily beautiful. On one side, the sea was coming in on large crested waves and on the other, the lake, large as it was, was as calm as a mirror. Both of them reflecting the same delectable blue as the sky. Gorgeous!

As we walked along, happily watching our young beachcomber doing his own thing, poking his nose into bits of weed and splashing around in rock pools, we allowed ourselves the luxury of just letting our gaze wander at will and, in so doing, took in the splendour of distant and majestic purple mountains, which stood off to one side and the more immediate sight of gold and blue and green-topped, wind-blown dunes, with, as an audio soundtrack to accompany the magic of such visual magnificence, there was the joyous sound of the gulls, who proclaimed their own pleasure in the day in their own inimitable way, combining with the sound of the surf to make it all so very special. A motion picture extravaganza! It really was a moment to treasure and, for Misty's sake, mainly, we stayed for as long as we thought sensible, in view of the fact that our final destination was still a goodly way off…and how easy it is to allow oneself to become distracted and sidetracked, even when you have a specific plan and destination…but then, what does it matter, anyway? We have all the time in the world and the freedom to let every second count.

And, just to prove the truth of my last statement, within only a few miles of Bertra Strand, we were intrigued by the name of yet another beach and just had to stop off and take a look. I mean 'Old Head Beach'…that just had to be investigated and, as I said…well, what's another half hour!

Half hour, I said! Make that about an hour. Misty found himself another of those lone trainers (and it still intrigues me as to why there is ever only the one), however, at least an extra twenty minutes or so was spent in trying to get him to leave the blessed thing where he had found it. Of course, there is absolutely no fun in that and so, he played the game, with a hint of satanic pleasure in those lustrous brown eyes, until he probably thought that he had strung it out for long enough and that maybe, just maybe, it may be wiser to give in and to graciously allow us to believe that we had won this particular round of this particular game.

It was a pretty spot, even so. Only small, when compared with some of the vast, sweeping stretches of beach which seem to go on into infinity but, there was a peaceful intimacy about it, with, to one side, a small jetty and slipway, which would no doubt, make it quite popular on the weekend, with small boats being introduced to the gentle waters of this pretty little bay.

Still laughing at the antics of our dear, daft dog…I mean, you just have to, don't you?…laugh, I mean. God love him. Anyway we decided that here, in this lovely wee place, was as good a place as any and, well, the time was about right, to break out the flask of coffee and as I busied myself getting the coffee poured, Jeff was quietly searching the car for something and had come up empty handed. Misty's water bowl was nowhere to be found. Water, yes…the container freshly filled up, this morning…but, no bowl. We could only conclude that it had been left behind somewhere on our travels and its loss was, quite seriously, a big deal. Either we find it or we buy him a new one, and soon. And of course, neither of us could have been positive as to when was the last time that we had seen it.

Duly refreshed…we had eventually poured water, direct from the container, right into Misty's jaws, which resulted in more water slopping down his chest than into his mouth but, at least he got some of it…..we set off once more and determined that this time, we would not get distracted and just set our sights on our prime objective…Connemara National Country Park.

Our way, from now on, definitely put from our minds any thought of becoming sidetracked. I mean, it was really quite stunning, as we travelled along the Doo Lough Pass, with Doo Lough, itself, a bright, shimmering, silvery, living entity, stretching almost endlessly, over to our right, with the light catching the gentle ripples which caressed the shingle shore…and the truly awesome magnificence of the Sheeffry Hills were as golden as any that we had yet seen, sweeping grandly into the distance, over on our left…hills which were as smooth as velvet, a deep tan velvet, a texture which could only have been achieved by eons of constantly nibbling sheep and even these sweeping hills were interrupted, here and there with the silvery mirrored surface of other lakes, of which there appeared to be many, nestled in some of the dips and hollows and rendered more brilliant with the light of the golden sunlight which brightened our progress.

Knowing my penchant for unusual Irish names…how about this one? 'Devil's Mother'. How delicious is that?…and it was actually the name of a 650m mountain, just near the Sheep and Wool Centre and just before we reached Leenane, on the N59, which road seems to form a ring all around the entire Connemara National Park. Everything is within the embracing arms of that road. The National Park, The Connemara Heritage and History Centre and two of the most magnificent mountain ranges…The Twelve Pins (another totally brilliant name) and the Maumturk Mountains. A vista to truly stun the senses. I mean, there really was no doubting that we were in Connemara country now, as we progressed along this wonderful road with Kylemore Abbey a glorious sight over to the right, situated up in the hills above Kylemore Lough and nestling in the splendour of the forest of ancient woodland which sweeps down the hillside, thus adding an air of romance and mysticism to a building which would have been more in keeping as the palatial abode of some great Prince.

Magnificence was everywhere. Whichever way one should choose to look, it was there, in your face, a gasp of enchantment escaping from ones lips quite unbidden and the road, in one particular place, just close to the abbey, was a veritable tunnel which was formed by the overhead canopy of the trees, their golden and bronze foliage a miracle of colour and the play of light and shade which patterned the surface of the road, as the sun found all and any chinks in the still quite thick covering of leaves, dazzled the eye with its scintillating mosaic.

Everything was gold and green, bronze and russet. Here and there, sparkling, tinkling streams frolicked over a bed of shiny boulders and the sheep, with their creamy little bodies full and bulging and with their little black legs firmly planted, doing, of course, their usual thing…chomping!

Just around a bend…what am I always saying?…was a waterfall. Right there, dead ahead. A glory of sparkling water, splashing and cascading and quite jubilantly hurling itself over the edge of a rock ledge as it has done, no doubt, like forever.

Finally coming over the Kylemore Pass, all I can say is…Awesome! Splendid! Magnificent!…and, WOW! (And just to add a wee cherry on the top, we saw a real Irish Gypsy Caravan. The old and original, horse-drawn type…and it was sooooo gorgeous).

And now, at last, just beyond Letterfrack, we were there. We had finally arrived at the place which, only this morning, at our usual meeting of the Board, was just a place on our somewhat dog-eared map.

Large, imposing signs marked the entrance, flanking both sides, so that the entry into this miracle of Nature was proclaimed from whichever direction one came…and the path to the Visitor Centre was bordered by a riot of tall and stately trees and shrubbery which added a touch of mystery as to where the path would eventually lead.

It led, as one would, of course, have expected…to the car park…and basically, that was it. Pathways led off in various directions and people who were boot clad were setting off, shrugging into backpacks, and laughing in the sheer pleasure of the anticipation of what lay ahead, as we pulled in and tried to take it all in at once…well, me, anyway.

As the sun filtered through the trees, we made the decision to have our snack lunch first…I mean, by the time we returned to the car, having explored all that there was to see, it would, no doubt, be too late and besides, we were both of us quite hungry by now. Misty got into the swing of things by reaching over from the back and poking his nose into all the foil-wrapped packages and hoping that eventually, some of it may just come within range of his mouth and with some difficulty, we did manage to get some water down his throat, again by, quite literally, squirting it at him from the plastic bottle. This, of course, led to water getting all over the place, us included, and a great deal of giggling and, well, at least some of it went where it was intended that it should go…down his neck. Throughout all of this pantomome, Misty wholeheartedly threw himself into the spirit of the thing and with the greatest of gusto and good will. I mean, he thought it to be a great game…and you know what he's like with water. Bring it on man!

Setting off, we were immediately impressed with the layout of the Visitor Centre and from there, well, it was possible to walk for as long or as short a distance as one was actually capable of achieving.

Just beyond the Visitor Centre, prettily gravelled pathways led off in many different directions, however, the main point of the exercise seemed to be the ascent of Diamond Hill, a vast lump of forest-clad rock that, although called a hill, looked to me to be every inch a mountain. I know that maybe I was being a bit picky but, take my word for it, that was no hill. You will accept that as being just my own humble opinion, of course.

Anway, apart from the argument as to whether it be a Hill or a Mountain, I was determined that, even if it should happen to be the very last thing that I ever did, I was going to make a very good attempt at getting myself and my diminutive little legs at least some way up that blessed thing…and in all honesty, the trails had been laid out in such a way that it was perfectly within my capabilities, even though it was but six months since my new hip was done. (And the other one left a great deal to be desired).

There were, in fact, four different walks…all colour-coded…ones choice being purely dependant upon ones own level of stamina and capability.

Starting at the bottom, there was the Green Walk. Green was really easy-peasy, being a gentle stroll and was entirely, more or less, all on ground level. From that, you could up the ante a wee bit by taking the Yellow route…now this one, this is a bit more like it. The trail is a quite steeply inclined pull until about a third of the way up Diamond Hill where it then cuts across the girth of the 'mountain' and the pathway follows a circuitous way back down again. Something with a bit of meat in it and that will do for me.

There then follows the Blue route, which goes just that bit, well, quite a good bit further, to about half way up and then, the ultimate Red route, which, needless to say, goes right to the summit and then back down again.

The fact that, not all that long ago, I would have been able to do the Red trail, matters not, at this point in time. That was then and this is now and, I'll tell you, when I completed that walk, with my Jeffy and my Misty, both of whom have good strong, powerful legs, I was just about as proud as I have ever been. It was a real big deal, for me…and I had done it. Needless to say, I was quite euphoric about the whole thing and well, let's just say that it will be quite some time before I forget that wonderful feeling of achievement.

Actually, I was probably just a wee bit full of myself, as we made our gentle way down…and the view from what had been our highest point was absolutely stunning (my God, what must it be like from the very top?)…the sun using its own Midas touch to gild the beige shale of the pathway and causing a dappled pattern, a mosaic of light and shade to criss-cross wherever the sunlight was filtered through the trees. Masses of autumn gold Rowan trees, grew prolifically, on either side of our path and the blood-red berries were as jewels which, indeed, could not have been outdone by the most lustrous of rubies. It was such a joy to feel at one with the countryside that lay all around us, especially having felt the adrenalin flow and ones heart pounding at the exhilaration of the climb and the feeling of new-found strength in ones legs. The birds seemed as though they were celebrating with me and the joy was quite mutual.

A tranquil moment shared, as we two sat, just for a few moments and felt the warmth of the rough stone bridge beneath us and heard the gentle ripple and tinkle of water from the small stream which flowed over rocks, barely a breath away, as it went on its way, passing under our momentary resting place as it did so.

Indeed, when we did arrive back down to the Visitor Centre, a celebration seemed appropriate and was achieved, in a small way, by stopping off at the lovely wee café and so, sitting at a table set out in the small, enclosed courtyard, where grew blossom trees which were bright with their late-summer blooms, we enjoyed our coffees and cakes and just allowed ourselves the small luxury of wallowing in the tranquillity of the mellow, sunlit afternoon, the peaceful, sweet song of the birds and the happy contentment of two people who could not have been closer, in heart or in soul. It was perfect…and quite unforgettable.

The magic of those gentle moments was even enhanced as, before we bade farewell to this Connemara garden of tranquillity, all the ladies who worked in the café came out to speak to us and started to make a huge fuss over you know who. Said canine immediately went into his now quite familiar 'superstar' mode, an attitude that he can adopt at the least provocation, and really turned on the charm…which caused even more exclamations of delight to be lavished upon the ever expanding head of our own rapidly becoming 'celebrity'. It was all offered as a genuine token of friendship and so it added that additional glow of warm contentment to what had already been a perfect day.

Perfect day or not, it was becoming quite advanced now and so, with happy hearts, we slowly made our way back to home ground. There was no immediate rush, of course and so we took the time to look and to appreciate every wonderful mile of our journey back to Tourmakeady…a journey which, once again, brought us through the pure Irish magic that is Joyce Country.

The golden panorama of the sweeping hills was stunning. The low evening sun casting shadows in all the dips and folds and hollows, created a vision of almost unbelievable splendour, especially as we rounded the bend in the road which put us on the home stretch. The view was immediate and full on as one hit the bend and the colours of hill and sky blended to give an almost exotic mixture of different hues. It was so breathtaking that we actually pulled in, both of us armed with a camera and both of us just hoping that the digital images would do at least some small justice to the images created by nature.

And then, we were home. Truly, all this beauty really is just a kilometer or two from the cottage. I mean, a few minutes, that is all…and one enters the very outskirts of paradise. Can't be bad, can it?

Needless to say, the golden glow of low evening sunlight, turned our own Lough Mask to shimmer and sparkle and, I tell you, I just felt so very fortunate to be, well, just to be ME as I stood there with my darling Jeffy and took in all of this amazing beauty and allowed fleeting images of our wonderful day to flash by the windows of my mind. Surely, it couldn't get to be much better.

Anyway, it will not be too long now, before I shall be trying to find all the right words with which to convey, to your ever receptive ear, the miracle that has been today…and now…well, dinner has been prepared and eaten and the fire is filling the room and our hearts with the magic of its flames. Logs are spitting and crackling and sending their cheery greeting towards the night sky…and the feeling is one of total contentment. The wine cellar has, of course, been raided thus adding its own special brand of excellence to the already mellow atmosphere…and now, here you are! Marvellous!

Today has been special, for so many different reasons but, all of those separate and yet, equally important reasons each merit, in their own way, my nightly offering of thanks to the source of all human pleasure, if only we would always take the trouble to find it…and appreciate it. On a personal level, it has been a truly amazing mile-stone. Maybe only a simple achievement but, to me, a towering and quite exceptional achievement…again, something which merits enormous gratitude…and that same gratitude goes to my darling husband, as much as it goes to any divine source. Jeff has seen the 'me' when I was at my lowest. He has seen me overcome the radical measures which had to be taken in order to achieve today's small miracle that I feel, quite justifiably proud of…and he also knows the pride of a husband for a wife who has made such a bold effort.

You really are a husband in a million, my own Jeffy…a hundred million…and I love you, with my very soul. If I have achieved any small success, my love, it is only because of you and the manner in which you have inspired me to overcome all obstacles.

God bless you and take my love into your own heart as you sleep. Rest well and tomorrow, we will be more than ready to find new adventures with which to fill our day with wonder.

Sleep tight, my Misty…my own dear funny face. You have had a good day and I know that it could not have been much more doggie-licious…I mean, remember those two lovely beaches…not to mention your climb up Diamond Hill. Sweet doggie dreams. We love you!

See you tomorrow. Goodnight, Ireland…and may God watch over your very special land, this night.

ⓐⓓⓓⓓⓓⓓⓓⓓⓓⓓⓓ

Tuesday evening…eventide…I do think that is such a lovely word. Eventide. And this particular eventide, as I wait for you, my very dear friend, to actually arrive, it proclaims that, with the inexorable passage of time, yet another day is fading and, ever so gradually, drawing to its inevitable close.

There is no dismay or feelings of gloom lurking in this dear wee cottage on this rather special eventide…far from it. In fact, to be honest, I actually quite look forward to this part of the day. You see, for me, it is a time for gentle reflection. A time for appreciating all that has, in the preceding hours, come together to make a perfect whole. All kinds of bits and pieces, just like the pieces of a jigsaw, which, when completed, create a picture that is very special and meaningful.

Today, I think that we have experienced all of the quite unique ingredients of a typical day spent on this enchanted Isle. Firstly…Scenery. Scenery of quite stunning splendour and magnificence and all of it enhanced by Ireland's own very special brand of Magic. And then, just to make sure, don't you know, as an extra bonus, one finds oneself being quite liberally sprinkled with an enormously generous amount of that rare and quite intoxicating Fairy Dust…the harbinger of all that is beautiful and, what is more, Romantic. Yes, there has been quite a lot if it about, today…romance, I mean and, as I sit here, in this quiet and tranquil evening twilight, with the fire burning merrily and sparks singing their cheery song to the darkening sky, I can still feel the rather pleasant sensation of a quite large amount of residue of said Fairy Dust. It must have been quite a heady dosage, to have lingered all day long and still be effective.

And now, I really am blethering and, as if by some prearranged signal, just at the right moment, here you are…so now I can really blether. In fact, I will probably step it up a few notches, before I'm finished.

Anyway, come along in and be welcome and, as all is ready to greet you…well, here goes!

Tuesday
29th September 2009

I don't suppose that I should complain when being awakened, even at a quite early hour, by a genuine show of love and affection…even though that loving gesture did leave me somewhat wet and soggy. For the last couple of mornings, I've managed to dodge the fervent and quite extravagant dose of ravishing from my hunky specimen of canine beefcake, however, this early morn found me quite unprepared and therefore completely at his mercy. Misty, of course. I mean, who else. Jeff's early morning affections are of a much less enthusiastic nature, although, only in as much as he uses just a little more finesse. Whatever, kisses are kisses, no matter from whence they may come or, in what manner proffered. Which cannot be bad…can it?

As I began the process of relieving myself of some of the surplus moisture, I could hear him clattering down the stairs, (Misty, not Jeff) all eager to get out and about. So much to do and so much to explore, don't you know! Anyway, the daily rounds of his own private meadow does have its good points as it keeps him occupied until such time as the smell of bacon and sausages wafts out to him and then he knows just where his priorities lie and he takes up his position by his breakfast bowl.

Just to deviate from the norm this morning, we didn't actually need to convene the usual meeting of the Board, as a unanimous decision with regard to our destination on this glorious, sunny Tuesday morning, had already been made.

Galway. Galway…there, I've said it again. I mean, how amazing does that sound? It positively oozes romance. Just the name seems to conjure up thoughts of love and romance…from every Irish love song that was ever written. (OK! OK! So I know what you're thinking…here she goes again. Lives in a little world of her own, that one. Silly old sod). Anyway, I don't care. There is absolutely nothing wrong with a bit of romance and, as there does not appear to be any age limit to being a silly old sod, even a romantic silly old sod, then there is no hope, whatsoever, for me. It would appear that it must be in my genes as it comes to me so naturally and I have absolutely no doubt that I shall still be as accomplished in the art of being a silly old sod, when they put the very last screw in the lid of my box.

So, with Misty happily digesting his 'full Irish' breakfast and now lying quite contentedly in his own half of the car…the biggest half, of course…and wondering just when this day's show was about to get on the road, we managed a reasonable amount of organization between the two of us, my Jeffy and I, and eventually set out towards Partry at a bright and early hour, with the sun up in her heaven and her golden glory all around us to set us on the right path, so to speak.

Before long, we were travelling through such a different terrain to that which we had already become accustomed. Gone were the gentle hills and the majestic mountains and shining lakes of Joyce's Country, only to be replaced by something equally as beautiful if not quite so stunning. Flat and grassy farmland was the main feature as we passed through some delightful small towns and villages, all with   intriguing names…Ballinrobe and Cross…with signposts to Inishmicatreer and Ballyhale…told you, didn't I? Wonderful names! Pretty farms and great herds of the gorgeous Irish cattle, which I have grown to love almost as much as the sheep and, oh yes, there were plenty of them around, also.

Way out, over on our right, we were, in fact, following the course of another of those enormous loughs, Lough Corrib, which begins just south of our own Lough Mask and which very nearly reaches Galway itself, with only a few miles separating the two stretches of water, Lough Corrib and Galway Bay itself.

Oh, how I had been looking forward to seeing Galway…or rather, Galway Bay. Like I said, I am, quite unashamedly, an incurable romantic and, well, the thought of it just couldn't get to be more evocative of all the dreams of Ireland that have, at odd occasions, filled my fancies with magic. Irish Magic…and well, I must say that my heart dropped down into my boots when, on the approach into Galway town, the traffic was just totally horrendous. It certainly was to us, anyway. I mean to become snarled up in all of that, especially being at a complete loss as to which way was up, or even down, would have been far too stressful, particularly for Jeff who, good driver as he is, does not need that kind of agro so, at my suggestion, we turned off and, well, I thought that all my dreams of seeing Galway Bay were done. Finished before they had properly gotten started.

But then, I didn't take into account the resourcefulness of my wonderful Jeffy. With all the love that is in his heart for me and a complete knowledge of every little thing which will either hurt me or make me happy, he had not given up on Galway Bay, no way and, after only five minutes, or so, there it was…yes! Galway Bay was there, full on and in my face, sweeping around the entire crescent of Irish land which forms, on three sides, the shoreline of this famous Bay.

Way out across the furthest side of these waters of lyrical magic was the stunning splendour of the mountains of The Burren, majestic and grand, as they reached for the sky…today, a sky of pale blue…peaks which showed themselves in purple mystery, in the tantalizing haze of middle distance. I mean, imagine the sun going down on all of that, with those very mountains as a backdrop. Wow! That could only be a celestial performance of quite astounding proportions. Just imagine the blaze of glory as the ocean reflects, in a perfect double imagery, the vibrant sunset colours. Truly a miracle which could not but enchant the soul and even then, the scene would become even more vibrant and startling as, second by second, the colours change, from orange to gold and from peach to pink, deepening and becoming ever more stunning as this heavenly orb slowly dips and then finally vanishes below the waters of Galway Bay. The fire extinguished, once again…at least until the repeat performance tomorrow, when, after this life-giving planet has completed its next circumnavigation of the Earth, hopefully, the entire spectacle will be played out once more.

However, before the fire is extinguished, this brilliant orb will have engineered a golden highway…an infinity, stretching out across tranquil waters. A highway along which the chariots of angels could travel in style, paved with ingots of gold…a highway of fantasy across which you could imagine yourself setting out on the journey to paradise, (no chariots for us mere mortals) indeed, to the foothills of those aforementioned mountains and finally stepping ashore where the rainbow ends. (Oh boy! There I go again! I don't know where it comes from…and you will probably be wishing that I'd left it in that place where the sun never shines)!

Oranmore and Kilcolgan, amongst other lovely names like Ballinderreen, were visible over on our left, with pretty wee islands likeTawin Island and Eddy Island, jutting out into the shimmering water of the bay…and then, the final miracle that had fulfilled my dream, the dream of walking along the shores of Galway Bay…Salthill. Salthill just had to be the most picturesque wee seaside resort that I have ever seen and oh, so absolutely perfect! I cannot begin to tell you…I was so happy, at that moment in time.

Oh, my darling husband…how wonderful are you? You did it! You found it for me. Thank you! Thank you!…and I love you!

Once parked up, I couldn't get out of the car quick enough. This was actually Galway Bay and here I was, as eager as any child, to see all that there was to see…which was so much.

The lovely promenade seemed to stretch for miles, in both directions. Broad and straight, with the beach running parallel. Galway and beyond, in one direction and, in the other, the beautiful, intricate coastline, the lacy doily kind of coastline, with its abundance of tiny wee bays and inlets and islands of all shapes and sizes, just off shore, which eventually winds its way along as far as Westport, indeed, all the way to Donegal, if you were to follow it far enough.

Direction was of little, indeed, of absolutely no significance whatsoever, to a certain furry person who, as soon as he was released from the confines of the car, shot off across the beach and was the first, well, the only one, really, to set a paw into the magic waters of Galway Bay…with, in hot presuit, a local dog who took a sudden interest in this new interloper and, within no time at all, they were dashing around, chasing each other in and out of the water and becoming bosom buddies, apparently for life. The two of them, caught up in their own simple doggie pursuits, made for a lovely vision of canine vigour, indeed, after about ten minutes of this boisterous game of who can run the fastest, my Misty completely out-ran his new bosom pal…a Golden Labrador…who finally ceded superiority to the 'big Irish' by flopping down onto the sand and looking, for all the world as if he might never get up again. At which point, we retrieved Misty, who, with absolutely no effort from us, had just had as much exercise in ten minutes as he would normally have had in a whole day. Not to mention the fact that he was now totally wet and sandy.

Heading in the direction of the small town area of Salthill, it was pleasant to just amble along, taking in the gentle ambience of this lovely little resort, with a quiet and leisurely stroll along the promenade. There were a few small shops and a café or two and a hotel, quite a big one, right on the front. I mean, harping on about the famous, lyrical sunset, again, wow…just imagine the view of the proceedings from the windows of that establishment. The fact is, this lovely wee place would be a perfect spot to spend some quality time. No fuss, just peace and tranquillity. A haven for the soul, if ever there was one. A panacea for all that might ail both the body and the mind. A curative. A salve with which to heal the wounds inflicted by life's wilful 'dirty tricks' brigade. That is the precious quality of this wee Salthill. But then, the same could very well be said of this entire country. Ireland is the complete package. The whole island is a veritable haven for any human spirit which may be in need of some TLC and also have a yearning for peace and tranquillity.

And, having said all that, well, as we made our slow and leisurely way back along the esplanade and to the car, my own soul was, I am glad to say, extremely serene, although I must admit to the fact that, as we walked along, I had one eye wide open, in order to take in as much of the quiet loveliness of Galway Bay as I possibly could, while the other was sharply peeled for the possible sudden emergence of that fickle Finger of Fate, that well-manicured celestial digit which might, at any time, decide to give we two mortals (and the big red hairy one) a prod between the shoulder blades and, just to emphasize the point, a stentorian voice decree that our magic carpet ride through this wonderful country must, if only briefly, stop here. A short hiatus in our journeyings. And strangely, the idea did not hold any great feelings of dismay for, as I have said, some quality time spent here would be very pleasant.

Arriving back to our trusty 'Magic Carpet', (Toyota Prius) I could not have felt any more thoroughly content and happy. I mean, for the last couple of hours, I had enjoyed the glorious vista of sea and sky, of alluring, distant mountains and the benevolent, gentle warmth of a mellow, golden sunlight, which has bathed everything with the touch of Midas…and I had done all of that in the company of my husband, my own special man, walking side by side, with Misty trotting ahead, ready and eager to investigate all and everything, with nothing too small or insignificant to stake some small claim on his canine attentions. It could not have been more perfect. My dreams of Galway Bay had been everything that I could have wished for, hoped for…thanks to my Jeffy.

Our plans remaining uninterrupted by some mischievous Diety, we took the time to break out the flask and had a coffee and then, duly refreshed, we set off once more, having already determined that we would carry on along this lovely coastal road and well, just see what happened.

Our progress was a slide-show of enchantment and delight as this highway wound its gentle way around the coast, bordered on the one side by the Atlantic waters, the very same waters that actually flow into Galway Bay and, on the other side boasted the beautiful rolling hills and the distant mountains of the Connemara. To use this term again, it was a magic carpet ride, indeed.

This entire corner of Ireland is Connemara country and, for the most part, if you but follow this coastal road for the full distance, I would wager that you would find very few places where there would be any lengthy stretches of road that were actually dead straight. As I have already mentioned and, I know that I have used the term many times before, it can only be described in like manner…like the frilly crocheted edge of a very ornate doily. But, what a joy to follow this maze of intricate twists and turns as the views out to sea are totally stunning. A profusion of tiny bays and inlets and offshore islands of every shape and size fill the gaze with wonder at the sheer beauty of it all.

The complete circuit would, of course, eventually bring you into the heart of Connemara, the spectacular Connemara, with its National Park and magnificent mountains…mountain ranges like The Twelve Pins and, just beyond them, the thrilling aspect of the Maumturk Mountains. The breathtaking beauty of which, we experienced only yesterday. The extremely lovely little village and bay of Roundstone is on this route of total splendour and, the view across to The Twelve Pins, from that wee place, is totally breathtaking. We didn't go up that far today but, we have seen it and, believe me, it is stunning.

On this particular day, a day when sunlight bathed our way in glorious golden light, (that celestial weatherman is certainly giving us some preferential treatment) we would be turning off this delightful coast road, long before getting up as far as pretty Roundstone and, by this moment in time, as said sun had reached and maybe even passed its noontime position over the yardarm, we set our sights on a perfect place to break out the butty box and, as you would only expect by now, it was only a matter of minutes from actually giving birth to the thought that the absolutely perfect place came along. Spiddal, which came complete with its own gorgeous beach…a fact that a certain canine had already noticed and was now more than eager to be the first one up and at it.

Taking stock of our surroundings, it really could not have been more perfect…a sun trap, if ever there was one and yet another quiet refuge for any slightly weary traveller in need of a wee respite.

Before we had even broken out the sandwiches, Misty was elbow deep in sand. I mean, he even managed to get it all around his mouth, God love him…and please don't ask me how but, somehow, he had achieved this unusual phenomenon. Probably trying to eat it, as nothing any more tempting seemed to be coming anywhere near to being close to his mouth…like a bit of boiled ham, or something similar.

We were only too willing, just to savour the tranquillity of this lovely spot and, no doubt, stayed longer than we had at first intended however, you would not have found me complaining…what?…Seasalt Vera objecting to an added infusion of the precious ozone drug? Don't be daft. And besides, it gave a certain furry person another opportunity to once again get himself thoroughly soaked before acquiring a liberal coating of fine sand. In this, he had some helpful encouragement, when he met and made friends with another doggie, a black Labrador and the pair of them instantly became bosom buddies…the second best friend this morning…and spent a good half hour seeing who could run and do 'handbrake' turns in the fastest possible time. In the meantime, I had a nice chat to the owner of Misty's new pal and we both agreed that this was far better than exercising them ourselves…just let them do their own thing, whilst we merely watch from the sidelines.

Finally, with a few pangs of regret, we gathered up our few belongings, cleaned off the dog and bade farewell to Spiddal. Thank you for your hospitality. It was lovely!

Sadly, we now left the coast behind us and the next two or three hours just sped by as we travelled through the glory of the Connemara…fleeting, yet everlasting memories of mountains and rolling hillside, strewn with myriads of lakes which shone in the afternoon sunlight, the larger and closer of them reflecting the deepest blue and which, like so many others that we have seen, were dotted, here and there, with little islands which supported their own flora and possibly, fauna. Tiny islands which I, for one, would not mind being marooned on. (Just as long as my Jeffy were with me to be my Man Friday and, naturally, I could not consider being anywhere without Misty, so I suppose I wouldn't really be a proper 'kosher' castaway).

Along the way, there were so many delightful villages or hamlets, as most of them were too small even to be classed as a village. One such was Derryrush. A few cottages, a pub…and then you had passed through it. Except that this wee gem of a place had a hidden, even more precious gem, sort of hidden from the road, unless you were, like me, with eyes all over the place, just looking for such hidden treasures. Turning down a narrow track, we were, all of a sudden, into the most gorgeous little harbour. It was so small…a tiny jetty and then a high seawall along both sides of which were boats of all sizes. Within the sanctuary of the inner harbour, were small boats, some with masts, some with small engine houses and all sporting their bold and vibrant colours…red and bright blue, teamed with white and then, moored on the seaward side of the harbour wall were the big fishing boats, with men pottering about the decks. It truly was a veritable picture postcard, with all the colours producing a perfect blend of blue sky, turquoise sea and the brightly painted boats. Gulls, glorying in the freedom of the sky swooped and cried for the pure joy of it as they swept across the water and the boats and the distant sound of mens voices, as they called to each other as they went about their work, all added to the very special ambience of the place. It was so beautiful that the temptation to linger for a short time just could not be denied and so, Misty was allowed to have a wander around and, needless to say, soon made friends with one of the fishermen and we explored all that there was to explore, whilst taking digital images which would be a lasting reminder of this unique wee harbour. Eventually, with a friendly greeting from some of the men on the boats, we continued on our way but, with special memories of a very special moment in time, spent at Derryrush.

Heading further into the mountains, the view of the quite remarkable Twelve Pins was stunning and then, with the direction of home now in our thoughts, we found ourselves virtually running alongside the awesome grandeur of the Maumturk Mountains. How small and insignificant one feels in the close embrace of these mountains. Awesome being the only way to describe their majesty…and, as always, sheep grazed the precarious slopes and fissures, their dear, spindly little legs, quite unbelievably holding them secure, although I shall never know just how they manage it. Little white dots, but oh, how I love them. Ireland would just not be Ireland without these endearing little woolly bundles.

Time was really getting on apace now and so, with regret, we turned our attentions in the direction of home…back to a scenic beauty just as stunning, with all the splendour of Joyce's Country on our very doorstep. Which still thrills and gladdens the hearts of we two travellers, each and every time that we come this way back to Tourmakeady.

With Derryneen and Maam Cross behind us, we were heading along the final leg of our journey, which would eventually bring us back to Lough Mask when, just at a bend in the road, we were treated to another small example of what I now call 'Irish Whimsy'. As we stopped at the crossroad, we would have had to have been totally blind not to have seen the quite large pub, Keane's Bar, which was directly in front of us. However, what actually caught our attention and, without any offence intended to the particular individual, was what appeared to be a bundle of old clothes. For reasons known only to those who may have placed them there, they appeared to have been deposited on the steps which led to the front doors of this fine looking establishment. Only, as it turned out, they weren't clothes…well, they were but, it just so happened that there was, in fact, a living, breathing (well, I hope he was breathing) man, lurking inside said bundle of clothes, who had, to all intents and purposes, been evicted at closing time and propped up in the doorway, with his back comfortably supported against the wall, in order to sleep it off, until opening time came around once more and, with God's good grace, he would have sobered up sufficiently in order to re-enter the establishment and proceed to start the whole process off again. It would have been well-nigh impossible not to laugh at the poor man's predicament, however, there was no malice in it, please believe that and it was, quite sincerely, accompanied with a wee prayer for his future welfare. (I just hope that when the night session comes to an end, someone will see that he gets home. I should hate to think that he would be spending the entire night in the same place that he had spent the afternoon).

A convenient wee shop, just up from the pub, gave me the chance to purchase a few provisions and, once again, I was reminded of the open-hearted nature of the Irish people. Two elderly ladies were deep in conversation as I entered but, instead of ignoring me and just carrying on with their talk, as would probably be the case back home, I was immediately drawn into their conversation, just as if I was a known friend and just from up the way…instead of being the total stranger that I was. They didn't have to do that. Why should they? They didn't know me…but that is the way of the Irish and it made me feel rather special and it is a feeling that I shall treasure. May God look kindly on these two dear ladies who made a stranger feel at home.

And then, we were almost home. The narrow lanes now were edged with the unique stone walling, which I noticed from the time we first arrived in these parts. It wasn't so much the stone but the shape of the stones…almost like round balls…and they just seemed to have been cobbled together quite precariously and yet, I would hazzard a guess that they have more than stood the test of time and all that the elements may have thrown at them over countless years.

Not far from home, we stopped for a short break, mainly to use up what coffee was left in the flask and, as we pulled into the small picnic area beside Lough Mask, I recognized it as being the same one at which we had made a brief stop, last Sunday, when we had been en route to Cong. And, well, you will hardly believe this but, there was Misty's missing drinking bowl…just exactly where we had inadvertently left it on Sunday. There was even some water in it still. It was, of course, a joy to find it but, apart from that, it was, and this was something of even greater importance, yet another example of life in Ireland. Not only do the people of this land have hearts as big as the ocean but, they are honest hearts as well.

It must have been somewhere in the region of 5.30 - 6pm by the time we arrived back in Tourmakeady and the evening light was quite spell-binding as we drove along the shores of the lake. The water had taken on an almost opalescent hue and the sky was just beginning to show a touch of pink and gold amongst the paling day-time blue. But it was the stillness which, because it was so profound, made it stand out all the more. A tranquil hush had fallen over the lake, with the only sounds being that of a gentle ripple and the occasional chattering of the ducks and the other water fowl who were fortunate enough to be able to call this beautiful lake 'home'. I mean, after the wonderful day we had just experienced, to come back to such an idyll, well…I could not think of anthing more ideal. It really was pure magic. A Technicolor landscape, as the varied shades of blue mingled with the greens and the golds of the mountains, gentle now, with the slight distance that we had put between us and them, but a truly heavenly back drop to the overall scene.

So, the day has drawn to its inevitable close but, what a day it has been and, as I take stock of everything…as I do each and every day of my life, not just when I'm here in Ireland…by offering up my thanks to all of those who deserve thanks, I find that, as always, there is so much to be grateful for. One can always be somewhat surprised, if you take each day on its own merit, just how much there can be in just a single day, that merits a word or two of thanks.

Today, as always, the man who makes the sun always shine for me, has my eternal thanks, not just for today but, for every day that we are together. Of course, he did earn my special thanks today, by finding a way around to the full, sweeping grandeur of Galway Bay, just when all seemed, to me, to be lost. He knew how much it meant to me and so, in typical Jeffrey fashion, he would not give up on it until he had made it right. Thank you, my darling and I love you…that love even greater as a result of all your efforts to make this day special. Goodnight my love and God bless you, always.

Sleep tight, my Misty. You too, have had a quite exceptional day…just let your wee head think of the two good pals that you made today and dream of the sea and the joy you had as you chased your mates around those golden beaches. May your doggie dreams be just as golden.

God bless everyone…and God bless Ireland this night. May a very special kind of peace lie over this land until the blessed light of another dawn transforms the ocean with its radiance and fills the land with its warmth.

See you, tomorrow! Bright and early, mind you!

◎◎◎◎◎◎◎◎◎◎◎◎◎

The shadows of a gentle and mellow twilight are now beginning to fill up all the wee corners of this pleasant and comfortable room…a veiled hint of mystery, with a flicker, here and there, from the dancing flames as they caress the living wood of the logs, making them spark and splutter and, as I sit here, with the ubiquitous glass of wine to hand and gaze into the ever increasing glow of those hypnotic flames, I could not be more content. The very measure of my serene contentment being a direct result of the special day that now, at this moment in time, I am so eager to relate to your ever patient ears.

Oh, I know that all days spent in this wonderful land of dreams come true are special but, as I sit here, waiting for your welcome knock on the door, in the warmth of the afterglow of the extra special magic that today has provided, (you see, it isn't entirely down to the alcoholic afterglow from the wine) I cannot deny that today has gone way beyond being just special. Try phenomenal!

I shall give you just one clue as to the essence of the day, indeed, a name. Just a name…Seasalt Vera. Veronica Hall's alter-ego. Need I say more?

Do look across the lake as you arrive. It is so ethereally enchanting at this moment, as I glance out in expectation of seeing you. A mist just as delicate and as fine as gossamer has turned what is always a beautiful picture into something that is now touched by an aura of romance. Fairy Dust is definitely in that whispy breath, that almost transparent mist and even the moon looks like a large opalescent pearl, as it tries to penetrate this delicate vapour. The gentle breath of angels, that's what it is…which is a nice thought to carry around with you so that whenever you see a fine mist, you will know exactly what it is and where it came from.

Taking into account, my exotic imagination…and completely ignoring same…it really is quite beautiful and you will, I know, be quite enchanted by the scene.

And now, here you are! Oh, how wonderful…now I can begin to try and unwind the tangle of jumbled thoughts and images which have all contributed to the miracle of today. You alone can help me to get it all sorted into some kind of sequence and order and my joy will be in not just being able to successfully untangle it all but, in the actual reliving of every minute.

Wednesday
30th September 2009

Just one glance from the window of our bedroom to an aspect of sunlit meadow and the vision of my two boys already out in the fresh, early morning air and going about their mutually enjoyed morning activities, was all that it needed to get me fired up and ready to propel myself into a part of the action.

It was a glorious morning, with not a hint of the delicate angel breath which had enshrouded the lake and the land with its ethereal magic, last night. No having to wait for the sun to burn it off…it had already gone.

No sooner said, than done…and I was down in the kitchen, clattering away with the pots and pans, with a merry rendering of some quite unrecognizeable song, which appeared to be issuing from me, obviously, as I was the only one present…and I was soon throwing bacon into one of the said pans and eagerly awaiting the return of my two loved ones, which I knew would not be too long, once the aroma of bacon, toast and coffee turned them in the direction of the kitchen, where a pair of loving arms were only too willing to give 'good morning' hugs to both of them.

The back door was open to let in this wonderful fresh and pure air off the lake and bird song also filtered through to me, as I was pottering about (just to shame my own poor musical efforts, no doubt) and well, how about that for just absolutely marvellous! A morning to rejoice in. A morning when all was definitely, positively rosy, to this particular lady.

Breakfast was the usual session of laughter and cheerful banter…and the usual battle to stop a certain furry person from demolishing all the bacon, right down to the very last rasher…if he ever got to be that lucky, that is. No way! Not a chance! His efforts, however, only made the breakfast table all the more hysterical and a great deal of innocent fun was had by all.

Of course, it goes without saying that the business of actually getting the Hall family threesome out on the road could never have been accomplished without the usual assortment of hiccups, cock-ups and, well, just the normal misadventures which always seem to occur whenever we three are involved in the proceedings. Anything in the least bit straight forward would just not be us…I mean, come on now, admit it. You would not expect anything else now, would you? No! I thought not!

One possible explanation could be the rather pathetic attempts, by me, naturally, of trying to navigate the rather tricky and murky waters of too many jobs with too few hands…and even Misty's generous offers of a helpful paw usually exacerbates the problem rather than being any actual assistance. Anyway, I found myself doing my usual headless chicken impersonation as I juggled with an attempt at writing some postcards with clearing up, washing up, making sandwiches and chasing Misty out of the kitchen after trying to nick the boiled ham which, in turn, led to him seeking another form of amusement elsewhere and finding said alternative entertainment in the act of nicking one of Jackie's shoes, thereby leaving the one lone survivor still sitting outside their front door like some small abandoned wee beastie.

Giving credit where it is due, he did come and present himself outside the back door, while brandishing this new trophy and waggling the thing at me as if he had done something exceedingly clever which, and here I made a huge mistake, resulted in the inevitable manic chase around the back meadow, in a futile attempt at retrieving said shoe. Oh, silly me! Not a good idea. The chase is all a part of the game, don't you know and when Misty then senses that the game is afoot, he immediately bursts into demonic activity, his eyes flashing and sparkling with the sheer joy of the contest of minds. While I become red in the face and thoroughly exasperated.

The obvious course of action is, of course, to totally ignore him but…I never learn! To just turn away from him and take no notice is the trick, you see. Once he realizes that nobody is playing, he will soon get bored with his once precious trophy and look around for something else with which to create an amusing diversion. I mean, I know all this but, like I said, I fall for it, every time.

We did, eventually, rescue the shoe (Jeff having joined in the chase, by this time) and it was just one more reason to give the cop shop a wide berth…again…as we later passed through Westport.

Jeff had hinted that our destination for the day was to be a surprise…a pleasant one, naturally but, with my own special preferences taken into account. (Another typical 'Jeff' thing to do…my wishes, my needs. Just whatever he feels will give me pleasure)! And, to say that he succeeded, just has to be the understatement of all time.

My premonition of 'something special' began with the usual tingle, that fizz that begins to pass through veins which are already flowing with about 80% sea water, as we were passing through Malrany (or Malleranny, or Mulrany) three different variations of the same name which we saw on various signs in the short space of time that it took for us to drive the length of the main street. For a start, Malrany could boast of having a beach that was to die for. Miles of glorious white sand and crystal-clear water, which was the breathtaking colour of aquamarine. All the colours, a glorious blend, came together to form a stunning picture. From the road, we were actually looking down upon it and, although it was not in the overall scheme of things that we should go down to it just at that moment, we both made a mental note to maybe make special time, to do just that, on the return journey. I mean, I was almost out of the car while it was still moving…you know what I'm like…but, wow, this was some beach. It sort of went on forever. However, a sign situated on the way out of this small town acted as sufficient restraint for me to remain belted into my seat. Malrany is not about to go anywhere!…not, at least, until later on today.

What lay ahead just about had me bursting at the seams…how do you do it, my Jeffy? Achill Sound and Achill Island…I mean, how scrumptious are those names? And these were the very places for which I would have given just about anything to visit, as we were travelling from Donegal, last Saturday. Do you remember? Well, Jeff certainly did. God bless him. But, honestly…those names! You can amost smell the sea, just by giving them utterance. Certainly, the Seasalt Vera part of my persona was as thrilled as little mint balls at the vision which instantly came to mind…a picture of open strand, sea and lighthouses. Oh, Jeffrey Hall, you are amazing! I don't know how you do it but, just drive on and carry me to what sounds, to me, to be total paradise.

And it was…paradise, I mean! Oh, Ireland, beautiful land of my heart! I love you more and more with every passing day. Is there no end to your surpassing beauty? I am now, more than ever, convinced that the answer to that question is no. Oh, I know that when it comes to seascapes, I'm already half way to my own personal form of heaven and need no further persuasion but, even the most unenthusiastic would be unable to remain unimpressed or unmoved. Beauty, in any form, has the power to move the soul and this land has more beauty than I could have ever dreamed of.

Having left behind Malrany, we were on the Corraun Peninsula and before long, the very image that had filled my mind, when I first saw the name, actually became a reality. There it was…Achill Sound. It was exactly as I had envisioned it…a vista that gave the impression of vastness…wide open and timeless. White sand stretching and reaching out for the distant water. I mean, how can one describe this phenomenon except to say that there was a totally endless quality to it with seemingly nothing to interupt the immensity of this panorama.

Gulls were everywhere, sweeping and swooping, great squadrons of them, their joy in being a part of this wondrous whole, evident in their strident calls, which were carried on the breeze off the open water along with the delectable aroma, the exotic tang of the sea…the great and glorious wide

Atlantic Ocean. This living entity which is and always will be, the only divide between Ireland and the great States of America.

Once on Achill Island, we were drawn to and actually took the tourist route, appropriately named 'Atlantic Drive'…and, it didn't need a degree in any kind of 'ology' in order to understand just why it had been designated a tourist route and why, consequently, it was chosen by every tourist coach driver worth his salt, as part of his itinerary. It was completely and utterly stunning. The great and glorious Atlantic was always in evidence, full on and magnificent and the obvious star of this particular show.

Our first stop was a drop down, not only in elevation but a drop down into a miniature bay that was only one stop away from being the most heavenly terminus. Small it may have been but a real gem. A half dozen cottages, which were dotted, here and there, around the sweep of the shoreline…and that was it. The bay itself, a horseshoe of protective rock formations and the usual white sand. (A heaven for lug worms, also, judging by the number, countless thousands of them, of the wee give-away curls of wet sand which usually proclaim their presence). This, dear friend, was Dooega. A name to create images of fancy, if you are anything at all like yours truly. You know, by now, of course, just where my whimsical fancies can lead me. (Into trouble, one of these days, no doubt).

Anyway, I was quite enchanted by our fortunate discovery of this wee place and, in no time flat, all the three of us were out of the car and scampering around the beach like three over-excited kids…or as much of a scamper as I was capable of accomplishing…with Jeff brandishing a long length of sticky seaweed at an ecstatic Misty, in order to try and distract him from the trainer (yes, another one) which his eagle eye had spotted, almost immediately, as it lurked amongst the shingle at the high-water tide line and I think we laughed so much that it was something of a miracle that I didn't get wet somewhere other than the places that the rain could reach. (Did someone mention knickers)?

The rain had come out of nowhere. Not in the least what we would have expected, after the glorious start to the day however, not to be in the least put off, we were still laughing as we hurled ourselves back into the relative dryness of the car and how lucky are we, I ask you, to be able to find such simple pleasure from merely a romp around a beach, nutty dog and all, and a bit of a soaking, to boot? As far as I am concerned, it couldn't come much better. Daft, it may seem but, money cannot buy it. It has to come from somewhere deep inside…some hidden depth…and, if you are lucky enough to find it, deep within yourself, then, you have something very precious. Thank god, my Jeffy and I have it in abundance.

How this husband of mine manages to find all these 'off the beaten track' kind of places, I don't know. I suppose it is just because he does just that…goes off the main thoroughfares and takes some hopelessly narrow track, at the end of which, we always seem to find the old crock of gold…metaphorically speaking, of course.

The next stop, by which time we had dried out a bit and the sun was back with us once more, was Keel. I mean, what can I say? For me, at least, it was another of those 'wow' places. Natually, in saying that, well, yes, it had a beach…a long and sweeping beach, which seemed to go on and on and on, like forever, (in other words, just your normal, average, quite spectacular Irish beach) said beach accessed by topping the rise of impressive sand dunes where the coarse dune grasses were lashed by a full on and in the face wind off the sea. A sea which was a deep and totally stunning, cobalt blue. White crested waves rolled in like a regiment of soldiers…rank after rank…it was Titanic, it was spectacle gone crazy. It was something akin to the treat which was so unexpectedly given to us last week, when we rounded the bend, just beyond Mullaghmore Head. It was vibrant. It was alive, as it rolled in, inexorably, onto the waiting shores of Keel. It was a riotous, surging, living thing which hurled itself towards the land in a rapturous frenzy.

We walked for a goodly way along this spectacular stretch of sand, with all of our senses alert to the blend of delights which the ambience of sea and shore had to offer. The smell of the sea, like exotic perfume to me, was in the air and the sound of surf and seabirds filled my head with visions of great ships and the freedom of the high seas, with mermaids on rocks and sirens luring these great ships in towards the land. (What do you expect?…I thought that I restrained my imagination rather well, actually).

The dark and satanic looking cliffs of Dooega Head loomed through the gradually clearing sea mist, creating an awesome backdrop to the ceaseless motion of the Atlantic surf and just off shore lay the small island of Inishgalloon, a rocky refuge and a home for all the countless seabirds which were, at that moment, making their presence well and truly known.

Having read all of that, you must have no doubts as to the state I was in. Totally mental, of course. Euphoric is one word you could use if, that is, you want to avoid hurting my feelings. Jeff would have used a much more appropriate word like, to put it mildly...BONKERS!

I was sooooo in my element...and, as for Misty, well, he was having the very time of his life. God bless his great big paws...paws which were leaving huge, dinner plate size prints in the sand, in patterns of ever decreasing circles and which were living proof, if proof were needed, that Misty was here. Saved for all posterity...or at least, until the next full tide washed all trace of him away. Never mind, old son. In your dear, doggie head, you will always remember and so, you will find your own immortality.

Lunch was partaken of in the car, which seemed like the best option. I mean, fine as it was and with the sun once again blessing us with its presence, it was still a bit too chilly to sit out, even in the shelter of the dunes. I mean, the wind was coming straight in off the Atlantic, when all is said and done. However, in saying that, we managed to derive the same amount of fun in the distribution of our simple picnic as always, with a certain large canine nose poking into everything, in the eternal hope that at least some small portion of whatever was going, might just find its way into the vicinity of his mouth.

By the time we left, Dooega Head no longer appeared quite so threatening and satanic. One final glance back, before heading out of Keel, showed it wearing a much kinder and sunnier countenance. The low cloud which had enshrouded it when we first arrived had now gone and the union of sky and sea was now clearly visible in a sparkling, deep blue horizon.

And so, farewell, Keel...until the next time.

Still filled with my usual daft elation at the marvels of Keel I remained in blissful ignorance of what lay at the end of the road which, even now, was beginning its inexorable climb up into the mountains and, little did I know it at the time but, Jeff had saved the very best until the last. I mean, there was no way that I could have ever dreamed that, the higher we progressed, up and up into these great, soaring hills, the road twisting and turning in ever more tortuous bends, that at the end of the line...literally, as far as you could go, without ending up in the sea...was a beach.

The higher we went, this small miracle of nature suddenly became apparent. It was miniaturised by the height from which we looked down upon it but it was incredibly beautiful.

The shape of this heavenly little beach was a perfect crescent of the purest white sand that we had seen so far. Water, as beautifully clear and aquamarine as any that I have seen on the Mediterranean, kissed the shore in gentle ripples, the leading edge of the flowing tide not straight but a perfectly formed scalloped pattern. Without a doubt, we had discovered true paradise in this dream come true. We had discovered Keem and, what a discovery! Keem Strand, this quite exquisite, sheltered bay, was to die for. Proof of which was in evidence as we eventually arrived down at beach level, in the shape of one of those tourist coaches, which, in the routine guided tour along the Atlantic Drive, had stopped here, in this small place, this precious jewel, hidden in the depths of the mountains…and the occupants of said coach were now strolling along the sand in groups, and marvelling, just as we were, at the sheer loveliness of the place.

The similarity to a beach which was also very special to me, for the simple reason that we spent quite a large part of our second wedding anniversary there, was immediate. We were in Malta and the beach was the jewel of Paradise Bay. I need say no more. The name was so appropriate, in Malta…and it fitted very well, indeed, here in this place of quite exquisite beauty, here in Ireland.

Oh, Jeff. This has been the golden crown to top a truly wondrous day. Thank you, my darling. How well you do know me.

Time was of no consequence in this place where one would not have been surprised to find angels walking beside you. It was like walking through a dream of what one may imagine heaven to be like. I really do believe that I could, quite happily have remained there, with my two boys, forever. However, if wishes were horses, even beggars would ride.

With nothing to surpass what we had already seen and marvelled at, yet we made one more stop before finally setting our sights on the homeward run. We still had some coffee left in the flask and a couple of chocolate bars so, coming upon a place with a name like Doogort, it seemed like a good place to spend ten minutes before the long haul home. It was, of course, another beach…and a very lovely one at that and we gave Misty his freedom to have one last run about and do his own thing.

The taste of the coffee proclaimed it to be well past its sell-by date but, at least it was wet and warm. Certainly, there was very little else with which you could give it credit and after finishing off the last chocolate bar, well, we just could not resist a quick look at what we knew to be just on the other side of the sand dunes. The whole thing should have taken no longer than fifteen minutes…tops!

Forty to forty-five minutes later, we just about managed to get our wet and soggy, though nevertheless, triumphant, indeed, positively jubilant dog, back into the car.

Almost like magic, just as soon as we set off across the dunes, our eagle-eyed copper nob had found himself another shoe…another trainer…a black one, this time, not that the colour of it was of any significance. This one, believe it or not, actually came complete with a matching wet and soggy sock.

I mean, I have to ask this question…again! How do these shoes (mostly trainers) manage to end their days, in solitary state, without their rightful mate, washed up on some forsaken shore, where daft dogs like ours consider them to be prize, indeed.

Of course, what did we two numpties do? Yes, you are absolutely right! We gave chase! That was all that Misty needed, if any encouragement were needed, to streak off like greased lightning, with eyes aglow and every fibre of his body all fired up for another great game.

A fine picture of manic, human lunacy we must have made to an observer who just happened to be in the vicinity at the time, attached to a metal detector and who, whilst doing his detecting, kept giving furtive, somewhat amused glances in our direction.

Just when I was beginning to think that we were destined to spend the night on this beach, somehow, Jeff managed to relieve our now very much 'in the doghouse' dog of his blessed shoe and, in all honesty, at that precise moment in time, I would have gladly sold him off for any offers around the 50p mark.

Some half an hour later, as we were well on our way home, I suddenly started laughing. Jeff gave me a quick side-ways glance and said…'What's up? What's so funny'? And then, of course, I just fell about laughing all the more and soon had him joining in as I painted a very graphic picture of the way we must have looked, we two great numpties, haring around like two headless chickens in overdrive, in hot pursuit of one gorgeous Irish Setter, with the look of the Devil in his glowing eyes and with a large, black trainer clamped between his pearly whites.

Of course, Misty, who had received the message, loud and clear, that he was not in good favour, as we unceremoniously hefted him into the car, now sensed that he was, with a bit of luck, out of the doghouse and once more re-instated into his usual position of much loved, pampered pooch and sort of grinned, albeit a bit sheepishly and the tail proceeded to beat out its usual rhythmic tattoo on the floor of the car.

Oh well…all's well that ends well…as the saying goes.

Needless to say…dinner was a bit late!

And there you have it! As yet another wonderful and quite memorable day draws to its inevitable close, my tale has been told and you, my dear friend, have heard me out, with your usual patience and stoicism…you have even given me the gratification of laughing in all the right places. All very therapeutic to my ego!

Now, you are gone and Jeff and I are sharing the quiet companionship of two people who also share a very deep love. Another log on the fire. Another glass of wine. Cosy shadows in the corners and daydreams in the fire. There could be a no more perfect way to end our special day. Soon we will be heading up the wooden hill. Misty has already gone up and, even downstairs, we can hear his snores…and smile…and imagine his innocent doggie dreams.

I feel that I shall find it difficult to fall asleep, tonight. There are so many images which will not be laid to rest in their rightfully appointed place…not that I want them to be. Thoughts of Dooega, of Keel and, of course, Keem. Undoubtedly, they are etched into my mind, never to be erased. And, as always, it is my wonderful husband to whom I owe every minute of this momentous day. As he does every night, he will sit for a while and study the maps, planning an itinerary which, from the first glimmerings of an idea to the final concept, he will have based upon what he knows will create a special 'Veronica' day.

Oh, my darling…you have soooo excelled yourself, today…and I do appreciate all the thought that I know you must have put into your plans for us, this day. It is, of course, just one more of the many reasons why I love you…and I love you Body, Heart and Soul. I love you with my life, indeed, you are my sole raison d'etre. God bless you, always.

As for you, Misty Hall, I am sure that your doggie dreams will be happy ones, this night. What a day you have had! I mean, all those shoes. (Three in one day, old son…not a bad haul). And, looking back on your escapades, I have to concede that your wilful but, hilarious naughtiness has added so much zest and amusement to an already wonderfully happy day. Sleep tight, dear funny face. We love you.

Thursday, tomorrow. So rapidly go the days. A measure, of course, of the happiness derived, from each and every one of them, by we three…The Intrepid Trio.

God bless us…God bless everyone.

ⓐⓐⓐⓐⓐⓐⓐⓐⓐⓐ

Mellow and Eventide…two words which have always pleasured me, greatly…and which so perfectly reflect the special ambience in this dear cottage, tonight, as I, as I do every night, anticipate your imminent arrival. An ambience which, in turn, reflects the tone of the gentle and pleasurable day that we have spent amongst the glories of both mountain and lake.

This morning, as every morning, as we, The Intrepid Trio set out on yet another adventure, our minds were as pristinely clean as blank canvases which only awaited the magic of beauty most spectacular, beauty as yet unseen, to colour it in with everlasting memories…and magic is what Ireland is all about!

Oh, there was no great stakes with regard to miles covered, today…certainly by comparison with yesterday and other days over the last couple of weeks, however, what a wonderful revelation it was, to discover the amazing and quite stunning scenic beauty which lay almost at our very doorstep, so to speak…and all it required was for us to seek it out. Well, seek it out, we did! To our delight.

Our immediate environs, around the very beautiful Lough Mask and the enchanting first fringes of the mountains of Joyce's Country, have already been a great delight but, what lay just beyond, well, it merely proved to us that what we had already been completely enchanted by, was, in fact, just a mere scratch on the surface.

And that's all I'm saying! I shall once again emphasize 'Joyce's Country' and add 'Connemara' and just leave it at that…for now. All will be revealed in due course and so, with as much patience as I can muster, I shall await your arrival…and I can't wait to get started….

And here you are! How wonderful! Absolutely perfect timing!

Actually, Jeff has, just minutes ago, taken Misty out for his nightly stroll along the lakeside. To be honest, I really don't know which of them enjoys it the most. Although, I expect that the peace and quietude induced by the gently lapping waters of the lake and the unique stillness of an Irish evening, would be an interlude of total bliss for my long-suffering Jeffy. A welcome, if only brief, respite from my incessant wittering! Bless him. Let him enjoy it while he can…and besides, he won't be too long, anyway.

In the meantime, do come in and take some comfort from the welcoming fire. Logs have just been added and so I hope that you will feel that the warmth of your welcome is just as real as that which emanates from the glowing embers of the fire.

Thursday
1st October 2009

I must confess that I seemed to wake up very slowly and languorously, this morning. For shame…and it being the first day of another month. It was enjoyable, though…a feeling of peace, comfort and serenity. Sort of laid-back, if you know what I mean.

My first thought was of Keem beach…maybe I'd been dreaming about it. I couldn't be sure but it wouldn't be at all surprising. I know that I shall never forget how very beautiful it was, as we first looked down upon it from our elevated position on the mountain road which ran down to it. So beautiful, almost like a dream in itself…pale, pale aquamarine water, white sand and that white, frilly, sort of scalloped edge to the gently flowing waterline.

Protected as it is, on three sides, by the mountains, it was such a striking contrast to the surging, white-capped waves which had been hurling themselves at the shore, completely unhindered and unrestrained, back in Keel.

The fact that my Jeffy was no longer lying beside me proved that, far from having been beamed up and abducted by aliens, that must be him in the shower. Of course, by the time that I heaved my lazy personage out of my comfortable nest and did likewise, he had already gone out with the large, red, hairy one and was, in fact, back and in the process of cleaning out the fire grate.

Shameful I know but I did, of course, say to you that this business of seeing the wonder of the breaking of the dawn and listening to the initial tuning up tweets of our feathered friends, prior to the full-blown concert, was, in all honesty, just a temporary novelty which would, in the fullness of time, die a natural death.

A loving greeting from my two boys, combined with the bright and cheery sunlight which was flooding through the open back door, only served to make me feel even more ashamed of my unfortunately normal reticence at rejoining the land of the living, first thing in the morning.

Misty was lying in his usual place, just outside the door, in a bright patch of sunlight, which only served to emphasize the glorious, lustrous gleam and glowing copper colour of his coat. Fortunately, that is where he remained, today. No forays into Pat's backyard or, heaven forbid, Pat's shed…and no more stolen shoes. Heaven be praised! The only thing to arouse his interest and inspire him to move himself was when the delectable and quite irresistible aroma of bacon and sausages wafted by the end of his nose and then, well, it took him all of about ten seconds to reach his nosh bowl.

Bon appetite, big boy!

It was such a joy to be out and about, today, as we eventually organized ourselves and got out on the road. A blue sky and a cheery, smiley, sunny aspect would have won over the most miserable of humours…and were we miserable?…not a chance!

Heading out along the lake, we took a road which turned out to be extremely narrow in places…narrow and tricky…however, it carried us into the realms of true Picture Postcard scenery. This was the true, quite unbelievable beauty and majesty of Joyce's Country which, up until now had remained undiscovered.

Up and ever upwards we went, way up into the very heart of the mountains, following a sign which proclaimed 'Joyce Country Drive' and, as we have discovered, on more than one occasion, these named scenic drives are so magnificent that they are not to be missed. I mean, take the 'Atlantic Drive' of yesterday!...and that is just to name one.

Having reached what appeared to be the highest point, the road eventually began to drop down, a gradual, winding descent towards a small village by the name of Leenane...just a tiny village really but, one of great character and loveliness. A perfect wee gem sitting as it does, by the edge of Killary Harbour. Somehow, it came as quite a surprise, to find this small haven of humanity, having just come across the barren, though very lovely landscape of the mountains, where, as usual, the only inhabitants were of the black-faced woolly variety...and what a perfect stopping point...a place to just take stock and to appreciate, to the full, the simple charm of this idyllic wee place.

So, stop, we did.

Needless to say, I made straight to the harbour wall, just to have a look what was on the other side...oh, my God, I'm getting to be exactly the same as my dog! What a view, though, as the water disappeared into the distance, with the sun dappling the gentle ripples which just barely ruffled the surface and the golden, sweeping hillside coming down to the very water's edge, where small meadow flowers grew amongst the much greener grass, closest to the water. Ducks fussed about, constantly chattering among themselves...these lovable creatures being such a delightful aspect of the freshwater lake areas that we have discovered so far...and oh, I do love the ducks. Sheep and ducks. What am I like? And don't even think of answering that!

Turning away from this magnificent scene, we paid a little more attention to the village itself, not that there is all that much to see...however, what little there is, well, it is quite charming. A pub, Gaynor's Bar. A small shop and a gorgeous little restaurant called The Village Grill and barely a handful of small cottages and that is about it...apart from a very enticing wee gift shop, which takes up the corner, just across from the pub. Add to that, the Sheep and Wool Centre...which could be of some interest if you should feel the necessity to gen yourself up on sheep and wool. (And before you actually say anything...yes, I did go into the Gift Shop and yes, I did buy a couple of items, or three. And yes, Jeff did know that I would be positively unable to just walk past this miniature emporium of all things delightful…and no doubt felt the odd stirrings of anxiety and a few rather painful tugs at his wallet).

Before leaving this lovely village of Leenane, we did notice that the only place which seemed to be quite busy…was the pub. And quite right, too! One cannot help but admire folk who so obviously have their priorities just right.

Following the road, as it wound its way through and out of Leenane, we came upon a quite large hotel, situated just off the road and with all of its many balconied front windows overlooking Killary Harbour and the hills beyond…I mean, how wonderful would that be, to spend a little time there, in this out of the way, peaceful idyll. Wow! That would do for me. Indeed, this entire area abounds with small, out of the way places, just like Leenane…especially in the part of the country into which we were now heading…Connemara territory! Now, that really is WOW country!

For miles and miles, our road carried us through scenic beauty which was such that you really didn't know what to look at first…or at least I didn't. It really was a matter of eyes on stalks and a neck that you could only wish had the facility to swivel in a complete circle, like an owl. The problem being that, whichever side of the road you just happened to glance, a small gasp of sheer pleasure would, without one even being aware of it, escape from ones most enchanted inner depths. To the left, it was mainly the golden and bronze-clad steeply sloping hills with, at ground level, a merging of vibrant green with bracken gold and sparkling, laughing rivers, which playfully chuckled and frolicked along their gently meandering courses.

 The blue of the sky would suddenly turn a lake into a blue mirror and, well, the overall picture would not have been complete without a good scattering of our wee woolly friends. White blobs with shy black faces, ever stoical and yet interested in all that goes on around them.

On our right hand, far reaching rock faces came right down to the road, verdant with green fronds of fern and ivy and oh, so many different varieties of rock greenery and, at one point…and here I did exclaim in pure delight…a waterfall. It was so unexpected and what a wonderful sight. Nothing mighty but a foaming, sparkling cataract of surging water, issuing from a fissure way up at the top of the rock face and sending a glorious cascade down and ever down until it sort of disappeared, somewhere beneath the ground, maybe to re-emerge somewhere on the opposite side of the road. It was impossible to tell, as we were passed it all too quickly.

Oh what a wonderful sight, as far as the eye could see and in whichever direction you might just happen to set your gaze. Just beyond the waterfall, we suddenly found ourselves driving beneath a veritable tunnel which had been formed by the spreading overhead branches of tall and stately trees which lined both sides of the road. The sun managed to find what seemed like millions of wee chinks and gaps in this beautiful, green canopy, which resulted in a glorious mosaic of brilliant lights and shades upon the surface of the road. Beautiful! And I was just exclaiming about all of this and, no doubt, driving Jeff nutty, when we came upon Kylemore Abbey. This, without a moments hesitation, definitely proclaimed, indeed, demanded that we stop and spend some time.

Kylemore Abbey, a vision of pale, silvery grey…and more like a castle, a fairytale castle, rather than an abbey. Even its very setting seemed to me to more accurately depict the environs of a fairytale dwelling. This magnificent building was nestled in the embrace of a steeply sloping hillside, stunning in its autumnal colouring and further enhanced by the stands of splendid, evergreen pine trees which skirted the lower slopes, at the base of which, they met a riotously flowing river, glinting and sparkling in the sunlight as the water passed over any rocks which just happened to find themselves in the passage of this flowing, crystal-clear water.

With my excitement reasonably contained, we parked up and, as we strolled across the bridge which spanned the river, we met our first Americans. There seemed to be about three tourist coaches which had been full of American visitors and they all seemed to be either returning to their bus or gradually heading in that general direction, just at the time of our arrival. OH BOY! That was all it took for these enthusiastic Americans to fall into raptures over you know who and for our dear, daft pup to find himself in the limelight again. Most people fall under his undeniable canine charm but, well, Americans seem to go absolutely nuts over him.

For a good ten minutes…and I mean, we hadn't gone more than a hundred yards…we stood and made polite conversation while different people made a huge fuss of Misty and, of course, had to have the 'Irish Setter in Ireland' souvenir photograph. With another one, just to make sure, don't you know…and can we have one of the three of you? And that was the way of it…and I do have to admit that even we were beginning to feel like celebrities at a film premier.

Needless to say, this copper-coloured, canine Adonis, just lapped it all up… preening and strutting his stuff and positively grinning, as he accepted all the acclamations extolling the great beauty of his beefcake manhood. (Well, boyhood. I mean, he is still but a baby).It was almost possible to see his head growing in size, by the minute.

Eventually, having spent so much time with a certain, fast becoming famous, Irish Setter, these rather lovely people with their so characteristic American friendliness, then had to practically run in order to get back on their respective buses without risking getting left behind and so, with a friendly wave to see them on their journey, we watched their buses pull out, our best wishes for a happy continuation of their European Tour still fresh in their ears…and we continued on our way, making straight for the Coffee Shop.

I can only assume that my Jeffy's trust in me has taken a turn for the better as he didn't so much as flinch when I, quite casually, of course, said that I was going to have a look around the Gift Shop and, I mean, it did look rather posh and on the expensive side. An assumption which proved to be entirely correct and which I discovered almost as soon as I walked through the door. However, thought I…there is no harm and, no charge, for just having a look! But then, it never, ever, stops at just a look, does it? Now, be honest. You always finish up buying something…which we did, of course. I mean, don't get me wrong. It was nothing that would actually bankrupt us but, at least we made a token purchase.

Trouble is, though, you see, while I was wandering around on my own, before Jeff actually came in to do a bit of undercover surveillance on me, I fell in love. Yes! It really was love at first sight. My eyes fell upon this particular item and devoured it and I knew that I just had to have this stunningly gorgeous piece of bronze. It was my Misty, you see. A truly magnificent sculpture, in bronze, of an Irish Setter at full stretch, leaping over a five-bar gate. Oh God. I just knew that I had to have it. Pretty, pretty please. I really have got to have it. It could have actually been modelled on Misty, even to the face…it really was him.

As we set out on the road again, I still couldn't get out of my daft head this most beautiful artifact. In the end, I just blurted it out to Jeff and, even though he was driving, I knew that what I'd said had registered with him, including the hastily mentioned subject of how much it cost and, well…you must know my Jeffy, by now. He merely smiled and said…'If it is still there towards the end of next week, well, we'll see'. If it hadn't been for the fact that he was controlling a fast moving car, I would have thrown my arms around him and hugged him. Instead, I merely smiled to myself and changed the subject. You see, I knew that from that one statement, what he was really saying was…'Yes! You can have it'.

I suppose some women would have just bought it and said nothing but, we don't operate like that, my Jeffy and I. Our money is all in one purse, so to speak and, if a thing costs more than just a few pounds, we always do each other the courtesy of running it by each other. Neither one of us has ever said no. But we both feel that it is only right.

With Misty in mind, we now began to think of somewhere suitable for him to have a good run. Time was getting on and, except for his 'superstar' stroll amongst his admiring American fans, at the Abbey, he hadn't been out of the car. Thinking along those lines directed our thoughts to the only place that would actually fill the bill. I mean, what else…a beach, naturally…and in this wonderful land of equally wonderful beaches, you never have to travel too far to find one. And so it was that, within only a very few miles, at a place by the name of Clifden, we joined a coastal road which boasted some of the most stunning Connemara coastline. When thinking Connemara, I always thought…mountains. OK, so the mountains and the surrounding beautiful, rolling hills and moorland are there, in all their true glory and magnificence, however, it somehow came as something of a surprise to us to discover these quite spectacular coastal areas. I mean, if we had paid sufficient attention to the map, it would have become immediately obvious because Connemara covers such a vast area. Whatever. It was still a beautiful sight.

Knowing me as you do, you know, by now, of my infatuation with Irish place names and this neck of the woods was positively awash with prime specimens. Ballinaboy, Mannin Bay and, the place where we finally stopped…Ballyconneely. I mean, how delicious are those? And from Ballyconneely, you could look out upon the gorgeous bay of the same name and across to the Connemara Smoke House, Slyne Head and Doonloughan. Names, names and more wonderful names. I will never become tired of seeking out these magically named places.

Ballyconneely…and what a gem of a beach. I don't know what it is about Ireland, but, as with most of the beaches, certainly all that we have walked along, the sand is so fine and, what is really the most striking feature…so dazzlingly white. It does, indeed, to use the same word again, dazzle the eye. And it is incredibly beautiful. Throw in water of the most exquisite turquoise and so clear that one could count every single grain of sand…and that not only just about sums up Ballyconneely Beach but all Irish beaches. Wow! Ballyconneely. Sorry but, I just had to say the name again. It's so amazing!

Far from being the only attributes of which this special Ballyconneely could boast, there was also a fantastic view…and if that isn't the most stupid remark I've ever made. I mean, this entire country is just one huge 'fantastic view'…just on the left and sort of slightly behind us, in the direction of the Connemara National Park, distant but, very distinctive, of The Twelve Pins mountain range and very imposing they were, even at such a distance. The reason why they had been so named was also fairly obvious, viewing them from this angle with all twelve points there for the counting.

By this time, the mutual decision was to make this our lunch stop. I mean, it could not have been a more perfect place and anyway, Misty was already half way to canine ecstasy by now, running along the waterline, scooping up huge amounts of seawater and, as a result, rendering himself sopping wet in the space of time that it took for us to bring forth the butty box.

For Jeff and I, it was a blissful hour, or so. What more could anyone wish for? Our simple lunch was despatched in no time flat, as we were, by this time, surprisingly hungry but, it was the quiet companionship, the easy-flowing conversation and the ever ready laughter, plus the obvious love which manifested itself in all of the latter, which made it all the more perfect. One of those moments when you really do want to stop the clock…just for a little while…and how often that feeling of wanting to prolong a special pleasure happens in Ireland. Reality always rather spitefully shoves its oar in though and so, with some small amount of reluctance, we packed up all our bits and pieces, dried off our now blissfully happy dog…I mean, the day had, at long last, started to run along his ideas of what constitutes a good day…and set out with no real destination in mind. Just see what comes along, in fact and, before we had gone very far, indeed, it was, quite literally, only within the space of a couple of minutes, that we came upon yet another purely perfect beach. It was, indeed, a very narrow track which led to it but, having seen the name of this beach on a small sign at the head of the track, we considered it to be well worth the risk of maybe getting stuck, or perhaps having to walk some way towards it. Dog Bay! Now then, how super, super delicious is that? See what I mean about names? God love him, our Misty's found himself his very own beach.

Needless to say, he already had his head sticking out of the car window, with a look of passionate ecstasy lighting up those beautiful eyes and well, we just had to try and find a space large enough to squeeze the car into. Not easy, with so many rather tricky, sticky-out, rocky outcrops all over the place but, believe me, just to look upon this quite exquisite beach, well, it was all worth the effort.

Having vacated the car and walked the rest of the way, we discovered that there was a way down to it, which we didn't actually take advantage of but the view down onto it, from our rocky elevation, showed off to its full advantage, the perfect sickle shape of it…and again, the ubiquitous pure white sand.

Another lovely name took us further on our way, Errisbeg…and then we were in Roundstone and I know that I have already made some passing remark about the loveliness of this small village and its pretty little harbour. A picture postcard village, if ever there was one. A village of quite exceptional charm and the most perfect vantage point to get an even more perfect view of The Twelve Pins. For me, in particular, with my artistic background, I was thrilled with the quaintness of the village, with boats tied up along the seawall, plus this most stunning view as a backcloth, it really was, is, an artist's paradise. Just to set up an easel on that shore and completely lose oneself in the joy of creating something of beauty…heaven!

Seasalt Vera was also most impressed by the resident seagull fraternity and by that I mean, well, they were so loud and raucous…in fact, just plain noisy…that my mind instantly (or, I should say, Seasalt Vera's mind) flew away to Cornwall. Cornish gulls just have to be the loudest and most raucous, certainly that I have ever heard…and I just love them and their jubilant arrogance.

I know that I said, earlier, that we didn't clock up any great shakes with regard to miles covered, however, once you get going they do seem to pile up, without any real sense of distance travelled and so we must have covered quite a lot, all things considered. I mean, by now, the day was well on the way to late afternoon and so, putting common sense before temptation, we quite rightly decided that now was, perhaps, the time to head for home…or at least, point ourselves in that general direction…much as we would have loved to have just kept going. As many miles as we had already clocked up, we still had almost as much again to travel before arriving back in our own Tourmakeady.

Without a doubt, we had enjoyed everything that Connemara could have given us, indeed, Connemara had lavished us with her own amazing brand of beauty. The most memorable being all the small, secret, hidden places. Unexpected delights which one had to actually seek out in order to find and appreciate their simple, yet quite staggering beauty. Purest gems, which could, so easily, be overlooked…passed by without even being noticed…like Ballyconneely, Dog Bay and Roundstone.

And so it was that a very happy Intrepid Trio returned to another wee gem…our own wee gem…and what a picture of lovliness it was, as our own delightful Tourmakeady welcomed us home. The lake is, undoubtedly, quite exceptionally beautiful, of that there could never be any debate but, tonight…well, one could only call it breathtaking. Yet again, we have been so very lucky with our choice of this idyllic spot to have as our base camp, so to speak. We made our decision purely from the website…and well, you takes your chances. We certainly have not been disappointed this time…nor have we ever been.

All of which was confirmed a hundred fold as we walked in through our own front door. It felt like home and the feeling felt so right. The perfect place to return to, armed, as we were, with a huge album of images, an accumulation of special, mental photographs, all taken on this truly magical day…they may be a wee bit mixed up and all over the place, right now, however, the joy will be in sorting this treasured hoard of special memories and putting them into the correct order. And that is where you come in, don't you see! You allow us, well, me mainly, if the truth be known, to live each special moment again and, what is more, get it all into the correct order…that and the pleasure of your company, which goes without saying.

With the inexorable passing of time, all of that has now taken place…you have been and gone and now…it is my very personal special time of the day. My own special treat before bringing the day to its final conclusion.

My Misty has stretched out his full, quite large frame, in front of the fire which means that no one else gets so much as a look in. The lights are low and the flickering firelight is sending lights and shadows across the ceiling and filling the room with something very wonderful, as a perfectly in harmony husband and wife cherish the final hour or so of this day. The last glass of wine and the quietly uttered words of reminiscence, as we select and mull over, some special moment that has made the day so memorable. A word. A touch. A feeling of mutual love. How could anyone, let alone me, ever wish for more.

Now, lying beside my beloved husband, I can do no more than thank God for all the happiness which, somehow, we have managed to cram into so few hours.

You have, as always, given us a perfect day, my darling, my Jeffy…perfect and quite unforgettable…for all the right reasons. You are so very dear and so very special to me, my love…and I do love you so much more than you could ever conceive. God bless you, always

As for you Misty Hall, well, what can I say about you, my own much loved superstar. You have been the best dog this day, but then, you are, of course, the best dog in the world…at least to me, your very doting mum.

Sleep tight, my handsome lad.

Finally, may God bless Ireland, this land that I love so much, this night and always. To each and every Irish heart, when tomorrow's dawn breaks, I wish you…

Gentle showers of sunshine and flowers,
and rainbows to colour your day.

See you tomorrow!

❀❀❀❀❀❀❀❀❀❀❀❀

If I could encapsulate the essence of this happy day and describe it with the use of just one word, that word would be 'laughter'.

From the earliest awakenings on this delightful Friday morning, The Intrepid Trio have excelled themselves when it comes down to their capacity for seeing the ridiculous in all and everything and thus falling prey to the usual bouts of manic, uncontrollable laughter. I mean, for heaven's sake, you know what we're like.

All things considered, it has just been one of those days…and all the more memorable for so being.

Yes. Laughter! That really does just about sum up this day and now, if I can lighten your heart by allowing some of that daft, but undeniably contagious commodity to rub off on you and send you, later, of course, on your way with a happy heart then, I will be more than content.

Friday
2nd October 2009

Breakfast was a jolly affair and the usual morning chaos…I mean, what's new…resulted in a lot of purposeless activity which succeeded, not one jot, in advancing our rather pathetic attempts at getting ourselves into some form of order and out on the road. Talk about three steps forward and two back!

For one thing, I seemed to be totally incapable of doing anything without laughing. I think I woke up with, as my mother used to say, my giggle pants on and that is never a very good sign…not if you want me to succeed in accomplishing anything even remotely sensible.

Misty soon realised that a lot of fun could be in the offing, as he very soon picked up on the vibes emanating from me and, with glowing eyes, did his best to help out…not that it really did, help out, I mean…and Jeff stoically left us to it by taking himself off, on the pretext of sorting out the car.

Notwithstanding, I feel that, in spite of everything, we did manage to achieve a quite creditable 9.30 (and I don't mean pm, thank you very much) when at last, we were, all three, seated comfortably, belted up (with the exception of Misty) and ready for the off.

Sitting back in automotive luxury, I settled down to enjoy the quite long run which lay ahead of us, sharing some laughs along the way, with a husband who, from past experience, realized that the most sensible thing that he could do, with regard to me and my obvious inane mood was, just to go with it…and so, the miles began to slip away behind us as we headed north and west towards Bangor and all of the many, quite stunningly beautiful islands and bays of the Atlantic coast…an area we just briefly visited, last Saturday, as we journeyed down from Donegal to Tourmakeady.

On that day, time was of the essence, of course, having a new cottage to locate, at least before it was considered, by our new hosts, necessary to send out a search party for us and so, we merely took the opportunity of making a short comfort stop, where we new there to be a beach, a quite exceptional beach, as it turned out, for his nibs to let off some steam and do a bit of exploring…all the usual doggie stuff.

You will perhaps remember that I made some reference to Misty, my own beloved beach bum and a certain trainer…and underpants. Yes, you've got it, those blue underpants. Ah! Yes! Now I can see that you do remember!

By the time that we actually arrived at the beach, the one just beyond Elly Bay, it was well towards mid-morning and as there did not seem to be any necessity to rush away from this delightful place and, it had taken us some considerable time to get to where we were, we gave ourselves over to the luxury of some quality time on this magnificent beach. It really is quite amazing. Like most Irish beaches, it is long and broad and wide open to the full sweep of the Atlantic and, with all of the justified reputation of this ocean, it produces some of the most fantastic displays of oceanic fervour. Seas which roll in towards the waiting embrace of the shore in squadrons of white-crested waves. Constant and unending. Wave after wave of surging energy. I can only assume that along this stretch of coast, these magnificent Atlantic shores, it is always like this. Today was just the same as it had been last Saturday and, I expect it will be the same tomorrow and all the other tomorrows…for as long as there will be a tomorrow.

Misty was in his usual element, rendering himself soaking wet in the time it took Jeff and I to walk a hundred yards. The water is the first place he makes for. God, but he loves the sea and what a joy it is to watch him as he races the waves and uses his ginormous gob, rather like the shovel of a JCB, to scoop up as much seawater as he can, sort of on the hoof, so to speak, with absolutely no slackening of his speed. Then, of course, comes the roll in the sand…possibly seaweed as well, if there is any of that wondrous, smelly stuff available to him…and then he will race ahead of us as if his very life depended on it, though not before he has come to us and displayed, with some small amount of canine pride, the disgusting condition that he has somehow managed, in nothing more than about five minutes, to render his doggie person. Today was no different than any other day. But, what does it matter. A bit of sand will soon brush off.

Having walked a goodly way, almost along the entire length of the beach, which was, indeed, a goodly way, we about turned and made our way, slowly and pleasurably, back to the car, where the flask of coffee suddenly seemed very tempting.

While we were enjoying said coffee, we were sitting in the car but, with all the doors open, while Misty shuffled around doing his own thing and, at that moment, I must admit that we were not particularly taking much notice of what he was up to until, well, I very nearly choked on my coffee and, at the same time, almost fell out of the car, laughing. Jeff did, in fact, choke on some chocolate biscuit crumbs as he, too, saw what I'd seen and burst out laughing.

And I know that you are probably going to think that I'm making all of this up but, it really is the absolute truth. Oh, my good God, not even I, with my ever over-active imagination …and you know, only too well, what I'm capable of coming up with… could have, even in my very wildest of fancies, made up something as totally unbelievable as this.

While Jeff and I were rendered quite incapable of controlling our hysterics, Misty just sat there, bolt upright and alert and with those melting-chocolate brown eyes of his positively glowing with a look of having achieved something quite exceptionally clever. His whole demeanour proclaimed that this had been no ordinary, run of the mill act of enormous intelligence. I don't think that I have ever seen him quite so inordinately pleased with himself…showing off and, in his own daft way, actually making a performance out of presenting to us his special gift, don't you know.

That gift being a pair of blue underpants.

Yes, you've got it…and I told you that you wouldn't believe it…they were the very same pair of blue underpants that Jeff thought he had disposed of, last weekend.

How Misty managed to find them again, well, I just have no idea and I don't really want to know. Just suffice it to say that I don't think we stopped laughing about it for the next couple of hours. This ridiculous picture of Misty would insist on coming back into my mind, no matter how I tried to block it out...the picture of my soggy, copper-coloured, lovable idiot, sitting there with eyes aglow and with this stupid pair of underpants dangling from his jaws. And every time I thought about it, it set me off again.

Thinking that nothing else could happen that could possibly be quite so downright ridiculous, we got ourselves as much under control as was possible, which wasn't much but the best that we could manage under the circumstances and in that 'what the hell, nothing can get much worse than that' frame of mind, we set off up the road to a place which just had to be investigated. I mean, Blacksod. Names again, you see...and how fantastic is that! Blacksod. That just has to take the biscuit in the Irish names stakes.

In fact, when we arrived in this wondrously named place, it was the most delightful small bay. It was quaint. It was pretty. Just a tiny harbour, with a few cottages, a few boats...and a lighthouse. And that, my friend, was the whole of Blacksod. (I just had to say that name again)...and I just loved it...or at least, my alter-ego, Seasalt Vera, loved it. But then, this is Ireland and it is these small, but enchanting, wee dots on the map that are the very essence of this enchanted isle. Indeed, some of the small gems which we have been fortunate enough to discover, sometimes haven't even been on the map...but then, in Ireland, small is always very beautiful.

It took very little time to explore as virtually everything that was Blacksod, could be seen with a single glance however, we gave it the attention which courtesy demanded of us. It was a pretty little bay and so merited at least some form of polite interest and as the day was now well advanced, we found, just around the corner, in fact, still within view of Blacksod, a stunningly beautiful little beach, with yet another super-delicious name, Doohooma, where we stopped for some lunch. This, as with Blacksod, was another example of small being special.

Suddenly feeling ravenous...and that is something else about Ireland...you become so enchanted and utterly bewitched by all that it presents in the way of scenic enjoyment, that you do tend to forget that it is, perhaps, many hours since you last ate and that now, you are absolutely famished...we ambled down the beach, found ourselves some comfy-looking rocks and made ourselves at home.

Doohooma was a wee treasure. It really was. Just a tiny, tiny, purest white-sand beach, in the usual sickle shape, with water so clear and translucent that it was possible to watch, with total fascination, the delicate, lacy fronds of bright green seaweed which floated, in a lazy sort of way, in the gentle flow of the water. For some daft reason, this delicate weed fascinated me. It was so fragile and, apart from the colour, could have been angel hair. (A punk angel, maybe)?

To one end of the beach were golden lichen-covered rocks, in wonderful formations, which ran straight to the water's edge and so, this was where we picked out our own personal rock, shaped to conform with the curvature of two individual bums, which gave us the ideal place to break open our humble picnic lunch.

The stillness was total bliss.

As we sat there on our rocks, like a king and his queen sitting on their thrones, we were quite strangely and overwhelmingly entranced by this stillness…a stillness which seemed to envelope us like a mantle…and I, for one, could not have been happier. It really was a very special and precious thing, this stillness. Not so much as a sound which wasn't one of nature, intruded on that unique stillness. We really could have been the last two people left on God's earth for all the earthly manifestations of humanity that were in evidence. OK, so there were the mere handful of cottages, back along the coast at Blacksod but still, the feeling of being completely isolated from the rest of the human race persisted. Not even a car passed us by on the road which led to Blacksod, indeed, which actually came to a dead end at Blacksod.

Jeff was close to my side, his very closeness a blessing in itself and Misty, that dear, sweet, innocent pup was doing his own thing, in his own doggie way, splashing through the shallow, crystal-clear water and pouncing on the gently floating fronds of the brown, shiny seaweed, which, because of its constant movement, totally fascinated him, which rendered his doggie person rather wet and which is, just a wee tad, understating his condition. Wet and sticky would just about cover it. So what's new? (A quick mental note…a good dunking in the sea for young Master Hall, before being allowed access to the car)!

So great was our absorption in the delightful surroundings and of the pleasure of the idle exchange of easy conversation between the two of us…and also, our pleasure in watching Misty playing…that both Jeff and I failed to notice that the tide was, ever so slowly and gently, yet inexorably, creeping ever closer and closer towards our feet. It was only when it actually began to lap around our shoes that it gave us the prod that we needed to shape ourselves and move a bit higher up the rocks.

Eventually, we began the process of packing up all our remaining bits and pieces and made our way back along this wee gem of a beach. There was no haste. There was no need for any haste…just a feeling of utter contentment causing our hearts to be light and sending our spirits soaring towards the blue sky.

Strolling with hands enjoined and with our bonnie (though somewhat soggy) lad trotting ahead of us, my Jeffy suddenly stooped and picked up something which he'd spotted, half buried in the fine white sand. When my love gave it to me, I was delighted to discover that there, nestling in the palm of my hand was a lovely piece of green agate, still shiny from the wet sand. But, what made it all the more special was the fact that it was formed, quite incredibly, in the perfect shape of a heart. Needless to say, for me it was more precious than the biggest diamond. A romantic gesture of love and, somehow, a fitting finale to this quite wonderful hour or so, spent in this wee piece of heaven.

It goes without saying that I still have the stone…and I actually carry it with me, always. A tactile, lasting memory of that one unforgettable moment among so many, spent in an unforgettable land…with, of course, the man who is my world.

Having done the very best we could with Misty's rather disgusting furry personage, we set off, back in the direction of Bangor. It was, by now, well into the afternoon and, well, we had enjoyed such a wonderful day. So, a hastily convened meeting of the Board made the earth-shattering decision that it would be best if we now slowly headed in the general direction of home. Not that there was any particular hurry. I mean, somehow, time had lost all importance. The peace and quietude of Doohooma still held us in its embrace and anyway, there was nobody who was going to be in the least bit put out, should we be a bit late in getting back.

Happy thoughts accompanied Jeff and I on the beautiful scenic journey home. From serene and peaceful water, we now travelled through rustic moorland with its stunning backdrop of the majestic Nephin Beg Range of mountains. Early evening sunlight gilded the upper peaks and turned the moorland grasses to burnished copper. Along the way were the hundreds of wee mounds of peat blocks, all stacked up neatly, in their cairn-shaped piles. It all looked so lovely, with the lights and shades created by the low sun, so much so, that I just had to ask Jeff to stop, thus allowing me to actually get out of the car and take some pictures.

Being absorbed in what I was doing, I was completely unaware of Jeff's activities during my short absence…indeed, I didn't even know that he had moved from the car. What can I say? When I returned and slowly became aware of what he'd been up to, well, I just fell about laughing. What first came to my attention, you see, was the fact that he was putting something, I couldn't quite see what, onto a spread out bin sack, in the back of the car. Oh Jeff! I know I laughed but, I could do no other than see the funny side of it. The 'something' turned out to be…three small blocks of peat. Stolen peat! He said that he wanted to see how it burned and that we could try it out tonight. I mean, for heaven's sake, he might have nicked more than three bits…might as well be hung for a sheep as a lamb, as the saying goes.

You know, I really do feel, very strongly, that we are destined to spend that night in Westport nick. What with my kleptomaniac of a dog…and now my peat stealing husband, well, there will probably be an armed escort of Gards waiting for us to make land, on our next visit, with one sole purpose in mind…send these three undesirables back home on the next boat…unless, of course, they kick us out before we have a chance to even think about coming back again.

Seriously, I must admit that I have never experienced the pleasure of sitting in front of a peat fire. It should be quite a treat. The lingering aroma of burning peat is quite a lovely thing, especially at this time of the year when fires are lit and the delightful smell finds its way up the chimney and into the atmosphere. The special ambience that it gives off is that of 'home'. Families sitting around the hearthstone. Love and contentment. A safe feeling.

Still laughing about Jeff's ill-gained booty, we arrived in Mulrany (the place with all the varied spellings of its name). It had been our intention of stopping off at this lovely town, on our return from Achill Island, the other day. Time got in the way, then…however, in our newly acquired laid-back frame of mind, late as it was, even today, we stopped off anyway…and, I can only say that I am so glad that we did. Mulrany beach could only be described as being quite enchanting…and yet another example of these wonderful Irish beaches that really are to die for. Some are small, some are large but, all are quite stunning…and this one definitely came under the latter heading. The prevailing weather conditions were so perfect, of course, in order to experience the picture postcard beauty of everything. The colours and the way in which nature had arranged the lay of the land (and the sea)…it was beautiful.

The thirty or forty minutes that we spent roaming around this gorgeous place just seemed the ideal finale to a truly special day. A day of beaches. Like I said…big ones, small ones, tiny ones, like Doohooma…but all quite amazing. A day full of precious memories, with this lovely Mulrany being a worthy part of it and, a day full of love and laughter. The laughter being the 'special' ingredient without which the flavour of the day would have been so much less than it was. (I don't think that I will ever be capable of remembering Misty's blue underpants without laughing).

In the fullness of time, we arrived back at Tourmakeady and, tired by now but, very well content with our sometimes crazy but, very happy day, we could now relax and enjoy the very special loveliness of all that we have, right here on our doorstep.

And there you have it. You have been so patient, as always. It never ceases to amaze me, the way you never show anything other than genuine interest in all my bletherings. Thank you…and bless you for it. And so, my tale has been told, for yet another day. My evening has been blessed with friendship (yours) and love (my Jeffy's) and now, it is the time for my usual round of giving thanks to all whom I consider deserve it.

Thank you God, for keeping us safe from all harm as we have travelled the roads of this wonderful land, today…not that there is all that much traffic to be concerned about.

Thank you, by darling Jeffy, for making it all happen. God bless you, my love. You are and always will be my best friend, my lover, my life. I love you.

I love you, too, my Misty. Sleep tight and may your dreams be sweet.

◎◎◎◎◎◎◎◎◎◎◎

My feelings, this Saturday evening, are almost beyond description. I feel like a big kid on Christmas Eve. It is not just any old Saturday evening, you see. Oh no! This particular Saturday evening is special, in as much as this is the day when, having spent the customary two weeks at our specially chosen holiday venue, we would now have already gone through the usual departure blues and be back home…and everything would feel as far away as ever. Almost like a dream.

BUT WE ARE STILL HERE!…and I know exactly what you are thinking and I know that I'm behaving like that aforementioned big, daft kid but, well, I suppose that is exactly what I am and always will be. (Remember ? Acting my shoe size, rather than my age)! In fact, it is with some pride that I admit to feeling absolutely no shame for my total disregard of the limitations set by the unfortunate fact of advancing years.

It's just that WE ARE STILL HERE! There, you see? I just had to say it again, just to make it seem real. Oh, behave yourself, you daft woman. It is real. We are still here in Ireland and nothing and no one can alter that.

Seriously, it really is the most amazing feeling to know that we have another whole week ahead of us, a week of more of Ireland's own, very special brand of magic and enchantment, before we have to, eventually, face that devastating moment of departure.

And I'm not thinking of that! We have been given a reprieve. We have been thrown a lifebelt…so just go with it, you silly sod and enjoy.

So, the fire is well laden with logs for the purpose of your welcome and a feeling of real celebration fills this small dwelling with a very special kind of anticipation. I mean, for me, especially, all I can say is that I can feel a very close rapport with someone who has just received a stay of execution.

The day has been truly blessed with additional meaning, somehow. It is as though we have been given a new start, a second chance. Even the weather has pulled out all the stops and done her best for us. Anyway, I can't wait any longer. So, here goes!

Saturday
3rd October 2009

Almost a soon as I opened my eyes, this morning, I felt a surge of electricity pass through me, as, with sheer joy, the realization suddenly dawned that, although this was the Saturday, the dreaded Saturday on which we would normally be leaving, WE WERE STILL HERE!…and would remain so for yet another week. A week filled with the Irish magic that makes your heart break, just at the very thought of leaving.

I remember shaking Jeff as though I were a woman demented while, at the same time bouncing up and down on the bed and babbling like an idiot, chanting some form of mantra to the general effect of… 'Jeffy, Jeffy. We're still here! We're still here, my Jeffy'.

Dear Jeff. My poor, long-suffering Jeffy. He merely muttered something about 'Yes, love. If you say so'. I mean, why can't I be so laid back and just take everything in my stride? For heaven's sake, I'm 68 years of age and should know better.

Daft old sod.

The thought of what might have been, only served to add more colour and zest to the normal, early morning routine, as I pottered about, preparing breakfast etc. Even the wild and windy elements, which sent a chilly blast through the open back door, as I let Misty out for his customary morning explorative wander around his meadow, could not dampen my feelings of elation. Let the weather do as it pleases! It can snow, for all I care! We are still here, in Ireland…and in Ireland, the weather is of the least consequence. Even snow would be just great. I mean, imagine the mountains covered in snow. How amazing would that be?

I did manage to muster a little decorum, as the morning advanced, although I was still well carried along on the great tidal wave of elation which would not, no matter how I tried, subside…not even a wee bit! And, I think we managed a very creditable time of ten o'clock as we got ourselves and Misty safely ensconced in the car and ready for the off….thankfully, not in the direction of Dun Laoghaire. No offence intended, of course, to the dear people of Dun Laoghaire.

The rather wild nature of the climatic conditions could, in no way, deter The Intrepid Trio, on this wonderful day. Like I said…let it do as it pleases. However, despite the early, extremely dismal outlook, as we were heading up the road, past the lake, although it was still somewhat blustery, it was brightening by the minute and already, the sky was clearing and there was, as the saying goes, enough blue patches to make a cat a pair of trousers…two pairs, in fact.

Just thinking along those lines, we can only be grateful for what we've had. I mean, it has been the most amazing two weeks, in more ways than one, however, at the minute, I'm thinking only of the weather. Unfortunately, as that is one thing which cannot be pre-arranged, you just have to hope for the best and, from past experience, purely because we are always ready to accept and make the most of whatever we are presented with, a rainy day in Ireland has always given us, The Intrepid Trio, some of the most fun-filled days. When we came on this trip, we arrived with a love of the country, and also, well prepared for some wet days. In this land of the emerald green, that green doesn't get to be so wondrously green, without the odd spot of Irish rain…and that is what I'm blethering about. Out of the two weeks, so far, only one day has been out and out wet…and we had a fantastic day! Bring it on, man…that's our motto!

None of that applied today, however. After the rather chilly start, the sun was positively sparkling off the waters of the lake, as we passed it by, water which was already reflecting the ever advancing blue and it gave the Midas touch to the mountains of Joyce's Country, by gilding the peaks and the undulating slopes in delicate, early morning gold.

Oh, how I have come to love these mountains!

The narrow road which leads from our wee cottage, winding, in a series of hairpin bends, up and up into those mountains was, somehow, especially stunning today…like I said, the feelings of being given a second chance has stimulated our reactions to more or less everything, adding extra colour and vibrancy. I mean, we have travelled this road a dozen times or more and yet, this morning, it was even more quite remarkably stunning.

The sky was, by now, almost all blue, a blue which provided a backcloth to the vibrant red and lush, dark green of the tall fuchsia hedge which flanked both sides of the road at this point. They seemed to tower over us, and the effect was a glory of sparkling ruby, as the residual droplets of moisture, a parting gift from the last shower of rain, glinted in the sunlight like diamonds. Millions of diamonds, it seemed to us, as they clung to their ruby-red hosts. One could only describe the overall effect as being absolutely stunning. They were in such great abundance, you see…masses of them. And I know that I have made mention of that phenomenon many times but, it is such a stunning road-side feature, wherever one may go.

Truly, there is very little that man could possibly produce that could ever come close to outshining the glories of nature. She has her own box of colours and they would be difficult, if not quite impossible to replicate.

It was a fleeting moment, as we passed through this quite amazing show of nature's own precious jewels but, it had a lasting impact and, even now, the memory is as vibrant as was the actual scene, on this very special Saturday morning. Again, the reason being that everything seemed to have been enhanced and more sharply outlined.

Our destination, today, was Cong. For reasons, many reasons, other than its association with John Wayne and the film 'The Quiet Man', it is a lovely wee village in its own right. Those quaint, narrow streets, with the river Cong running right through the middle of it and, well, just the gentle atmosphere of the place. Although, I must say that I can very well imagine John Wayne chasing Maureen O'Hara through the streets of Cong, as I have seen the film countless times and recognize so many of the places where certain scenes were filmed. That is one of the many attributes, indeed, one of the beauties of Cong. Although these memorable scenes from the movie were filmed, in this village and its environs, way back in the early 1950's, nothing has really changed. It is possible to recognize certain places and particular details and experience that strange déjà vu feeling of having seen it all before.

Anyway, I have, for all the reasons just given, grown extremely fond of Cong and today, it was so charming, just to stand on the wee bridge, just across from 'The Quiet Man' cottage and lay ones hands on the sun-warmed stone and just absorb the tranquil sounds of water tinkling across its own bed of small rocks and the accompanying song of the various birds, whose homes are in the tree canopies of the nearby Cong woods.

Today, with the sun warm on our faces, we stood on this small bridge and did what most tourists do…we had our picture taken, by a complete stranger, in between the two red markers, fastened to the stonework of the bridge, which mark the boundaries between two counties…County Mayo and County Galway. It's a novelty and most people try to stick out their legs, thus putting a leg in each county. We merely moved in close to each other and smiled nicely…thus leaving the two markers quite clear for all to see.

After a coffee in one of the few, rather sweet tea shops which are so charming, in themselves, we gave ourselves over to thoughts of the big, red hairy one, who, much to his disdain, had been left in the car. We had promised ourselves the luxury of going into one of these lovely tea shops and, well, he just had to remain behind, even though I think it hurt us more than him…just the thought of leaving him. Hence the reason for our now quite famous flask. It means that we can stop and have a coffee, wherever the fancy make take us…and keep our boy with us. I don't think we ever used the blessed thing until we got Misty. Now, it is the first thing we do when off on an outing…fill the flask.

Dear Misty. He never bears any grudges and so, as soon as he saw green grass and a river full of fast flowing water, I think any slight feelings of resentment were immediately forgotten and his eyes lit up. Dear, daft dog…it takes so little to make him ecstatically happy.

It really is such a tranquil place to be, with the old, noble stonework, or what remains of it, of the old Cong Abbey, now mellow with age, blending with the green and well kept lawns which roll away, in a gentle slope, down towards the river as it follows its ancient course. And, as we crossed the small, narrow bridge, which spans this part of the river, it felt so wonderful to find ourselves once again on the fringe of Cong Woods. This was where Misty could now go daft. Pathways which meandered through stands of a mixed variety of trees, went on for miles, all depending on how much time and stamina you had at your disposal.

Misty was about as agog as any canine could be, as he chased around, the scent of rabbits in his nose and the occasional muddy puddle to jump up and down in. Everything done in true Misty fashion. Dear, lovable, great daft lump. So pure of heart and loving…of life itself and of the whole of human kind.

And then a miracle happened! And all that this great, daft numpty could do was to stand there, like the prize idiot that I am…and stare…quite literally with my mouth wide open. It was a split second occurrence. A microsecond only…and then it was gone.

Before you begin to wonder just what on earth I'm babbling on about, as is my wont, let me just explain. We had come out of the woods and had returned to the side of the river. Jeff and Misty had wandered off and were just ahead of me and I was just standing by the water's edge, quite enraptured by the pretty effects of the lights and shades which the sunlight created in the fast flowing water…and then, it all happened so quickly, you see.

So taken was I with the river itself, I was in no way prepared for the sight, fleeting yet pure magic, of the gleaming salmon which suddenly erupted from the water. It leapt and actually left the water, high and arching…a truly astonishing sight and, with water sparkling as it dripped from this gleaming, shiny-wet body, it arched its back and seemed to wiggle its tail and then, almost before you could believe that you had actually seen it, it fell back into the water. An action that was so gracefully executed that it caused only the barest ripple.

And again, I ask the question…what did I do?

What this great numpty did was to just stand there gawping, for heaven's sake! I mean, I could have got a photograph in a million. All it needed was some sign of life from me. You know…knock, knock. Is there anyone in there? I mean, I was actually clutching my small, digital camera in my daft, useless hands. But then, let's get real here. This is me that we're talking about, so what else would you expect.

Great, daft, stupid, silly old fool! (Me, of course…I mean, who else, that you can think of, fits that description)?

When I caught up with Jeff and excitedly told him of this wondrous sight, we went back to the bridge and stood for what seemed like ages, hanging over the bridge rail, both of us with our eyes peeled but, not a chance. There are some things for which you never get a second chance…and this, unfortunately, was one of them.

Even now, looking back all those months, the vision of that arching body, with scales gleaming in the sun and the glistening droplets of water that cascaded from it as it sort of hung there in mid-air, just for that microsecond, forms a picture in my mind that is every bit as vivid as it was at that moment in time. (And, if my memory serves me right, I swear that this elusive fish winked at me, just a split second before becoming once more submerged in the fast-flowing waters of the Cong river).

Content, now that Misty had enjoyed a good run, we left Cong behind us, reluctantly, for, as I said, I have developed a great fondness for this dear village. However, with all of next week still ahead of us, I know we will be back again.

Anyway, I don't know if that fish played any part in this…I mean, we are both extremely partial to a bit of nice salmon…however, the urge to bring out the old, faithful, butty box, quite suddenly, seemed of the most dire emergency. I, for one, was now acutely aware of the fact that I was famished.

We came upon the perfect place for our alfresco lunch within just a mile or so from Cong…I mean, you never do have to look too far, when every way you turn, the scene is like a picture postcard. Anyhow, this particular idyll proclaimed its whereabouts with a sign, just at the entrance to a narrow, unsurfaced track which eventually wound its way through a glorious, quite dense belt of pine forest…The Ardnageeha Forest, to be precise and the trail seemed to go on forever, leading deeper and ever deeper into what appeared to be the very heart of the forest. With every twist and turn, we expected to come to something of an end to it and then, just the other side of the last twist in the dirt track, there it was…wow! Truly a picnic area to die for. It was only small, three or four tables with benches but, it was where those benches were placed that made the difference between being very pretty and being down right gorgeous.

We pulled in and just stood for a moment or two, to get our bearings and just to take it all in. The picnic area had been set down just at the fringe of the tree line and an additional touch of pure magic was that the land, at this point, sloped down towards the dappling edge of one of the larger lakes in this area…Lough Corrib. In the conditions which prevailed today, it was breathtakingly beautiful. As always, the blue of the sky was replicated in the water…a perfect match…and the myriad of small islands which were dotted, here and there, right across this great expanse of water, were all kitted out with their own mini-forests of trees and colourful flora. But, it was the size of the lake…truly one of those which are more like and inland sea. Certainly, with the naked eye, it was impossible to see to the other side. The water merely blended in with the sky, over on the horizon. Indeed, the sparkling, sun-glittering waters seemed to stretch away into infinity.

Oh, bonnie Ireland. You never fail to serve up a veritable feast. A banquet of all that is beyond belief. And it is always there and so easy to find. There is no artifice, no coyness…all you have to do is seek and it is just waiting to welcome you and stun what senses you may have left. In my case, as you well know…not very much. However, I still have eyes to see and the ability to positively devour all of Ireland's most generous largesse. A special largesse which she offers free of charge to all those who appreciate beauty in all its forms.

Bathed in warm sunlight and having fortified ourselves from our humble sandwich box, (nothing as luxurious as salmon, unfortunately) we set off to enjoy the truly magnificent surroundings in which we had, purely by chance, found ourselves. The views across the lake were totally stunning. Viewing it all, as we were, from a slightly elevated position, we were able to see for miles along the length and breadth of this magnificent lake and still, there seemed to be no end to it.

Finding a path, which was barely noticeable amongst the ground level undergrowth of moss and ferns, we discovered that it descended to the level of the lake water and culminating at a quite lovely, small beach. Again, it was one of those idyllic wee spots where peace was paramount…a peace that was only interrupted by the very gentle lapping of the water as it touched and caressed the pebbles of this secret, shingle beach. And I use that word 'secret' because that was the way it was. It was not in ones face…you had to look for it. I mean, we didn't even know it was there, until we came upon it by chance. Yes! Our own secret beach. (Though I expect that every man and his dog has done and thought the same thing as us, long before we arrived on the scene and made our own stumbling discovery of this hidden treasure). Still, I will always think of it as being our own.

Just to the rear of the beach, the surrounding forest of ancient pines came down to the very edge of the shingle and stood in solid ranks, forming a sheltered backdrop where one could rest awhile. There was even a small stone shelter…nothing fancy but, in keeping with its natural surroundings, containing a simple wooden bench on which to do just that. Ahead, the bluest of tranquil waters and behind, darkly dense, the forest. Cool and damp and lush.

The pines seemed to draw us like magnets. The stillness was a solid entity, with just the wind to rustle the pines and the occasional snap of a twig underfoot. The ground was so soft that it was like walking on the most luxurious carpet, only this carpet was leaf mould and moss…the most luscious, vividly green moss that I have ever seen. It seemed to grow everywhere, even up the sides of the tree trunks and there were forest plants that were all totally new to me as they grew out of this carpet of velvety moss in an unbelievable abundance. Delicate, lacy fronds of fern grew like fragile, emerald-green fans, holding aloft their own pretty foliage, just to add that extra touch of class.

And just to add a little extra colour, Mother Nature had used her vividly charged paintbrush to put, here and there, a few daubs of yellow and red, orange and cream…and these were but a few of the variety of beautiful toadstools which poked their pretty heads from beneath a lovely, leafy fern or from the mossy base of a tree trunk.

It was a veritable lush, green wonderland and within less than five minutes I knew, without the least crumb of doubt that, here, in this fairytale forest, we were in Leprechaun Territory. Indeed, there was more than one occasion, as we progressed further and further into this dense and silent forest that I heard a sweet sound that was certainly not the sound of any bird that I had ever heard. Oh no! It was, if you will get my drift, more like a merry, tinkling laugh. A giggle, more than a laugh, actually…and I know, just as surely as I know my love for my Jeffy, that happy, sparkling, merry eyes were following every step of The Intrepid Trio.

OK! So, now you can scoff…but, it is true! Honestly! If you want to see for yourself, well, all you have to do is allow yourself to believe…and, I promise you that you will not be disappointed.

Time seemed to stand still in this magic forest, its all consuming silence enveloping us like a mantle. So entranced were we, that we walked much further and ever more deeper into the trees than we had intended. The ambience, the magnetism of the place seemed to hold you and lull you into a sense of unreality. However, we did turn back eventually, as the same distance that we had walked already, had to be retraced, every step of it, in order to return to where we had left the car.

This had been a magical experience…a place where there just had to be fairies and leprechauns…not to mention that elusive pot of gold. That, my friend, could have been at the base of any one of these tall and elegant pines. Indeed, we could have walked past it and been totally unaware. Maybe, when I heard that merry, tinkling laughter, that was what had amused our little friends…just the fact that we had almost stepped upon it and just not noticed.

And now, you really must be having very serious doubts about the state of my mind. (I mean, Jeff must always be having those very same doubts, poor man)! However, scoff ye not. They do exist! Honestly! Apart from which, I know that when we finally got back to the car, I was fully aware of the fact that I had been well and truly pelted with those fairy-dust bombs (I mean, where there are leprechauns, there, also, will you find and be enchanted by, these exquisite jewel-like beings)…and what a gift. A gift to treasure. A gift of love and a gift which is so generously bestowed upon all who just have the courage to believe! (And besides, there was something strangely glittery adorning Misty's fur coat, as some of it landed on him. I mean, it sure must have come from somewhere)!

Just before we left this enchanted forest, we took the time to study the area map. It was just by the place where we were parked and maybe it would have served its purpose more, if we had bothered to study it before setting out. However, we can't all have brains, although, I must admit that I was surprised that Jeff hadn't given it a dose of looking at…my Jeffy is well into maps. Whatever…what we did discover and this was really interesting, is that this beautiful Ardnageeha Forest, if you walk far enough and for long enough, actually meets up with Cong woods, the very same where we took Misty for his run, only a few hours ago. How about that? Cool!

There seemed no great urgency, once we were on the road again. I think we were both still just rather incredulous at the idea that we were still just exactly where we were…and by that I mean, still in Ireland. I'm sure that this feeling, a feeling that every day is a bonus, is going to flavour every day during the coming week. Which won't be a bad thing. It will just make each day all the more precious.

Time was not an issue and so we headed back towards Joyce Country although certainly not with the intention of heading for home. Today, we just wanted to lose ourselves in the majesty and the sheer stunning beauty of these mountains and now, with the feeling of having all the time in the world, it was a luxury that we could well afford.

Over the last week in this area we had, by now, become so familiar with everything that we could now take time and be a little more exclusive, a little more discriminating and single out particular places…in fact, as I said, wander off the beaten track and, well, just lose ourselves and give ourselves over completely, to the spendour and the magnetic attraction that these hills seem to possess. They almost seem to beckon and invite you to walk the pathways and hidden trails…and there are so many, secret, hidden places which can only be discovered by allowing oneself to just follow wherever these hidden trails may lead. So much can be easily missed when merely following a road and traversing it by car….a treasure here, an incredibly beautiful view down into some unexpected valley there…all of which could be passed by in the blink of an eye and not even be noticed.

Apart from which, our digital photograph library grew by the second.

It's strange how, after so short a time, I have grown to love these mountains. I was just the same last year, surrounded as we were, with the grand and imposing Caha mountains. I mean, you know me sufficiently well by now, to know my almost manic passion for anything connected to the sea and, I know, that I have mentioned this quite often, of late but, there is also a deep, deep part of me which immediately feels at home and at peace, when in the embrace of mountains such as these. They can be bleak. They can look wild and fearsome but, they can be soft and mellow. With which ever guise they may choose to adorn themselves, I always feel a sense of belonging. Maybe I read 'Wuthering Heights' too many times when I was a very impressionable adolescent. Those Yorkshire moors and sullen, wind-swept hills must have had at least some influence on my young mind.

Basically, what I need is a wee stone cottage with sea to the fore and mountains to the rear…total heaven! Just as long as the cottage is big enough to accommodate all three of us. Even the perfect haven of total bliss, the like of which I have just described, would mean nothing if I could not share it with my own Jeffy and my gorgeous, nutty pup. (Dream on)!

By the time we found ourselves back to the blue welcome of Lough Mask, we again took ourselves off the given path and went up to acquaint ourselves with Maire Luke's Bar. As with many other things, we had merely driven past this lovely old pub, maybe a dozen times and just glanced up at it and maybe, made some remark about the splendid position it held, elevated as it is, high above the road and with, as we were to discover, absolutely breathtaking views across the lake…views which seemed to go on forever across this seemingly endless lake.

This dear, solid stone edifice seemed to nestle, quite smugly, in its unbelievably lovely setting, with beautifully laid out gardens and rustic tables…gardens which sloped downwards towards the blue waters below…and standing there, with an expression of delight on our faces, we could not believe this quite stunning panorama which opened out before us from this elevated and extremely delightful garden setting.

Charming! That just about says it all and, apart from the beauty of the outside, charming is such a perfect word with which to describe the interior of Maire Luke's…and what a welcome! As we entered, there were, already, a handful of locals who were either sitting at the bar or sitting over by the window…a window which was filled with the magnificent view over the lake…and we were, as is the way of things here in Ireland, made to feel immediately welcome. Our accents, of course, gave away our Englishness but that only served to enlarge the welcome which these dear people offered to us so openly and with such generosity. Even 'mine host' took time for us and quite genuinely seemed to enjoy our long and illuminating conversation. For us, it was extremely enlightening as he was so very knowledgeable of the area which, for the past week, we had thought of as home. Indeed, when he introduced his son to us, we were delighted with the depth of knowledge and the easy eloquence that this young man possessed and this, in effect, was the reason for our rather extended visit.

We were so absorbed by this young man's pleasant and interesting narrative that he completely held our attention and our genuine interest in all that he had to say. Indeed, it was this same young man who actually told us that Lough Erne was the longest in Ireland and, apart from that wee piece of information, he seemed capable of rattling off the size of each lake in the area…so many miles wide and X number of miles long.

In this most genial atmosphere, time went by in a most pleasurable way and one Guinness led to another, (for Jeff) and the same applied to my wine. However, when we did, eventually, drag ourselves away from the friendship of these dear people, it was with a feeling of enormous warmth and well-being…and not merely because of the alcohol!

Just as we were leaving, I happened to glance at the clock above the bar and that flutter of joy ran through me once again as I realized that, at this moment, or as near as makes no difference, if we had been returning home today, as would have normally been the case, the ferry would just about be pulling out of Dun Laoghaire and heading out into the Irish Sea towards Holyhead. She was in fact, doing just that but, we were not on board! WE ARE STILL HERE! I still can't quite believe it!

And now you must be thinking, 'Oh my God. Are we going to be hearing this every five minutes, every day for the next week'? No! No! I will calm down, eventually, I promise… and I also promise to make every effort to make it sooner, rather than later.

Leaving the pleasant atmosphere of Maire Luke's and bidding farewell to those dear people, left us feeling sort of special. That's what they do, you see…these lovely Irish people. They make you so much a part of them that it does make you feel as though you just have to be the most special people on the planet. It's a nack they have…a gift…but there is no contrivance about it. Their open-hearted generosity is as genuine as it can be.

Wallowing in this cocoon of Irish good fellowship, we followed the course of the lake, our road home running just alongside it, every inch of the way. Our arrival back home, to our dear wee cottage, was blessed with the gentle peace and quietude of a normal, Tourmakeady evening…and that peace remained with us as we settled down to enjoy an evening which so reflected the character of the day.

The stout stone walls of this small dwelling were saturated in the warmth and love of its present incumbents and, as always, that feeling of shared love dispelled any latent, evening chill and filled up all the corners.

Somehow, I feel that I have even more for which I need to give thanks, on this day than any other. Next week, we have been given a second chance to fill every tiny corner of our hearts with the magic that is Ireland…and we will take advantage of each and every 'bonus' day by making every second count. The Intrepid Trio's own motto.

And now, as I lie beside my dearest love, safe within the security of these stone walls, walls which have withstood the power of nature for many countless years, I can only say thank you, my darling, for giving us this extra week. I know you did it just for me, knowing me as well as you do and knowing how it would break my heart to have to leave this land which I have grown to love so much. It will have to be faced, eventually but…not yet! Thanks to you. I love you, my Jeffy, beyond all earthly things. My love is yours, forever. You are my love. You are my life.

Dear, loving and faithful Misty, I know that you have not had the chance to run in the sea or dig in the sand today. Apart from that small, shingle beach, at the edge of Lough Corrib, there have been no beaches for you or, for that matter, for you mum but, I do believe that you have been content. God love you, it takes so very little to make you the happiest dog in the world. Dream your own happy, doggie dreams and God bless your honest heart.

⓭⓭⓭⓭⓭⓭⓭⓭⓭⓭⓭

Today has had a sort of surreal quality to it, a feeling which has persisted right through the day and has, if anything, added an extra dimention, making everything stand out in sharp relief, if you know what I mean…colours appearing brighter, bird song even sweeter. There has also been a feeling of gentle reflection on this happy Sabbath which again, has persisted throughout yet another special day. Both of us have felt it…only the big furry one being as alert as ever and ready to immediately spring into action at a moments notice, should the reason for such bold action become necessary. Something which the dear, daft dog considers to be his bounden duty. Always ready to offer a helping paw, so to speak. Dear Misty. I do love that big lump!

As I wait for you, this evening, I have been sitting watching the tranquil magic of the lake. There is a moon this evening, which has transformed the gently lapping waters into a silver mirror and it really is quite ethereally beautiful…and so peaceful! Just at this moment, a soft and ever so light and gentle mist is beginning to form, just over the surface of the water. A gossamer veil which, by the time I look at this same view again, will have disappeared…evaporated by the warmth of the morning sun.

Just occasionally, the breath of a gentle breeze rattles the fronds of the palm tree which stands just beyond the front door, standing against the moonlight like a giant, feathery fan.

All is ready for you, as it always is and then, we can exchange thoughts, one like mind with another and I will relate the tale of our day's adventures and I know that you will listen with your usual kindness.

Do stop and stand, just for a moment, as you come to our door. It is a sight which sends a shaft of joy into both heart and soul.

Sunday
4th October 2009

The pure, luxurious joy…and before I go any further, I can hear you saying 'Oh God, she's off again'!…of the gradual realization that we were still here, (I wasn't wrong, was I)? still here in this cottage that I have grown to love so much and, still here in Tourmakeady (and I swear that I shall not refer to this particular topic, ever again, honest to God) brought with it such a surge of happiness that I wanted to leap out of bed and just shriek, while, at the same time jump up and down like an idiot, just for the sheer joy of it…regardless of how absurdly ridiculous I may have looked…and at my age, I certainly would have looked totally ridiculous. A completely certifiable loony, in fact. Not that there was anyone about, which was probably just as well.

Jeff had saved me from my Misty's over enthusiastic, early morning demonstration of just how much he loves me so, instead of doing my undeniably infantile whirling dervish imitation accompanied by his mate, the screaming banshee, I simply lay back, for a few moments only of course, and just let the full wonder of it fill me up to the brim…filling my heart and lifting my soul into the realms of pure ecstasy.

Just as if God were pulling out all the stops, to give this day an extra special send off, my first glance out of the window revealed an absolutely perfect morning. Pure, bright, early morning sunlight lit up our small but, glorious piece of this treasured isle and turned it into a haven set in palest autumn gold.

The lake sparkled and winked its greetings to the morn and ordinary colours seemed to take on a richer vibrancy. Misty was, of course, in his happy place…lying, quite contentedly, in a patch of warm sunlight, his coat a glory of burnished bronze, shimmering against the verdant green meadow grass. All of this I assimilated in the matter of seconds that it took for me to galvanize myself into instant action.

I could hear Jeff downstairs, raking out the dead ashes from the grate and, just as swiftly as I could, I disposed of the mundane things like showers etc, at record speed…record speed for me, at any rate…and then dashed down the stairs into the loving embrace of both husband and pet pooch. (Yes! Misty actually does make a pretty good attempt at doing just that, with his long graceful forelegs doing their utmost to accomplish this task).

The mood of the day was one of laid-back contentment. I had recovered some sense of decorum and I think we had both succumbed to the all pervasive atmosphere of Irish magic and also, to the quietly reflective and deeply grateful appreciation of this perfect day. Not to appreciate it would be nothing short of a sin. I mean, in this, the most glorious early morning of this very special Sabbath, the little world of The Intrepid Trio could not have been more fantastic. This was as good as it could get. As good as anyone could ever expect it to get!

Breakfast out of the way, a few small chores were soon despatched and we made some small effort to come to a decision about how to spend this special day. For some reason, Jeff seemed to have a quiet determination to head out into the Connemara and, I mean, I could not argue with that. You know how I love those mountains…and so, Connemara, it was.

Of course, just the name, Connemara, covers quite a vast area. You could lose yourself up in those hills and mountains, purposefully, I mean, for a whole week and see something amazingly different each time. It is an area of extreme beauty and so quintessentially Irish…which means, without a doubt, scenic splendour of quite breathtaking proportions. Just unsurpassable, in fact!

I do truly believe that, wherever one may travel on this planet of ours, there could be very little that could possibly compare with the quite glorious spectacle that is Ireland…especially the extra special brand of the quite spectacular that abounds in this area called Connemara.

By now, of course, the road was familiar, although, nonetheless enchanting for all of that. There, once again, as pretty and captivating as ever, was the waterfall. Still chuckling and gurgling as it splashed its way downwards to embrace the waiting rocks at its base and the leafy curtain of green and lacy fern fronds and the deeply rich and shiny foliage of the ivy, still sparkled with a myriad of diamonds as the sunlight caught and held every minute drop of water and turned it into a precious jewel. Today, we knew it was there and were able to prepare ourselves for the special magic which comes, somehow, from laughing, scintillating natural water features. There is something so happy about the sound of splashing, gurgling, running water…but then, you are now fully aware of what any kind of water can do to me. It can do very strange things to me…and that's a proven fact. Very strange indeed.

Once again we drove beneath the tunnel of trees, with its dappling, ever changing mosaic of sunlit reflections which patterned the surface of the road…and then, we were turning into Kylemore Abbey! I immediately knew the reason why we were turning into Kylemore Abbey…and I just couldn't believe it.

Oh Jeff, my love! I should have known!

At that moment, as we drove into the grounds of the Abbey, I knew why he had been so keen to come out this way…and my heart very nearly burst at the seams, so great was my love for this wonderful man who is my husband.

He had brought me here for one purpose, you see…that purpose being the purchase of the thing he knew I wanted more than anything…my beautiful bronze Misty. Remember? The lovely bronze sculpture that I saw on our previous visit to the Abbey. Why it should have come as such a surprise when he turned into the entrance to this place I don't know because I know him so well, you see. He never forgets anything that I have expressed a liking of or a desire to possess…be it small or expensive, as this particular object of my desires was. Now maybe you can understand when I say that I am the luckiest woman alive…and that is the honest truth!

When I finally emerged from this glorious haven of all that is delightful…and extremely expensive…clutching my beautiful artifact , my lovely sculpture, as if it might suddenly disappear in a puff of smoke, my joy was such that I could barely contain it. So much so that I very nearly gave in, to the almost impossible to deny temptation, of doing my jumping up and down bit. However, with some small effort, I managed to control the impulse…I must be mellowing a little in my old age…and merely flung my arms around my Jeffy's neck, almost throttling the life out of him, in the process.

Besides, after his enormous generosity, the very least that I could do was to restrain myself sufficiently so as not to show him up, as I constantly do, on a regular basis.

Looking around me, everything was, or appeared to be, startlingly brilliant. No doubt a combination of my previous early-morning euphoria and the more recent excitement over my new and expensive acquisition. The sky seemed to have become, all of a sudden, a more intense blue and the facing hills wore an even more resplendent attire, with the copper, russet and gold like a velvet gown which had been decorated, here and there with the pretty white polka dots which were, of course, the ever present sheep. Still chomping, of course. I mean, what else would they be doing?

Loath to relinquish my treasure, Jeff took it from me, very gently and kindly, of course and put it in the car, with the request that I do the same with myself…and so we turned out of Kylemore and headed up into this russet and gold paradise, until we felt as though we had reached the very top of the world.

The view over to The Twelve Pins was a shock, as the sheer majesty of these superb mountains hit fully, dark and magnificent, their great bulk against the sun which made them stand out in sharp relief.

Just a little further on we took a very narrow track, off to our right, which just seemed to disappear into the hillside. Intrigued by the legend on the sign on the stone wall running alongside the road…'Connemara Loop'…well, we just had to see what that was all about. For all we knew, it could have been something of nothing, indeed, it did look to be even more of a goat track than some of the others that we had previously ventured up, however, never to be deterred, up we went and in all honesty, with each foot of elevation that we gained as we rose higher and higher into the mountain side, the track seemed to narrow correspondingly, until it really was becoming a little unnerving and I was beginning to have grave concerns as to whether or not we would be able to go on much further and, what was more important, what we might just encounter if we did carry on.

Nevertheless, we pushed on. The very fact that we could see the occasional, isolated cottage, way off in the distance suggested that it must be accessible. I mean, there is no way that you could live here, in this isolated mountain side, without having some form of transport and one would only assume that the mode of transport would be of the motorized variety.

Without a doubt, the views from this ever increasing altitude were stunning and that is very much an understatement of the obvious. Breathtaking! Magnificent! How easy it is to run out of descriptive words in this country where there is something of the most incredible beauty around every bend in the road. There I go again…the bend in the road thing. But it really is true.

From our elevated position, there was nothing with which the wide open vista could be marred. The main range of mountains were a glory of majesty and solemn grandeur, the many peaks standing sharp and intricately defined against the skyline. Views across towards those mountains gained added colour and attraction by the addition of blue water, water which was only visible, in the forground, from this higher plane where we now were. Indeed, only a few minutes after entering this mountain-goat trail, we passed a tiny bay, barely large enough to hold, within its sheltering arms, a half dozen, or so, small boats, which gently bobbed in the slight swell which, in turn, sent ripples up onto the small and, I do mean small, sandy beach.

Obviously, with a name like 'Connemara Loop', with emphasis on the word loop, the track that we were on must, in the fullness of time, finish up somewhere, having eventually completed its circuitous route around the mountain, however…we were never to actually find out, one way or the other.

The more we went on, the narrow trail became even more frighteningly narrow and that was when we decided to concede defeat and, taking the cowards way out, looked for and finally found just one place where there appeared to be sufficient space to do about a twenty-point turn, in order to maneuvre the car into a position so as to be able to return the same way that we had come. No doubt we would have been OK but, it was me, rather than Jeff who eventually chickened out and didn't want to take the risk of getting completely stuck.

It was, admittedly, something of a white-knuckle ride but, there was absolutely no doubt that it was worth sitting on the edge of ones seat for. I mean, views such as we had just experienced were truly remarkable and quite indescribably stunning. Maybe we should have carried on however, if we had done so, we would have probably missed something equally as spectacular…and that is something we were destined to discover in the none too distant future.

Once down on the ground floor again, we just allowed ourselves to be carried along by instinct and happenstance, a luxury which eventually opened up a whole new stage upon which nature could play out her role with drama and with a backcloth lit by natural sunlight. A backcloth painted in colours which so delighted we humble humans who just happened to be fortunate enough to be granted free tickets for this splendid show.

The first wee place of interest, at which we made a stop was Rinvyle. Coming upon it, again, just by following a bend in the road, revealed a small, shingle beach and a castle. Yes! A castle. Not a very big one, I have to admit but, a real castle and one which dated back to the 15th century.

In fact, this particular happenstance could not have been more perfect. Dear Misty. He is such a perfect gem when travelling in the car, not so much as a peep out of him as he lies, perfectly content to gaze out at the passing scenery, just as if it actually meant something to him. In this case, it did mean something to him, in as much as he could smell the sea. That's all it needed for him to stir his bones and, once he hit the beach, that was it…a fastly disappearing streak of copper-coloured lightning. I suppose he must have been more than just a wee bit desperate to uncross those long and graceful legs of his, with which he was now pounding the shingle along the water's edge. Total manic, canine activity.

As Jeff and Misty capered around the beach, I found and made friends with three very amenable ponies. They took great interest in the new, queer-looking human who was interrupting their morning relaxation and gave every inclination of having a desire to extend the hand, or, should I say, hoof, of friendship. Which was very nice.

I have always adored horses! I shall always adore horses so, this was an unexpected treat to be able to offer fond greetings to these three lovely creatures. Strangely, there appeared to be no restrictive boundary to prevent them wandering off, however, they obviously had absolutely no inclination to do that and were perfectly happy to graze away the pleasant morning with just an occasional break from feeding, in order to stand, with noble heads raised, to consider the beauty of the scene which lay before them.

Eventually, I thanked my new friends for sparing me the time of day and they, with a nuzzle from a soft nose and a gentle whicker of farewell, turned and went about their own business, once more. So I did likewise.

Having rejoined the two youngsters on the beach…I mean, Jeff just about regresses to the age of 12 when scampering around a beach with his dog…we strolled back in the direction of the car, only to be hailed and greeted in the bright and cheerful Irish voice of a man who was just coming out of a cottage, just by the castle, in the company of a dog which made even our Misty look small…a huge Newfoundland.

The ensuing ten minutes of genial conversation was so typical. Our Irish friend was, within minutes, talking to we two strangers as if he had known us all his life…and the two dogs were doing likewise. Poor Misty. It is only very rarely that he comes upon a fellow canine who is bigger than him…in fact, in all honesty, I rather suspect that this was a first. Not that he was at all intimidated. It is all one, with my dear, daft pup. He offers love and lifelong friendship to whomsoever, human or canine, small or large, who should happen to come within his range.

Bidding farewell to our Irish friend…and Sheba…we had a quick coffee and then set off to follow this road of enchantment once again and this time, we found ourselves deep in picturesque valleys and small, equally picturesque villages. People who dwell in these villages, live out their lives, at peace and in constant view of the most famous mountains in Ireland. I mean, just the word, Connemara, is Ireland! Today, they were looking over places with names which could only be Irish. One tiny village bore the name of Tully which, in turn, ran into Tully Cross. This last one could have come off the shiny lid of the most exclusive chocolate box. (Remember, yonks ago, when you could get boxes of chocs in these large, special edition boxes? Usually around Christmas time).

Almost the entire village consisted of small thatched cottages, almost like doll's houses and all absolutely identical. A whole row of them, all with their welcoming brightly painted, red front doors.

With the surrounding scenery and the distant mountains standing sentinel behind them, the whole presented a scene which must surely enchant even the most cynical of souls…and then, we were climbing up into these sentinels of the valleys, where the land was eventually taken over by the great outcrops of rock which formed the bases of these mighty massifs and, throughout this pleasant interlude, yet we still had no real idea of what we would encounter further along our way. It was a magic mystery tour, all the more interesting because we were now on previously, untracked road.

I must say, it is rather fun, just following ones instinct and allowing the fickle finger of pure chance to dictate the course and direction in which the day may go.

This choice of fickle chance now carried us across wild and rather desolate moorland. It seemed to fill our vision and the soaring peaks rose ever higher the further we went, becoming more grand and imposing, their majesty overpowering everything else. This was real Connemara heaven!

While we were crossing this wide open and quite desolate stretch of moorland we came upon something which really did proclaim the fact that heaven really did exist in these remote hills…and it really was the very last thing that anyone would have expected to find, out here, in the middle of nowhere.

And I really mean that, when I say, right in the middle of nowhere. All around us were the towering hills…and sheep. Nothing else…except the church. Yes! No jest intended here. A small Catholic church. Our Lady of the Wayside. It felt like finding an oasis in the middle of the Sahara desert…and so very beautiful.

Just in front of this precious jewel of the hills was a space for cars to pull in, if they should so wish, along with the invitation to stop and enter this precious, road-side haven and take a quiet moment for contemplation and prayer…which is what I was absolutely compelled to do.

On entering, it was, indeed, a sanctuary of peace. A peace so profound because the silence was total. The doors, of course, were unlocked…as they would, no doubt remain unlocked, day and night…and the interior was lit by nature's own light as it filtering through pretty stained-glass windows and also by the myriad of votive candles whose number I immediately increased by another three.

In this haven of peace, this shrine which seemed almost sacred, I knelt and offered up a prayer of thanks to God and to Our Lady, in front of whom I had placed my candles and then, both Jeff and I signed the visitor's book and left with a deep feeling of tranquillity filling our hearts.

I don't think that I shall ever forget that moment in time. A fleeting moment but, a blessing from God, spent in that wee church which nestled in the isolated splendour of the Connemara hills. A haven indeed, for any troubled soul. A haven for all who have some small amount of faith.

From the very first, early beginnings of this day, I felt that it was going to be special and, up to now, it has far exceeded any ideas that I may have had with regards to what one would term 'special'…and even now, although we were, as yet, completely unaware of it, fate had one more special trick up its sleeve…something so breathtaking, especially to yours truly, that it sent me into the realms of total, uncontrollable, land of the loony-tunes ecstasy. I mean, considering that we were in the middle of the mountains, it did come as something of a shock…albeit, a nice one. But then, so did the church. I mean, what can I say except that, well, this is Ireland…and this lady never ceases to amaze.

Taking a quite innocuous looking off shoot, which seemed to wind its way through another hillside, we could not believe our eyes when, just as we topped a small rise, there, in all its full and majestic glory was the sea. Large and stunning and magnificent. Blue water, white-capped waves and, a white-sand beach which just had to be the most striking and splendid beach that we had yet seen…and we have seen many. An infinity of beach with, away in the distance, mountains which caught the full munificence of the sun and stood out against the pale blue backcloth of the sky in golden glory.

I don't think that I have ever exited a car, any car, at the speed with which I exited this one today. I mean, the sight of those white-crested waves, rolling in as if there could never be an end to them, was more than I could take in and the only way in which I could express my feelings was to do the very thing which, twice before, on this quite remarkable day, I had managed to hold at bay…I let out a banshee shriek. I could no more have prevented myself from doing it than I could have prevented myself from breathing. Then I was jumping up and down like a demented lunatic.

Poor Jeff. Fortunately, at that moment, there was nobody else in sight. Even if there had been, I know that I would have had to let it go, regardless. As it was, he managed, with some small amount of difficulty, to restore some semblance of sanity to his totally deranged wife and we made the decision to stay here. Have some lunch and then walk and explore.

The very act of eating at least calmed me down a bit and also gave us the opportunity to really take in the true magnificence of our suroundings. It really was breathtaking. A seascape which could only have come from a Divine source. Whichever way one chose to allow the eye to wander, it was really quite unbelievable. Colours blended into each other to give the most perfect effect. Blue on blue, as the sea touched the sky. The whitest of fine sand, mile upon mile of it, or so it seemed, which, in turn picked out the crests of the waves and the occasional puff of cotton wool cloud. Then, off in the middle distance, those mountains…The Mweelrea Mountains…aglow with the precious gift of the sunlight.

This was Lettergesh! A name which will forever stay in my memory.

With regard to names…the name of the mountains which watch over this heavenly strand, was but the tip of the proverbial iceberg, when it came to my somewhat whimsical ideas on that subject. This entire coastline was a catalogue of quintessentially Irish names, for example…Kinnadoohy, Killadoon, Crump Island. Not to mention Inishdegil More and Tonakeera Point. I mean, be honest now…just how full of Irish magic are those names.

I was still in a state of total euphoria but there was a rather special visitation, from a small and rather enchanting local, which momentarily silenced my continuous wittering and focused my attention completely on its own, dear wee self.

As Jeff and I were quietly enjoying our humble lunch, whilst anticipating the pleasure of getting up close and personal with that incredible beach, a tiny sound, a very babyish meow, drew our attention to the wee ginger nut which was sitting just by the car and gazing up at Jeff with blue eyes which were as round as saucers and focused on his sandwich.

A few kind and gentle words from Jeff precipitated this minute furry bundle right up onto Jeff's lap with one very small paw waving about in indication of his desire for a share of said sandwich.

To say we were quite enchanted, well, you will be able to imagine the scenario and, when we introduced Misty to this tiny example of what should have turned Misty into a frenzy, we were quite touched by his gentle, almost tender manner and the way this great, daft lump of ours almost kissed the tip of the tiny nose. I must say that the wee soul had, or seemed to have, absolutely no fear of this large dog. They looked at each other, sort of eyeball to eyeball and appeared to have become life-long buddies.

Talk about David and Goliath. Even now, months down the line, the thought of that brief encounter brings a smile…plus the fact that, as we made a move to head off down the beach, we were unable to get rid of him.

Eventually, he took up residence beneath the car and, fortunately, by the time we returned, some hour or more later, he had gone.

The time spent on the beach was timeless and unforgettable. The two of us walked, hand in hand, while Misty did his own thing in his own fashion. He was in his element when he found, discarded in a large rock pool, a very badly burst football. The fact that it was burst mattered not a jot to our boy. Oh no! Its condition allowed him to get his big gob around it, after which he paraded up and down the beach, showing it off to anyone who may, or may not, have been interested. When he got tired of that, he took to tossing it into the sea and catching it again when the waves sent it back.

Very reluctantly, we slowly sauntered back, Misty now bored with his ball. As we drew closer to the shingle bank which topped the sandy beach, there, struggling down the steep shingle was yet another kitten. A different colour, this time and before we knew it, the two of them were eyeing each other up and then, quite literally, began playing together. It was a charming sight, although, at the same time, ludicrously funny, purely by virtue of the quite enormous difference in size and as they sauntered along the wet sand, sort of side by side, the David and Goliath similarity became even more pronounced. The two heads were turned to each other…one gazing fearlessly up and the other looking gently down. I could almost hear Misty saying to the wee one…'Do you come here often'?

We later discovered that the two with which we had made acquaintance, were, in fact, only two of a larger litter belonging to a cottage just further up the shingle. They also had a dog, which explained the obvious lack of fear of our Misty.

Anyway, it was an unforgettably charming experience and one which added colour to an already amazing day.

Now, it is at an end, this wonderful day. We are back in our own small dwelling in Tourmakeady and we are allowing ourselves to wallow in the feelings of quiet contentment which have so greatly coloured these special hours of the day…at least to Jeff and I.

You have been a joy to have in our home once more, as we have exchanged a tale and a loving hour in each other's company. Now I cannot but thank God for a day which has been a blessing, in so many ways, for each member of The Intrepid Trio.

Some things stand out above others but, for me, at least, it has to be the small church, way out in the wilderness and, it goes without saying…Lettergesh Beach.

If ever you have excelled yourself, my darling, you have certainly done so today. You have given all of us a day which will live in our hearts, forever. Thank you, my love. It sounds so little but, it means everything. Just…thank you!

If I could have a wish granted right now, it would be for a far greater eloquence than I already have at my disposal and then, just maybe, I would be able to find words which would truly tell you of how much I love you, my Jeffy, my husband. As it is, my own humble words will have to suffice…and that love will live forever.

Dear Misty. What a great, gentle lump of canine beauty you are…beauty to the eye and beauty in your innocent soul. There is not an ounce of aggression in all of your large, furry person. I was proud of you today…and I love you, too. Loads!

And so, farewell, just until tomorrow,
Goodnight…and God bless.

◎◎◎◎◎◎◎◎◎◎◎◎

There are so many occasions in ones life when maybe, there has been a really wonderful event that you would love to relive or a place which you would just about give anything to be able to revisit but, for whatever reason, somehow, never had the opportunity.

The content of this day and the quite special way in which we chose to fill these precious hours has, without any premeditated intention, set a precedent for the coming week…this extra special 'bonus' week.

You see, that is exactly the enormous privilege that we have been granted…the chance to relive the special moments and to revisit all of the exceptional and quite special (special to us) places by which, over the last week and, for whatever reason, somehow left a lasting impression on us. To pick and choose is not an easy task by any means, as everything that we have seen and experienced has been so full of Irish magic as to leave us with a lasting impression. However, there are some which really do stand out, especially to me, or rather, to my other half, Seasalt Vera…needless to say, those are within sight, sound and smell of the sea.

Today has been the fulfilment of a wish which I could never have hoped to have granted, in as much as I have been able to see, once again, an area of this unique part of Ireland that is absolutely redolent of all that is of the sea. In other words, my own personal idea of heaven.

Anyway, I shall say no more…not until you get here. You will then understand what I'm wittering on about.

Monday
5th October 2009

Having been blessed with a peaceful and thankfully, more dignified start to the day, at least for the past few days in fact, for almost a week now, it came as something of a rude awakening to find myself being given the Misty treatment again, as I gradually became aware that it was, in fact, morning…and at a much earlier hour than is considered to be decent, at least by yours truly. OK, so it was about 7.30…to me, 8 o'clock would have been thought of as being a little more civilized.

I do have to concede that it was a lovely morning and that I should have felt myself privileged to have still been alive to experience such a lovely morning. I mean, when you get to my advanced years, to be actually still breathing, at the start of yet another day is, don't you know, extremely reassuring, however…I quite openly confess to being totally in love with my comfy bed at the hour when my pet pooch deems it time to be up and at it.

Now you will understand why I admit to being guilty of so much hypocrisy on the many occasions when I have been extolling the magical glory of the sunrise…I don't see it very often!

All of that aside…there was I, curled up in a pleasing and very comfortable position, in the lovely warm place just vacated by my Jeffy, when, splodge! There was the wet and extremely cold nose shoved, with much enthusiasm, into my left ear. As I squirmed and laughed, the dear, daft dog took that to be a sign of approval and promptly intensified his ministrations.

With no other option, I accepted the fact that peace had just flown out of the window and that the day was well and truly under way…and that was when I remembered our little conversation, last evening, with regard to our plans for this very gorgeous Monday and, with that thought in mind, it immediately galvanized me into frenetic action, with ablutions and dressing being achieved with record speed. Even managing to descend to the kitchen in matching socks.

By now, of course, my rude-awakener was out back, sunning himself and sniffing the air for the scent of any rabbit which may just be foolish enough to stray into the vicinity of his big nose.

What a joy, as we set off, at the quite respectable time of 9.20, with the air pure and fresh and with a pleasing sparkle glinting off the lake…and to think that I could have missed all of this if my boisterous alarm clock had not done his duty so energetically. (Not much chance of that…if Misty hadn't done the job, Jeff would have done the necessary with little or no regard to my dignity).

The road was now familiar but lost nothing in so being. Out through Mulrany and once again onto the Corraun Peninsula and all the delights of Achill Sound and Achill Island. I fell in love with the wide open aspect of The Sound at first sight and it pleasured me not a jot less on this, my second and more detailed inspection of it.

Everything felt so fresh and pure. The light was, as before, quite remarkable, with a brilliance that was almost luminescent and, as if welcoming me back, the gulls screeched and swooped in a glorious exhibition of seagull ecstasy.

Our first stop was Dooega…it just had to be. This tiny bay had remained in my thoughts for reasons that are not immediately obvious. Yes, it is a pretty wee bay but, I have seen nicer…however, for me, it has that special something and that is why I wanted to see it again. Today, there was no sudden downpour to spoil the view of Dooega Head and Clare Island, the like of which sent us, shrieking with laughter, back to the car, on our previous visit and, as an added blessing, we didn't have the need to spend about half an hour trying to retrieve a lost trainer from the unrelenting jaws of the big, hairy one.

The peace and tranquillity were totally unmarred by any adverse conditions this morning and it was, in every way, a perfect idyll.

Still very much under the spell of this lovely morning and revelling in the luxury of this trip of nostalgia, this 'bonus' ticket to ride, it was hardly a surprise to either of us to find ourselves en route from Dooega to Keel. This entire area from Achill Sound right across to Achill Island is just a paradise for anyone like me who just lives and breathes anything to do with the sea and Keel is the epicentre, as far as I am concerned with, as I did my best to describe to you last week, its combination of magnificent white-sand beach, that sweeping swathe which seems to go on forever and the mighty Atlantic Ocean, rolling in on crested waves as only the Atlantic can. The beckoning embrace of that charismatic ocean and the surrounding cliffs of Dooega Head and Achill Head had the drawing power of a magnet and we seemed to be led there by a power much stronger than our own…at least in that direction although, just as we entered the outskirts of Keel, we were diverted by a sign which we had, in fact noticed, last week but, did nothing about it. Being one of those little brown signs which, usually, lead one to something of particular interest, we decided to rectify last week's omission and go have a look see.

The Deserted Village. That was the legend on the sign and that alone was intriguing enough for us to take the appropriate lane which diverted our thoughts from all things nautical and sent them up into the hills which rise above the town of Keel. For me to allow myself to be steered away from the sea, just to look at a pile of stones, was a measure of the way that we were both equally attracted by the whole concept. The Deserted Village. I mean, there really had to be a fascinating story about that…and we were more than glad, even before we had actually had a chance to really look around properly, that we had followed our instinct.

Apart from the mystery surrounding this particular pile of stones, the view across both town and ocean was well worth the deviation however, this pile of stones was so much more than just that…a pile of stones…and certainly very much more than I had imagined it would be. In fact, I found myself, as usual, soaking up the atmosphere of the place. I seem to have the unique qualities of a sponge whenever I find myself in and among any ancient pile. I immediately felt, somewhere deep down inside myself, something of the essence of what this place had once been. Indeed, I actually found it to be just a wee bit spooky.

Just to wander around the remains of this once thriving village, a community of real people…families, neighbours, friends…and now, their only legacy, the only testimony of the fact that they had existed being in just these few remaining stones. These had once been their cottages, their homes. Now it was just fallen masonry…and yet still recognizable as houses, houses divided into individual rooms, rooms in which these people had lived, with fireplaces where pots had boiled and from which warmth had penetrated the fabric of these humble dwellings. Real people, just like my Jeffy and I, had lived here…lived and loved, laughed and cried…and then, for whatever reason, had just walked away, leaving to the ravages of nature, a deserted village, an abandoned way of life.

Standing amongst the ruins of this by-gone existence, I could feel a deep sense of melancholy. It was almost a tactile thing which hung over the remains of this devastated village. The total desolation seemed to be deeply entrenched in each and every stone that still stood as living proof that men, women and children had once inhabited these dwellings.

I mean, what happened to these people? Who were they? Where did they go? So many questions which, I must confess, gave me pause for thought for quite some considerable time after we had left it all behind. Deserted, but now at peace and with the sunlight of this Monday morning in the 21st Century, warming the stones and maybe, just maybe, lifting the veil of unease which had, at first, been an almost living entity. I certainly felt it…and my heart went out to the souls who had once walked in this place. God willing, these people, these very real people, who had lived and worked some kind of a living in these hills had…and I hope this with all my heart…gone somewhere where they eventually found peace.

All of which was of absolutely no interest to our four-legged Irishman who, with his ever-questing nose and acute sense of smell working overtime, knew that he was within sniffing distance of a beach…and nobody was doing a damned thing about it!

I mean, come on folks! Let's get real here…what's the hold up! And even if my boy had been granted the ability to speak the Queen's English, he could not have been more eloquent. Those dark-brown velvety eyes held such a child-like look of reproach that it was almost funny. Although to laugh would have been quite unforgivable.

Those same eyes however, quite literally lit up with sheer canine joy, some moments later when he hit the beach at turbo speed, sending sand flying in every direction, before heading off into the shallow waterline wet stuff and proceeding to scoop up as much of it as he possibly could in that huge gob of his. I can only be extremely grateful that he has now developed a modicum of sense in that daft head of his and come to understand that to swallow it is not such a great idea.

Much to Jeff's acute embarrassment, something which, to his misfortune, he is well accustomed to, I have to concede that my own behaviour was not much more dignified than that of my nutty pup. I mean, it was glorious! The sun was sending sparkling prisms of light off the deep cobalt and turquoise sea and the incoming waves were deep and curling and topped with frothy white foam which, as they hit the beach and exploded, sent myriads of diamonds glittering into the air. Needless to say, I soon lost any residual feelings of Deserted Village gloom and reverted to my usual Seasalt Vera persona and behaved, quite shamelessly, accordingly. Much to the dismay of everyone else…including Jeff.

Strong, fit young men, clad in wet suits, were engaged in what seemed to me to be a quite hazardous occupation, as they took advantage of the prevailing conditions. The flow of the surf was, to them, absolutely perfect for their purpose, which was Kite Surfing. We watched with admiring interest and some excitement as they skilfully handled these flimsy-looking devices…for myself, the interest being tinged with some small amount of wistful nostalgia for a youth which was long gone. Forty years ago, who knows. I rather suspect that I would have enjoyed pitting my strength against that of one of natures most powerful forces…the sea.

Leaving these young adventurers to enjoy their battle of strength against the waves, we set off towards the one place which had been formost in my mind, as we set out, this morning. Something even more special than that which we were now leaving…KEEM.

To me, this hidden gem, lying within the embrace of the surrounding mountains, just has to be the most perfect oceanic idyll that I have ever seen…with just the one exception and that exception is, as I told you previously, Paradise Bay, on the island of Malta. Apart from the climate, the two are almost identical, the similarity being obvious to me from that first moment, as I looked down upon it from the elevated mountain road. Even today, on this magical return visit, it still had the power to thrill me. It may have something to do with the way in which it is accessed…the climb up into the mountains, which then reveals this vision of pure beauty down below, followed by the steep descent to sea level. There is also a kind of intimacy about it and the privacy that is provided by the mountains which protectively enfold it on three sides. If you happen to be blessed, or cursed, depending on ones own views on the subject, it could be so easy, with an imagination like mine, to imagine oneself completely alone and marooned on this white beach…and rejoice at the thought of it. And what I wouldn't give to have the chance!

As if to bring my daft head…silly old fool…out of my fantasy of deserted islands and being marooned with Jeff on this lovely secluded beach for like, forever, all of a sudden, low cloud seemed to come out of nowhere and settle like a watery mantle, over the tops of the mountains, which, in due course, let drop their full load onto this hapless wee beach and the few souls, us included, who just happened to be at the furthest end of the beach and furthest from any sort of cover.

Wow! It was terrific! Coinciding, as it did, with a tide which was fast coming in, we screamed with laughter, all the way back. I mean, we were absolutely soaked within minutes and there suddenly seemed to be water everywhere, even where there had been none just a short time before.

Apart from the rain, streams now appeared where minutes before there had been only empty channels, streams which now had to be waded across, being too wide to attempt a running jump. Rocks had to be scrambled over and wet feet were an inevitability. So, no one ever died from a bad case of wet feet…not that I know of and the entire fiasco was soon rendered even more deliciously farcical as hilarity took complete control. We laughed like loonies and jumped, quite purposely, into any accumulations of water that crossed our path and remained totally unperturbed by the fact that we were, by this time, thoroughly soaked, from top to bottom.

For once, Misty was not the only one who had to be given a good dose of seeing to, by the time we got back to the car.

There was one other lasting memory of this hilarious episode which will always remain. You see, even after we had finally cleared the beach and returned to the car, there was one last person still remaining, down on the beach.

This solitary man, clad in a business suit and highly polished shoes, was just standing there, rain pouring down upon his well-dressed shoulders and slightly balding head and he clearly seemed to be having a great debate with himself as to how he was to get himself across a particularly deep stream of water which was becoming ever wider and even deeper by the minute. If he was hoping to come upon a passing life raft, he would be sadly disillusioned…and believe me, if he stood there for very much longer, that is exactly what he would be needing…a life raft.

We were gone and away, before he finally reached the comparative dryness of the car park…that is, if he ever did. I mean, for all we know, he may still be down there, as we didn't actually see his eventual escape.

By the time we got back to Keel and on ground level again, wouldn't you just believe it? The sun showed her face, albeit, somewhat sheepishly and a little watered down from her usual glowing countenance, just as if nothing had ever happened. It was as if that short, sharp downpour had never happened…apart from the fact that we were still just a wee tad damp.

It's funny, but I can't quite get out of my head that guy on the beach. I mean, why just stand there when the obvious thing to do was to remove the shiny shoes and stuff them into his pockets. He may even have enjoyed reverting to his boyhood and having a paddle, with his trousers rolled up. At least it stopped raining and, if he waits long enough, the tide will go out again.

By now, unfortunately, the afternoon was beginning to positively gallop by and, as you will recall, distance on this return journey just has to be taken into account, so, this was, perforce, the end of the road. But, how lucky am I? It is not often that one has the opportunity and the privilege of doing what we have done today. We have been given an enormous blessing just to have been able to revisit this wonderful part of the Atlantic coastline which had become so special to me from that first visit. Now I have even more memories of this wonderful place. Achill Sound…that name will always breathe the sea and vast open space, into my very soul. Yes! It really was wonderful. Same place, new and different memories.

Jeff had planned this day…planned it with love, plus the added advantage of his profound knowledge of me and of what makes me happy…and it could not have been more perfect, consequently, there were no feelings of sadness, as we about turned and headed back. Our thoughts were happy and we were both pleasantly content to leave, as leave, we must. I mean, we could not stay there forever, unfortunately. We still had the anticipation of a very pleasant journey ahead of us and so, the miles passed, quite unnoticed, as we both settled down into our own private reverie, our own private place.

Just as we entered the town of Mulrany, another of those wee brown signs caught Jeff's eye. 'Spanish Armada' was the white-painted legend on this particular brown sign and so, with some small amount of curiosity, we set out in search of the Spanish Armada. Following this sign was like following a paper trail that went on and on for ever…and the further we went, there was still no sign of the promised Spanish Armada. Every time we so much as went around another bend we hoped…and we hoped. I mean, I don't know what either of us expected…and, daft as I may be, I certainly wasn't expecting to see the entire Spanish Fleet, at anchor, in line abreast, all along the coastline.

When we finally discovered the 'Armada', it was on a bronze plaque attached to a stone monument, just off to the side of the road, overlooking the sea. It depicted the positioning of each ship of the line as they had lain, just off this stretch of coast, way back in what ever year it may have been. Just a bit before my time, anyway. Although, only just.

I have to confess that it was all just a wee bit disappointing. No ships. No Errol Flynn. Nothing! Just a bronze plaque. Oh well. Never mind. You can't win them all. (Besides, we left Errol Flynn back at that castle in Donegal, waving his sword about and scaring all the tourists).

After our visit to the invisible Armada, we could not resist a last, quiet stroll along Mulrany beach…purely for Misty's benefit, don't you know. I mean, it had absolutely nothing to do with the fact that I could not let a beach as lovely as Mulrany go by me without at least putting one foot onto the crystal sand. Both feet were managed and we spent a pleasant half hour of more, with Misty trotting around, doing his own thing and poking his nose into all kinds of stuff that could only be of any possible interest to him…or another dog.

How mellow it was, with the evening sunlight gilding the hills above this small town. The sun was lying low now and so it was the time of long shadows and secret hollows. Just the final touch of perfection with which to

257

round off this lovely day. Home was not too far away now and so, we returned to the peaceful and equally mellow tranquillity of our own Tourmakeady.

For both Jeff and I, this has been a truly memorable day and now, in the loving ambience of this small cottage, we anticipate the advent of a memorable evening.

What can I say, my darling? You have put so much of your love for me into the planning and the execution of this special day…and you must surely know that I appreciate it. You are proof indeed, if proof were ever needed, that love can be shown in oh, so many ways. And you shower that love upon me every single day and in every single way conceivable, from a husband to his wife. In other words, my darling, you spoil me rotten.

God bless you and never doubt my love for you. It's a love that, like all the memories we have made today, will never fade.

Sleep in the deep peace that can only be found in the land of doggie dreams, my Misty. You will always be my big baby and for one so young, you are faithful and true and the best four-legged Irishman in the world. Your mum loves you, too.

And so, as one day comes to its inevitable close, I anticipate tomorrow with joy and we three, The Intrepid Trio, will grasp each minute and make it our own, as always.

God bless everyone.

Until tomorrow, may God keep us all safe from all harm.

๏๏๏๏๏๏๏๏๏๏๏๏

Having embarked on this, our own personal trip of nostalgia, as two weeks in this land of magic and beauty turned the corner into three, we could not have imagined the special kind of joy that this small act of indulgence could have brought with it. It has been like embarking on a short but, very sweet, voyage of rediscovery, just as if we had stepped into a gently bobbing wee boat, pushed away from the bank and then, well, just allowed our small craft to follow the flow of the stream and see where it would carry us. Now, yet another twenty-four hours has passed by in what would seem to be just a fleeting moment, with each and every second filled with this unique pleasure of anticipation and nostalgia. A re-acquaintance. A reunion with another old friend.

Today, that special nostalgic reunion was with Cong. Just to walk the 'Quiet Man' highways and byways of this small village, which is positively steeped in John Wayne memorabilia and absolutely redolent with the very spirit of the man, is a very special treat. All of these criteria were the reasons which endeared it to me in the first place. I know that I fell in love with Cong on that first exciting day of exploration and discovery as we exchanged the magnificence of County Donegal for the gentle beauty and rolling hills of Joyce's Country, in County Mayo.

I mean, John Wayne! Wow! You, my friend, are now looking at his number one fan…and I mean, big, big time! The real deal, you know. (And if I have seen the film 'The Quiet Man' once, I must have seen it a dozen times). Seriously, the pleasure of our re-acquaintance with Cong was no less, this time around, than the new and vibrant excitement of our first visit, indeed, I do believe that it was actually enhanced, as familiarity replaced novelty.

However…that is all I'm saying, just now. The time for more detailed explanations will wait, at least until you are here to listen. The anticipation will be all the greater and the reminiscence will only be more flavoursome.

Tuesday
6th October 2009

Well, the weather forecast for today was wet and windy. Not that we were in the least bit daunted by such a prospect. A bit of precipitation has never bothered us unduly, something of which I think we have more than given reasonably respectable proof in the past…I mean, The Intrepid Trio and all that…however, it was a pleasant surprise to open the curtains this morning and discover that it was reasonably fine. Dull, it may have been but, at least it was dry and, I would even go so far as to add that there was also a soft glimmer of sunlight which was doing its best to show through the gloom. Can't be bad!

Lifted by the promise of fair weather and after the usual early morning manic activity, (although I did manage to escape the over-amorous advances of my daft but quite adorable dog, today) which is something of a hallmark when assessing the average day in the life of the Hall family threesome, we were, in fact, almost ready to hit the road, so to speak when, for a pleasurable twenty minutes, or so, I got into conversation with Jackie Shannon. What a lovely couple they are, Pat and Jackie and, with their working hours being somewhat flexible, we have had the quite genuine pleasure of getting to know them, over the past two weeks.

As was the case with some of the other delightful cottages at which we have stayed, the owners have not been in evidence, said cottages being tended, in between visitors, by appointed caretakers. In fact, I think the only other time when we had the pleasure of meeting the actual owners was last year, at The Old Pub Cottage, way down on the Beara Peninsula, during which stay, we were fortunate enough to get to know the O'Shea family.

The more I talked with Jackie, the thought occurred to me that I suppose I should be suitably grateful that our family kleptomaniac has not been on any noticeable thieving sorties recently…unless it is that Misty's obvious predilection for nicking anything that he can, within reason, get his paws on, has rendered the inhabitants of the main house a little more vigilant with regard to what they leave lying around. (We still maintain a discreet distance from the pretty wee cop shop in Westport, however. I mean, there is no point in adding tempation into a fate which can, if possible, be avoided).

By the time that we bade a 'good day' to Jackie, the prevailing conditions had improved enormously and the day was now extremely pleasant indeed, which gave an added lift to spirits which were already quite adequately elevated to begin with.

This wee boat of ours, in the shape of our Toyota Prius, on which we had, with the intrepid spirit suitable to The Intrepid Trio, embarked on this delightful trip of nostalgia, was now drifting downstream towards Cong…and, as far as I was concerned, that was reason enough for the feeling of euphoria on which I was now floating.

I guess I fell in love with Cong from day one, besides which, it has such a lot going for it which suits our particular needs. There is the village itself, of course, which deserves merit in its own right but, for someone with an ever-eager young dog who needs entertaining and exercising, the Cong River and the extensive reaches of Cong Woods couldn't be more perfect. Definitely much favoured Misty territory!

For devotees of the film 'The Quiet Man', amongst whom I count myself, I was overwhelmed by the aura of the movie which lies over the village. There is so much that is instantly recognizable as one wanders around the village and the grounds of the old Abbey…especially down along the banks of the flowing river…so much so that it is almost possible to imagine the imminent arrival of the film crew and, just maybe, the big 'Duke' himself, with that shy half smile on the, what was then, young face of this very special man.

Crossing over the small bridge which spans the river, before it leads one into the cool depths of the woods, I must admit that I did, momentarily stop and lean over the rail, with my eyes scanning the clear, green depths of the fast flowing water…just in case, don't you know. Sadly, there was no trace of my salmon, which is such a shame. Obviously, my one brief sighting of that elusive but very beautiful fish will have to suffice and the thrill of that quite astonishing, split second in time, will remain with me, always. With instant recall, I can see that gleaming, arching body as it leapt out of the water, with iridescent, sparkling droplets cascading and mingling in the air, before this wonderful creature once more disappeared into the protective waters of the river. Gone! A fleeting moment in time. A fleeting moment of joy but, etched in my mind forever.

Lingering in the village, sort of stretching it out as much as possible and loathe to make that final move towards departure, we mingled with the other tourists. They seemed to consist of, incredibly, so many different nationalities, yet they were all, in their own way and for their own reasons either paying their own homage to the memory of the Big Man, or merely enjoying a very picturesque wee village.

With some small amount of reluctance, we eventually made our way out of Cong…travelling no more than a matter of a few hundred yards outside of the village …to the anticipated delights of Ashford Castle. For whatever reason, we didn't pay it much, if any, attention as we passed by the entrance to the castle, on previous visits to Cong. To be honest, Jeff and I, well, we are not really 'castle' people, however, with this particular castle, I must say that we were pleased that we had made the effort, as it turned out to be a pretty impressive castle. The fact that it is now a hotel and, I would hazard a guess at it being a very expensive hotel, does nothing to deflect from the fact that it is, or was, a real castle. I have to say that I was seriously impressed.

Ashford Castle could not have been set in more attractive grounds. Not that this was the way it would have looked in days gone by. I mean. the beautiful gardens were obviously a very modern addition. Nevertheless, it was a lovely sight, as the silver- grey walls and turrets of the castle rose from the gravelled paths and the green, sloping lawns, which sloped away down to the clear blue waters of Lough Corrib and, as you wander along these crunchy, gravelled pathways, which bisect the lush, well-kept lawns, they lead you past an old and very quaint boat house and then, into the cool depths of a belt of mature woodland which follows the shoreline of the lake, giving splendid views, across the water, of the far side of the castle.

Misty was now in his natural element, of course. Forest paths are great, man. I mean, there is a whole wealth of doggie-licious smells to be found in a forest…only of even remote interest to a dog, of course…but, in this wee forest there was the added bonus of gentle, shallow water, in which he could submerge as much of his large, furry person as was possible, with the sole purpose of becoming a completely undesirable, anti-social, soggy mess.

Emerging from the woods and retracing our steps back towards the castle, we found ourselves suddenly accosted by this delightful young black Labrador. She appeared out of nowhere, or so it seemed, streaking across the lawns towards the object of attraction…our once glowing, shimmering Irish Setter…whose present condition was definitely only suitable for contact with his own kind. With but a brief greeting, of the doggie kind, of course…a quick sniff to the private quarters, in other words…and they were off, the pair of them, like greased lightning, having apparently become friends for life.

No sooner had the two of them become reasonably acquainted, these new bosom buddies were joined by two more dogs, both of them black Labradors, again…and the four of them just went daft. Four wonderful examples of glossy, healthy doggie-hood, having the very time of their lives.

Whilst all of this canine bonding was in progress, Jeff and I soon got into conversation with the two respective dog owners. Both were Irish of course, in fact, the young lady who was the owner of Labrador number one, actually worked at the castle. The other guy lived close by and so, within the space of maybe, half an hour, conversation flowed, easily and pleasantly. Talk is easy when that exchange of pleasantries is with these sincere and honest, open-hearted people of Ireland. A wonderful people who are, without doubt, this country's very heart and soul.

Having finally sorted out our respective dogs and achieved some semblance of order, once more, we all went our separate ways but, this brief encounter had left us with a nice feeling of 'life couldn't get to be much better' and so, it was in this frame of mind, with happy thoughts and light hearts that we rounded off our visit to Ashford Castle.

All of this doggie bonding and general socializing had left us feeling the pangs of hunger which, all of a sudden, began to dig its teeth in and, as we were so close, it seemed the obvious thing to do to seek out that special place, on the road out of Cong, which would be the ideal place to break out the butty box.

Considering the rainy forcast, the sun dazzled the eye as it sparkled off the waters of Lough Corrib and our spontaneous alfresco lunch was all that one could have wished for. With the sun warm on our faces and the gentle murmer of the whispering pines, as their upper branches caught the light breeze off the water, plus the reciprocal, gentle lapping of the lake itself, all combining…it was a positive caress to the ear. First thing this morning, something as absolutely perfect as this would hardly have seemed possible. OK, so the food may not have been five-star but, it tasted like the proverbial manna from heaven, under the present circumstances and in such a place.

Fed and watered, we looked for the pathway, the almost hidden pathway which leads down to the small shingle beach, right down at the water's edge and taking advantage of the bench which was ideally positioned, just above the high-water line, we lolled back (in a most ungraceful manner) and allowed the warm, sunlit ambience of this quiet and peaceful and, totally deserted (except for us) place to embrace us and, just to spoil the picture for a moment, to give the big hairy one yet another opportunity of getting an even larger part of his anatomy soaking wet. That dear, daft dog! God love him…he just loves water, whether it be contained within the confines of his drinking bowl or running freely in lake, river or ocean. Even a puddle of reasonable proportions will send him into paroxysms of canine delight.

After the bright, benevolent glow of this unexpected sunshine, the deep, dark depths of, what I have named, Leprechaun Woods, seemed, by comparison, even deeper and darker. Once again, we were taken by the quite unique, almost tangible moist, green, lushness of these woods. The vibrant, verdant variety of moss and fern and the delicate colours of exquisite fungi…and then, from somewhere, maybe from the hidden recesses of dark and mysterious root caverns or from amongst the great patches of red and white-spotted toadstools, came the gentle, almost, but not quite, audible tinkle of merry laughter, drifting on the silent ether towards our always receptive ears. It was but a fleeting whisper of sound. A brief susurration…and yet, it was there! And we were just as equally sure that our plodding, human progress was being followed by the twinkling eyes of the mischievous gigglers, as we were led?…were we being led? …deeper and deeper into these magic woods where miniature rainbows could lead the unsuspecting wanderer to the illusive pot of gold which, legend promises, is the reward that awaits all of those who have the courage to believe.

You don't believe a word of all that, do you? Well, scoff if you must but…it's true! Honestly! On my life, I swear that it is true. And, all you have to do to find out for yourself is to open your heart and believe.

Anyway, the thought of their harmless presence was actually quite comforting and…Okay! Okay! So, before you say a word or have any ideas about sending for the wee men in white coats…just think about it. And, having thought about it, you do have to admit that it is a perfectly delicious thought, in fact, enchanting could be a better word and besides, who are we to scoff at things which are beyond our comprehension and merely dismiss the whole idea, out of hand. I mean, one only has to remember the old saying, that 'There are more things in Heaven and Earth' etc. etc. etc.

And there! There it is again! Don't you hear it? That sweet, almost musical chuckle. Surely you must have heard it, that time. And is it any wonder that these mischievous, happy wee souls are laughing at us? Of course not. Their amusement is, no doubt, at the expense of we poor, daft, mortals who have no more imagination than we deserve to have.

Emerging from the secret depths of these verdant woods, we sat on our bench again and allowed ourselves the luxury of pretending that we could make time cease to exist, a fleeting moment when we could escape from reality, in a glorious haze of dappled sunlight and gently lapping water. Prisms of light caught the eye, winking and blinking, as we enjoyed this timeless moment of peace and tranquillity and drank in the quite exquisite beauty and boundless aspect of this almost endless infinity of water that is Lough Corrib.

Almost as if we were emerging from a trance, we eventually stirred ourselves and threw ourselves into a little gentle activity by clambering over the quite rocky left-hand shore of the lake, where it wasn't just pebbles but was, in fact, liberally strewn with large boulders. There then ensued a lot of shrieking and outbursts of laughter, as I tried to make my diminutive and slightly aged legs straddle some of the wider gaps between rocks or do a bit of a scramble over some of the bigger ones until, with a certain amount of triumph, I got there in the end. The 'there' being a miniature peninsula, a wee sticky-out bit which poked itself into the waters of the lake like a small finger. Jeff, my beloved half-mountain-goat Jeff, had arrived long before me but, my pride in my achievement was none the less for the somewhat tardy arrival.

This, of course, led to a photo-shoot, just to prove, don't you know, that yours truly had actually managed to perform this wee bit of a scramble, which, just a few months ago, I would not have been in a position to even think about, let alone actually accomplish. Photos were taken and poses were struck and arms were waved manically in the air…even a bit of jumping up and down was thrown in, for good measure.

So, what's new!

With a certain amount of genuine surprise, we gradually became aware of how far we were into the advancing day, which was immediately accompanied by a vague feeling of sadness at the so rapid passing of yet another day. The feeling was very real but, it was also fleeting. The residual memories, the gentle echoes of today and all the ones preceding, will always remain just as fresh as they ever were and, well…today, as with every day this week, is a bonus.

Coming down to earth, as you do, as indeed, you have to do, we dragged ourselves out of our pleasantly dreamy state of reverie and, with the idea of a few basic essentials in mind, stopped off at a small town by the name of Ballinrobe. Pretty little place with, which was the general idea, a small supermarket.

Caught up, we may have been, in the magic of make-believe and fantasy, at least for most of the day indeed, the heart and soul of both of us may still be loitering around in there somewhere, yet, the more base-level demands of an empty stomach dictated the necessity to provide for our future sustenance and so, some few small provisions were purchased which will, hopefully, see us through until the end of the week.

Once back in Tourmakeady, the early evening was far too lovely to just ignore it and so, with a special place in mind, we pulled into a small cove edging Lough Mask and just absorbed the tranquillity, whilst talking over all that had made the day so perfect. It was still and it was tranquil, in among the secluded pools of the lake-side, where the delicate susurration of reeds stirred by a gentle breeze, together with the almost ethereal ripple of the water, were all that intruded into the perfection of total peace.

Sitting in this pleasant little spot, lulled into a beautiful feeling of complete lethargy, Jeff suddenly proclaimed the desire for something a wee bit stronger than tea and, once the idea had taken a hold, we hot-footed it or, to be a little more refined, we hastened to the nearest pub, which was Paddy's Thatched Pub.

You can but imagine our dismay, when we discovered that it was closed…as was Mare Luke's. Honestly! Two Irish pubs, actually shut. It almost, but not quite, unbalanced our sense of equilibrium. I mean, how could the world ever be put to rights again when two local and very Irish pubs were shut. (And don't we all do it? You must have done it yourself! Although it is fairly obvious to anybody that a place is actually closed, we still manage to attempt shaking the door off its hinges, just in case, don't you know. The door may just be stuck. As if).

Salvation was still to be had, however.

Not to be daunted, or done out of our immediate desire, we headed for the other end of the village, where we knew there to be another pub and…Lo and behold! Alleluia! A welcoming light shone forth from the cosy interior of The Lough Mask Inn.

Oh, I expect that the others will be open for business later this evening, however, now is now and so, the availability of some light refreshment, before the delirium of devastating thirst sets in, plus the genial company of some of the local male population, made for a very pleasing couple of hours…not to mention the savouring and enjoyment of the consumption of a quite respectable quantity of some of Ireland's finest and very special nectar…Guinness!

Now, sitting within the warm and comforting ambience of this small dwelling which has become so very dear to us, the all-embracing aura of love, the flickering flames from the fire and the sweet bouquet of a good wine combine to fill our hearts and all the secret corners of this stout cottage, with an abiding serenity and contentment. It is one of those rare and very special moments when you know that life just could not get to be any better. Certainly not for me and that's for sure. Everything which fills my world is here, close to hand and more precious to me now, than ever before.

Jeff and Misty are in their accustomed place by the stone hearth, from the centre of which, logs splutter and send sparks glowing up the chimney, in a greeting to the night sky. This is the nucleus of any home, the hearth stone and Misty has found his place, pushed up as close as close can be to his dad, his full, quite considerable length stretching across the entire hearth, or almost. And there you have it. There, in one package, so to speak, is my entire life. The man I love above all else in life and the big, daft, wonderful dog who gives his trust, his quite unconditional love and his honesty, so unstintingly.

How lucky can anyone get? I ask you!

Thank you for today, my darling. As always, you have made it special. Just as you make every day special, merely by being my husband.

And dear Misty! What can I say? Dry, at last, for maybe the first time since this morning. God love you. Anyway, you are safe, now, in the warmth of the love that will always be just for you. You are a good dog…the best…and I know that God will always find a special place in His heart for such a faithful soul.

◎◎◎◎◎◎◎◎◎◎◎

Of all of the places in this land of mystery and quite extraordinarily spectacular beauty, there is one word, one name, which sums it all up and is, all by itself, so quintessentially Irish. That word, that name is Connemara and on this lovely, early autumn day, it has been a journey of sun, sea, laughing rivers and glowing, towering mountains, the like of which is and, can only be, unique to the Connemara.

If you will…and I hope you will…just allow me to take you back there, I know that you will derive as much pleasure and enchantment from the experience as we did.

Now, as we enter into the eventide of this very special and unique day, a day of Irish magic and the majesty of those soaring peaks and laughing, gurgling rivers…of lakes as still and as perfect as mirrors and of seas as blue as the sky which, in a blaze of glory, united themselves in that limitless horizon and filled our hearts with indelible images which will remain with us for the remainder of our lives.

Anyway, come…take comfort by the hearth. Yes! That's it…that chair just by the fire. And now, I shall begin a narrative which will be a special joy in the telling. It is my hope that you will be able to see it so clearly that you will be able to follow in our footsteps, every inch of the way.

Wednesday
7th October 2009

I really must begin this day with a small confession. I was not exactly the first one out of the nest, this morning…in fact, I was running quite a wee bit late and so, it was a somewhat flustered and flummoxed, extremely contrite me who hurled myself down the stairs to the loving greetings of both Jeff and Misty. (So, what's new? I can hear you say).

Jeff's was enthusiastic, if a bit sooty, as I had interrupted his morning fire-monitor duties, that of clearing out the grate and then re-setting it, in readiness for the welcoming fire which will be your visual sign of a warm welcome, in more ways than one, when you arrive, this evening. Still, sooty or not, it was an embrace that was most welcome and for which I would fight off the Devil Himself…or anyone else who may venture to block my passage into the arms of my Jeffy.

As for Misty…well, Misty's greeting was short, sharp and done and dusted within the space of time it took him to offer a quick lick to one of my hands and then, he was off and out. I mean, there was far more urgent and important stuff, which was only awaiting the arrival of him in order to get it all sorted, out there in his own little meadow, than wasting precious time in over-excessive expressions of his canine adoration of his daft mum. Still, it's the thought that counts, I suppose.

Indeed, the first thing which immediately brought a smile of quiet joy to my face (apart from the sight of my own, darling Jeffy's sooty face) was the quite enchanting sunny tableau of Misty, lying in his accustomed patch of sunlight, by the open back door, with his eyes deep, dark brown, dreamy pools, as he contemplated his idyllic environment.

Having persuaded the incumbent electric cooker to produce a reasonably edible breakfast, we momentarily put our heads together…in other words, we had our usual morning meeting of The Board and, with a unanimous show of two hands and one large paw, made our choice of destination for the day, a direction in which to point and steer our small craft, the good ship 'Happy Days', on this very unique journey of nostalgia. A journey, or, maybe I should say voyage, which is, I might add, passing at a goodly rate of knots…just to keep up with the nautical jargon, don't you know.

Connemara. Just the mention of the name opens up a kaleidoscope of unbelievable images, all of which, when put together to form a whole picture, become the unique paradise that is the Connemara. The name symbolises and is the very essence of Ireland. Everything that the mind and heart could imagine of the beauty of Ireland, is in that one word.

And it is all there, just waiting for you to seek it out…and, with an early start, seek it out we did.

Even while still on 'home territory', so to speak, the hills were a joy on this absolutely perfect morning and so, instead of taking the road to Leenane, we took the single track road, off to the left, which climbs steeply and in a series of sharp, hairpin bends, up into those glorious mountains of Joyce Country.

Through Maum and then on to Maam Cross, small villages which were even too small to bear such a grand title and ever onwards with, as our constant companion, the great, sunlit massif of the Maumturk Mountains.

Enchanted as we were by the stunning display of golden autumnal colours which swept the hillside in ever-changing hues…colours which changed, quite literally, by the second, as small, insignificant white clouds passed across the face of the sun, we were suddenly brought down to earth, in a rather brutish way, which successfully landed us firmly, from any remote and fantastical place we may have previously been, back into 21st Century reality once more, with the unexpected appearance of a bin waggon. This incongruously out of place monster was, at the same time, the cause of some quite unseemly hilarity. I mean, it was rather funny, under the circumstances. There we were, just us, the bin wagon and…nothing else. Except the incumbent sheep population.

Quite honestly, of all the totally unimaginable things which could have appeared before our eyes, we could not have been more taken aback if it had been a flying saucer that had just plonked itself down in front of us.

Obviously, even in paradise, they have their designated bin day!

And there then ensued the contest of minds as to who gained the right of road in order to continue on their way…the thing was, you see, the bin wagon was just a tad bigger and heavier than us.

Flippancy aside, it felt to us as if these mountains, which we have come to love with a passion, were putting on a special display that was just for our benefit. The day could not have been more perfect. It seemed, to us, that Mother Nature was pulling out all the stops in order to leave a truly lasting image in the hearts of we two humble souls, of Ireland at its most unbelievable best. At that moment in time, there was not so much as a small puff of cloud to mar the perfection of the sunlight or a mere whisper of a breeze to stir the moorland grass or create so much as a ripple on the mirror-like surface of the lakes.

At one particular point, where the length of the mountains ran parallel with a large lake, the mirror-like image was so profound that it was almost beyond belief. It played tricks with ones eyes causing the necessity to blink every few seconds, in order to re-orientate ones vision. The image was so perfect, in every minor detail that it really was almost impossible to differentiate between the solid and the reflection.

Even later on, when examining the pictures which we took of this amazing phenomenom, it was still quite unnerving and, even on just a photographic image, still had the ability to affect ones vision.

Thinking about it…I mean, what are the odds on ever seeing that again? What are the odds on that peculiar and quite unique combination of prevailing conditions ever being so perfect, ever again, in order to achieve such a miraculous phenomenon. Something as insignificant as a mere breath of wind would have rippled the water and totally shattered the illusion. Yet another example of what I have just said. I really am beginning to believe that this special performance is just for us.

Freedom of choice seemed to go out of the window as the morning advanced. It was as if some unseen force was guiding us, steering our passage and dictating our road.

Without thinking about it, we found ourselves on the road which passed the dear little church of Our Lady…the haven, the tranquil refuge, out in the wilderness of the mountain moorland…said road eventually leading us to Lettergesh.

Maybe it was She, Our Lady, I mean, who led us there…who knows. All that I am sure of is that it was, without me actually realizing it, the one place that I wanted to be, at that moment and on this day.

Of all the beaches, in this land of beaches made in heaven, Lettergesh is, for reasons which I would find difficulty in numbering, very special to me. So many memories. So much happiness. So many simple but, amazingly happy associations, all of them wrapped around the three of us. My Jeffy, my dog and, me…and this beach. Memories to hold and to cherish and, cherish them I do, of the two souls who are my life.

For a day in October, the sea put forth her own show of perfection, as she preened in the reflected blue of the sky and added just that little bit of sparkle that was strictly her own, as she sent happy, laughing waves frolicking in to caress the soft, white sand, each one wearing its own decorative tiara of diamonds.

We both stood, quite transfixed by the eternity of perfect loveliness which stretched out in front of us and seemed to go on forever. An infinity of blue and turquoise, dazzling white and, as infinity was suddenly brought to an abrupt end, the golden glow of the ever magnificent mountains of the Connemara, which stood proudly, off in the middle distance.

Suddenly, the spell under which we had both been held, momentarily, was shattered by the flash of glimmering copper as a certain furry person leapt into action and legged it down the shingle and on to the beach. In the split second that it took for him to achieve the world record, Jeff and I were still standing there with our mouths wide open. However, not to be outdone, I soon followed suit and, letting out a shriek, caught up with and did my best to emulate my daft dog…closely followed by a slightly more laid-back and infinitely more dignified husband.

With all of us now deposited on the sand, it was impossible not to be stunned by the panoramic vista which lay all around us. Lettergesh is, in just one word, spectacular.

Gorgeous as was the view, it was also impossible not to delight in the antics of our young beach bum. God love him…his face and his eyes were aglow and he was frantically trying to do everything, all at once. I mean, for heaven's sake…holes had to be dug in the sand. Seaweed had to be grasped and shaken and prodded at anyone who was unfortunate enough to be in his close proximity…which was us, of course. And then, well, he just had to get into that water! That was the ultimate joy. A dog can do so much when there is such a boundless amount of this glorious wet stuff.

Jeff and I watched all of this with the adoration of a proud mum and dad and, lost in our own happiness, as we walked along, hand in hand, we didn't particularly notice the precise moment in time when he became bored and began to search for something else with which to amuse himself. This new alteration to the scheme of things only became apparent when he came trotting back to us, brandishing the same large, white and black, busted football, which had so diverted him on our last visit. He'd found it floating, well, not exactly floating, as it was somewhat deflated, in a rock pool which had formed around an outcrop of rocks, just further up the beach. Rock pool being something of an understatement. In reality, it far more resembled the moat that you would normally find surrounding a castle.

This reunion with his old and precious source of amusement kept our daft dog happy for about another ten minutes and then, as before, boredom set in and the ball was dumped and off he went in search of pastures new. (Or, something else with which he could make a general nuisance of himself). Unfortunately, it was not just us who then found themselves at the mercies of a young and extremely exuberant Irish Setter. Not that they seemed to mind all that much. After all, they were all very young and seemed to find the whole episode, enormously amusing. Or so the shrieks of laughter would have had us believe.

Way up at the furthest end of the beach, Misty had eyeballed a group of youngsters who, along with a Spaniel, were playing their own water-sports and were, from all accounts, thoroughly enjoying every moment. Of course, it would never even occur to Misty that his presence may not be required and so, once he had spotted them, he once again broke the three minute mile and immediately joined in what had, until that moment, been a private affair. A great deal of splashing about, with water flying every which-way, combined with shrieks of laughter, led us to believe that we would not be too unpopular, as we finally caught up with our young charge and, in the end, both dogs and humans spent a very pleasurable ten minutes. Indeed, because of the obvious fearlessness of the young Spaniel towards the water, Misty, still a little unsure of the sea, ventured further out than he would normally have done. So, all ended in a very amicable way and we bade them all farewell and headed back the way we had come.

Misty, by this time, was totally unrecognizable as the glorious Irish Setter that we had brought out with us. Still, it will all come off with a bit of a rub down and, well, he had enjoyed the best of times. For heaven's sake, what's a bit of sand! His eyes still glowed…with health and with sheer canine joy. That is what really counts!

There was just one more thing which occurred, just before we got back to the car…and it sort of finalized this magical couple of hours in a way which could not have been planned.

Misty was trotting some hundred yards, or so, ahead of us when he suddenly stopped and, with head bent low to the sand, well…it almost looked as if he was talking to something, only for the fact that dogs don't talk. Well, not in the way that I'm meaning…and it was only when we got a little closer that we could make out what it was that was the focus of his attentions. It was, once again, one of the wee kittens from the cottage along the shore. The tableau which was being played out before our eyes was, to say the least, unusual and, totally hilarious. A more unequal couple you would have been hard pressed to find. As the last time, I could not help but think of them as David and Goliath. However, there was also a quality about the whole thing which was strangely beautiful. Little and, not just large but, enormous, yet, there was not even a suggestion of fear in the little and, there was not a scrap of aggression in the enormous. They were at peace with each other. A bond had formed between them almost and I felt strangely touched. Once again, it was as if the wee kitten had come out, with the sole purpose of saying farewell. It would be nice to think so, anyway. I really am a silly old sod, aren't I?

Making ready to get on our way again, this episode that had touched me so much, mirrored my own feelings as I stood by the door of the car and looked back.

I knew, at that moment, that I would probably never see this idyllic spot, ever again. To my shame, tears came into my eyes and I was powerless to stop them. In the days, the weeks, even the years ahead, all of this would still be as it was at that moment and yet, I, we, would not be here to see it. It was a moment of childish emotion but, it was real and it hurt far more than I would have believed possible. So could be measured the special place that this small part of this magnificent country that is Ireland had found in my heart.

And then, despite my stupid, emotional behaviour, I had to laugh! You see, as I took that one last glance back, to the beauty of Lettergesh, one small object caught my eye…the deserted and abandoned football! Out of the tears came the welcome laughter and, strange as it may sound, the thought of that poor, abandoned ball will always remain with me…and will always be a testament to the fact that 'Misty was here'!

The laughter sent us off in a happier frame of mind. I think that both of us had felt the tug to our heartstrings at the thought of leaving Lettergesh, for good. So, not to be dismayed, off we went, back into the mountains. Nothing mattered all that much, indeed, it was quite liberating to just let wilful chance dictate our direction and steer our course.

Soaring peaks beckoned to us to raise ourselves up to meet the sky and lakes shone like glass, in the unbelievable endless sunlight. Rivers laughed and chuckled to themselves as they frolicked over boulder-strewn beds, at one minute gurgling beneath a rough stone bridge, the stone warmed by the sun and the next, cascading over a hanging ledge and creating a miniature waterfall.

Our unseen guide took us through some breathtaking scenery but then, this is Ireland and, even with no set path in mind, something quite mind-blowing is usually to be found, just around the next bend in the road. Today, we were guided to a small harbour, called Cleggan…and I do mean small. Yet, there was enough of apparent interest, to cause us to make this our lunch stop. Time was of no importance, not on this day and we were keen to explore.

Boats, large and small, were tied up around the harbour walls but, it was around the slipway that we soon discovered the main source of livelihood to the men who ply these waters…crabs. And when I say crabs, I mean monster crabs. I have never…and I don't imagine that I shall ever again, see crabs as large as these. They were like dinner plates and their claws were as big as my hand. One thing was for sure, it rather took the gilt off our poor, modest ham butties. Oh boy…what I would have given to taste some of that succulent crab meat! Dream on!

Still, it was a pretty wee bay. The views all around were quite stunning. Purple mountains loomed in the distance, a modest distance which added a sense of intrigue and mystery and, just offshore, a collection of small islands were tantalizingly close enough to spark off sufficient interest in maybe taking advantage of the ferry service. Just the names would have been enough to intrigue me. Names like Inishturk or Inishlyon.

So much beauty, encapsulated in just one relatively small part of this beautiful country and yet, it would be possible to wander the hills, the moors and the mountains of Connemara for a whole week and still find an abundance of hidden gems such as this wee Cleggan. The passage through this land is always a joy but, the discovery of some of these small, off the beaten track places is treasure trove indeed…and well worth any small measure of inconvenience in the getting there. Not that there was any such inconvenience in reaching Cleggan.

How quickly the time had passed today and, without actually being aware of it, we had put quite a lot of miles between us and Tourmakeady, since leaving there this morning. Taking into consideration the time factor, we knew that we had reached the outer limit of our range, and so, not entirely saddened but, with a touch of nostalgic melancholy, we turned our wee 'boat' towards our own shores.

Happenstance carried us along the Kylemore Pass and so, it needed very little persuasion to stop off and have a coffee at the abbey. In fact, what we were doing was just trying to eke out the day as much as possible. Any excuse, just then, would have been gratefully grasped, if it only prolonged the afternoon by so much as a half hour.

Notwithstanding our childish attempts at making the day last forever, those futile efforts were of no avail and, as nature took care of itself and did its own thing…the world continuing to turn etc, our day did, at last, draw to its inevitable conclusion. The planets will not cease to rotate just for our benefit, that's for sure. It has been special though. Somehow, everything has been completely perfect…and in all the right ways. Even the weather! I mean, for October, it has been as balmy and as golden as a summer's day, which has, in the ideal order of things, added vibrancy of colour to all our memories of this day.

Dinner was a feast of warm and loving conversation…the food wasn't bad, either. Then there was the ceremonial lighting of the fire and the happy, quite silly, really, pleasure of the sparks and the crackles, the flames and the dreams. Definitely dreams for young Master Hall! As I speak, he is flat out! Totally. (And snoring)!

And now, as I go back over some of the more personal moments of today…the emotions, the love, the joy of companionship…I can but thank God for all the blessings of this day…indeed, all the blessings of my life…the chief of which is the man beside whom I now lie. My love for you, my own Jeffy, has reached a whole new level, over the last three weeks, today especially. You mean more to me than ever and our deep and eternal love has become all the more precious. God bless you, always, my darling.

Poor Misty. He hasn't so much as stirred, ever since he discovered that the fire had been lit. You really have had quite a day, young man and you have so much to fill your doggie dreams, this night. God bless you, too, funny face.

The days are passing at a frightening rate, now. Tomorrow is Thursday and the end is almost in sight…but, not quite! Tomorrow, we will not allow any thoughts other than happy ones to spoil those precious hours. We have to make each and every one count…every second.

God bless you, everyone, wherever you may be…especially the people of this land. And take fair warning, The Intrepid Trio will be out and about in full force, tomorrow so, well, you know that can lead to all kinds of trouble.

Sleep tight!

ⱷ౦ⱷ౦ⱷ౦ⱷ౦ⱷ౦ⱷ౦ⱷ

Dear friend, in all fairness, the only decent thing that I can do is to give you advance warning that this evening you will be walking into a total miasma of doom and gloom. Oh, it's all my fault. I mean, who else would be so daft.

But, you see…it's Thursday evening, which means that tomorrow is our last full day. Jeff, of course, is taking it all in his stride, as he always does, so at least that is one lonely tick on the positive side and proves, yet again, that one of us has some sense…and I know that I have said that before, indeed, more that once, I expect. I just didn't indicate which one. Still, anyone who knows us will know that it isn't me and that's for sure.

But, I can't help it! I cannot help who I am or what I am, even if that persona happens to be a big, daft kid. (Can you believe a daft, old sod like me, positively sulking)!

Oh, for heaven's sake, woman! Behave yourself and for once, act your age and not your shoe size. This is not the right occasion to behave like a four year old! You should consider yourself to be the most spoilt and extremely fortunate big, daft kid on the face of the earth. I mean, you have just spent three wonderful weeks in this land of dreams and you should be giving thanks, instead of bewailing your impending doom, to the man who made it all happen in the first place and who, at this precise moment, is having to put up with your long face.

So, that's it! All done and dusted. I have given myself a good ticking off and that's the end of it.

Let us make tonight extra special. Your presence will lift the melancholy of impending departure and we will live, once again, the time just gone and rejoice in it… and look forward to the pleasure of things yet to come.

Today has been another wonderful day of special joy revisited and the October sunshine has blessed us once again, accompanying our wee boat as it flowed a bit further up the stream on today's voyage of reminiscence and farewell.

Apart from which, a certain furry person has, this very day, become two years old. Two years! Where has it gone? It seems only yesterday when that three week old pup placed his tiny paw on the side of my face and sort of claimed me as his own. Dear Misty. What a joy you have been to us…and, no matter what, you will always be my big baby.

So, tonight there will be no gloom. On the contrary, we will make this night one of celebration. Tomorrow is another day and we will not think about anything other than love and friendship and of the enormous wealth of both that are present in this house, tonight. These stout, stone walls must have absorbed into their very fabric, so much of the love that has been and still is present in this humble dwelling that it will probably remain there forever.

The wine has been opened, in order to take the air and we will make it a real night to remember…as memorable as the day has been.

Thursday
8th October 2009

'Happy Birthday to him, Happy Birthday to him'…and if you think I've gone ever so slightly potty, I can reassure you that I have not. The birthday boy, himself, got things rolling in his own ever-loving fashion this morning and, because it was his birthday, well, I hadn't the heart to admonish him and so I just let him get on with it. I just wish that I wasn't quite so ticklish.

And before you start to get the completely wrong idea…No! It was not Jeff! There would have been no resistance offered if it had been Jeff, of that you can be sure. Which leaves just one more guess as to the identity of the over-amorous culprit. Yes! The birthday boy! Our great daft dog.

Happy Birthday, funny face!

Two years old! Oh, my Misty…it hardly seems possible but, there is no point in denying it…our baby is growing up!…and that, of course, makes all of us two years older. However, we won't think about that. There is no point in depressing ourselves, unnecessarily. You are as old as you wish to be…and you know, from experience, what I'm like.

Oh, glorious, glorious morning! I mean, what is happening, here! I know that October can be a very lovely month, if you're lucky but, wow, the last week in particular, has been way over and above the norm. All I can say is, that we must have earned ourselves a few extra brownie points, somewhere in the overall scheme of things, which has been of some small influence with the lovely angel first class who just happens to be in charge of the weather.

In between tossing the bacon around a pan, catching toast in mid-air, as it hurled itself out of the toaster and making sure that our Misty, who is ever the opportunist, didn't nick the sausages (birthday or no birthday) I have actually taken some time to look out on this absolutely perfect morning and marvel at the unique, early morning, Irish stillness, as it hangs like a blessing over a lake which looks like a silver mirror, with, just here and there, the diamond sparkle of sunlight on the gentlest of ripples.

The only sounds to break the stillness, although in all honesty, these sounds don't so much break the stillness as accentuate it, were gentle, subtle sounds…the tiny chirp of a sleepy bird. Little twitters, just to let you know that they really are awake and the piping calls of water fowl as they begin their day, calling to each other from the reeds at the edge of the lake…and as I took all of this into my heart, in a vain attempt at keeping it there forever, I was overwhelmed, momentarily, with a feeling of total panic…devastation, for want of a better word.

I can't do it! Leave all of this, I mean. OK, so devastation may seem like a rather strong word to use in this context, especially with regard to Jeff but, let me tell you, it is not even remotely strong enough to describe my feelings.

Help!

Why do I do this?

I mean, I come to Ireland, full of joy…but with the full knowledge that, in the end, it will only break my heart each time that I have to leave this land that I have grown to love so much.

Anyway, that is more than enough of that! For heaven's sake, just look out there…and what the hell! Today hasn't so much as been touched yet…not to mention tomorrow (and I would very much rather not mention tomorrow).

We are The Intrepid Trio…and do we let things get us down? Not on your life! The Intrepid Trio never buckle under the strain, we grab life by the usual bits and give it a jolly good shaking. So, come on you guys…let's make every second count! Starting with my Misty. OK, young Master Hall…extra sausages, birthday boy!

Being the penultimate day when we could actually take advantage of this special privilege which we have been granted and indulge ourselves once more with another short voyage of nostalgia…and, taking into account the glorious weather, our choice was not a difficult one to make. Apart from which, it being a special occasion, it was a choice which immediately met with the approval of a certain furry personage. If I wasn't mistaken, I'm almost sure that when he heard the words Bertra Strand, his eyes positively glowed. You always hear people say of their dogs…'Oh, he understands every word I say'…well, this one does. I swear to God, there really is a real person in there, somewhere and one day, I will find the zip in that Irish Setter suit.

You will, of course, remember our previous visits to Bertra Strand, which has become for me, personally, a firm favourite which runs a very close second to Lettergesh. Indeed, it became a favourite haunt, for all of us, from that very first time when, having passed through Westport, we were simply exploring the immediate environs, sort of familiarizing ourselves, so to speak and came upon Bertra by chance…and what a happy chance that was.

Alright then, everybody…all aboard the good ship 'Happy Days' (daft idea, I know but, well, it seemed appropriate) and we were off, setting sail for Westport, with spirits high, despite the gathering gloom in the shape of a small, insignificant cloud of melancholy, which would keep trying to depress us by settling just above our heads and which was immediately dispelled once we were on our way. Indeed, laughter was to be the order of the day and that, only a few miles up the road as we were quite delightedly amused by another example of those eccentricities which I dub 'Irish whimsy'. Indeed, you do not have to travel too far in Ireland before you come across something or other that will instantly raise a smile…even a chuckle or two. This was a simple thing but, whoever thought of it has a similar sense of the ridiculous as I. Thank God I'm not alone!

Entering the main road from our own narrow, country lane, just on the left-hand corner was a farm, with quite extensive grounds and many out buildings. Just by the side of a barn, which just so happened to be nearest barn to the road, there were dozens of black-plastic covered bales, which had all been very neatly stacked.

Ok, so, what is there to appear so strange, let alone amusing about that, I can hear you say. I mean, even back home, in Delamere, the sight of plastic covered bales is a common sight and one which does not even create so much as a raised eyebrow. But then, this is Ireland. Let us not forget that this is the land of Irish humour and Irish whimsy…and some guy with the sense of humour of a Leprechaun had joyfully adorned the rounded ends of all of these bales with merry smiley faces. Created in white paint, on the black, shiny plastic, they were totally amazing. Oh, what a joy! I mean, how delicious is that? We almost fell out of the car laughing…and I imagine that those cheeky, smiley faces brought a smile, indeed, a chuckle, as I said before, to all who passed that corner, on that day…and every day.

Passing through Westport and hastily crossing ourselves as we passed by the Police Station (I mean, there is no point in taking any unnecessary risks…you know what I mean? A little divine intervention never goes amiss) we were soon turning onto the single track road which led to Bertra Strand.

Dear Misty. Almost the very second that we turned onto this side road, my big, darling beach bum raised a questing nose and, having inhaled the doggie-licious smell of ozone, immediately became alert, with his daft head sticking out of the car window, as if he were riding shotgun on a stagecoach and the rest of his body coiled like a tight spring, so that he could be ready to spring (so sorry about that) into action the very second that we released him from the confines of the car.

A special birthday treat, my big boy. Enjoy!

Which he did, of course…in spades.

Bertra is just like every other beach on the entire Irish continent…in as much as it is absolutely breathtaking. An infinity of white brilliance, with the Atlantic Ocean rolling in on white crested waves and, if you allow ones gaze to glide over this blue and shimmering water, purple hills add their own touch of mystery to the scene, away over in the middle distance.

But, this is not all that Bertra can, quite justifiably boast about…it has the added feature of tall and stately sand dunes which rise up at the head of the beach and form a ridge all the way down its full length. You will, of course, remember all of this from that first visit when, I have no doubt, I went into my usual realms of fantasy, in my completely inadequate attempt to describe and do justice to, this quite unique place.

Today, we chose to walk across the sand dunes and, from the slightly more elevated position, it was possible to see, all in one go, the special feature of this beach. From up on the dunes, one can see, to the left, the glorious Atlantic, hurling itself at the shore in its usual frenzy of adoration of the land while, at the same time, to the right, look upon the quiet, still, mirror-like surface of the large inland lake which lies on the further side of the dunes. Today, with the prevailing colours being a combination of various shades of blue…I mean, just look at that sky…it was impossible not to gasp in sheer wonderment at the full, panoramic scene which, at that timeless moment, lay before us in all its glory.

Strolling along, with the sun warm on our faces, we were quite content.

The mood of the moment was one of absolute peace. I mean, it would be difficult to feel anything other than at peace, in these sublime surroundings.

The birthday boy was always some way ahead of us and yet, he knew just exactly where we were and occasionally stopped, just to ensure that we were still there. He always does that. No matter how far ahead he may wander, if that distance should be considered, by him, to be too great, he will stop and sit and wait until we catch up. Today, Jeff and I were happy just to let him wander, poking his nose into the clumps of stiff dune grass, or digging himself a quite satisfactory hole in the sand…and, when he is indulging in this particular doggie pastime, to be standing in too close proximity is not a good idea. Jeans become caked in sand and trainers finish up being the unfortunate receptacles of about half a ton of the stuff.

On this morning of all mornings, I seemed incapable of just walking…I kept stopping and staring. I mean, I'd just stand there, like an idiot (no rude remarks, please) just gazing out across the expanse of white sand…and the sea and the sky…all of which were so magical as they, each in their turn, showed off their summer-like colours on this blissful October day.

I can't say that my mood was exactly sad, rather it was introspective. I was trying, in my own way, to cram it all into my head…despite the squillions of photos that I must have taken…in the vain attempt at keeping it in there forever. Sometimes, that slightly melancholy frame of mind can do just that, making the memory a more lasting and indelible one.

Before going down onto the beach, we looked for and found, a nice sandy hollow, up on the top of the ridge and we just sat there. Maybe a half hour went by, yet we were in no hurry to let go of this precious moment. My Jeffy and I were both absorbed by our own thoughts yet, our closeness was stronger than ever. It was almost a tangible thing, as if one could reach out and touch it…and it was inordinately special.

I suppose I have left you in no doubt as to my feelings with regard to leaving Ireland. I mean, I've done enough moaning about it, however, I do believe that, at that moment in time, as the two of us sat, side by side, close in body and in mind, Jeff was feeling some of the same sadness that was now beginning to take a stronger grip on my heart and, looking around us, at the sheer beauty and magic of all that lay before us, I just could not bring myself to accept the inevitable or even so much as contemplate leaving it all behind.

Oh, shut up, woman!

Lifting our minds from the reverie which had, for a time, held us in its thrall, we seemed to, quite simultaneously, heave ourselves to our feet…a somewhat greater heave on my part, my nether regions having gone more than just a little bit numb…we set out on the return journey, coming down from our sandy roost and taking to the beach for one last walk along its full length.

The tide had only recently gone out, leaving, in its wake, firm, damp sand and, what was of the most joy to Misty, great rock pools, full of clear, deliciously enticing water, sufficiently deep for him to have a good old splish and splosh and more than deep enough to just generally immerse himself in. The end result being, one totally sodden Irish Setter.

Definitely a two towel job, when we get back to the car. One to remove most of the moisture and any surface muck, the other to do the final drying off.

On that particular subject, what a revelation it has been since we became the proud mum and dad of our big, sloppy canine. I mean, going on holiday now, has to be planned like a military operation, especially when it involves the stuff that we take with us and the final loading up of the car. When finally stocktaking, there is more essentials packed for the big hairy one, than there is for the two humans. For example…towels. At least a half dozen big ones. Then there are blankets and his large bed (I mean, large dog, needs an equally large bed). After that we pack sufficient food to last him for the duration (it eliminates the necessity of always looking for pet shops), plus his leads…various…and his brushes (though why we bother ourselves with those, I can't imagine. I mean, he is barely clean and dry for more than a few minutes) and last, but by no means least, his assortment of toys. Yes! Toys. He his still a baby, after all. What room remains, in the interior anatomy of the car, is for our stuff. Although we do have resource to the roof box…the coffin-shaped recepticle which has proved to be quite amazingly capacious, fortunately.

Still, no regrets. I mean, when he looks at us with those eyes which, to me, have an almost human quality to them, how could anyone harbour even the smallest regret. OK, so, gone were the luxury holidays abroad and the posh hotels yet, we have experienced so much joy from this great lump of loving, faithful, loyal dog that, in all honesty, I have no inclination to look back. This is our life, now…and that dear, daft dog gives us his all, in a love that is totally unconditional. All I have, is all I want. I have my man, the best husband any woman could wish for…and I have my boy…and that is all the happiness that I shall ever want or need.

Arriving back at the car, complete with soggy canine, we were just getting started on the clean-up operation when the people in the next car made themselves known to us. They had been watching, with some amusement, our efforts to restore our wet and sandy dog to his former glory, well, as near as possible. Their own dog, a spaniel, was looking on with the look of total disdain for a young sprog who still had a lot to learn. It was a look which said it all. 'I know all about that, my lad and, in my time I've done it all. You won't find any flies on me, youngster'….God love him, I expect that he had, indeed, done all of that…and probably received a good rollicking into the bargain.

As one does, the conversation covered most of the major points in the lives of both of us and this elderly couple, who, it transpired, were fairly local, living no more than about twenty minutes drive from this wonderful, Seasalt Vera paradise. I mean, my envy knew no bounds. Not that I begrudged this enormous priviledge to these lovely people. Total strangers, they may have been but, as is so typical, the open-hearted friendship of the Irish people, was not one jot less sincere when it was offered by these two gentle, elderly folks.

I felt that it had been a great privilege to have been given the opportunity of meeting them and their acquaintance seemed to put the final touch of pleasure to a very pleasurable morning. OK, so we hadn't done anything particularly earth-shattering but, it was special to us, which was all that really mattered and, as we discovered long ago, it is almost always the simplest of pleasures which provide the most lasting memories and give the most happiness.

With an almost physical wrench, we did, at last, walk away…or, drive away. Reality won this small battle of wits, in the end. I mean, choice didn't even come into the equation. Not really. If it had, there would have been no choice to make. We would be staying put! Anyway, before we could change our minds, we set off in the direction of Westport.

We were, by now, hungry enough to roast a sheep and, as it had actually been our intention to spend the afternoon in this lovely town and become a little more intimately acquainted with it, we were soon set on getting there with as much haste as was seemly. After that, today was the day when we would really hit the town and, as well as fulfilling our need for sustenance, we would do the one thing which really smacks of 'going home'…purchasing the things which make a holiday complete. In our case, small gifts for friends and special treasures for our own home. The no doubt daft trinkets, which serve to immortalize the happy memories of a special time and a special place. We all do it , don't we? And it is a thing which always carries with it a mixture of pleasure and a hint of sadness, purely because one always leaves it until the last minute. (I remember as a child, having no money left, by the time souvenirs were being purchased. I always seemed to spend every penny of my small amount of holiday spends, almost by the end of the first day).

Before taking some of the weight from Jeff's back pocket by lightening his wallet, purely by virtue of the fact that we were both famished, food was the first priority and so we searched for and eventually found a suitable establishment where we could get that sheep onto a spit. Attacking our lunch with all the voracious enthusiasm of two people who had not seen food for at least a month, our attention was suddenly diverted from what was on our plates, to the enchanting, sweet strains of music which had begun to drift in to us, from just outside the entrance door way. It was the romantic and evocative, unmistakable sound of an accordion, the sort of sound one associates with the street cafés of Paris, which both enchanted and delighted everyone who was within earshot, as this unseen musician began on a beautiful medley of Irish tunes and then led us straight into the romantic Mediterranean sunlight of Italy, with songs which sent Jeff and I winging back to places like Sorrento, Capri and Sicily…all of which brought back echoes of romance for both of us.

By the time we had finished our lunch, he had gone. Completely disappeared. I was hoping that he may have had a CD on offer…as some of these street musicians do. Still, the lingering strains of his delightful accordion, remained with us for quite a long time afterwards.

And so, with music still in our ears, we got down to the serious business of shopping and as my Jeffy would definitely agree, I never have any problems with spending money. It should have been an extremely satisfying and pleasurable task and yet, somehow, there was not the enthusiasm in it as there should have been, even when we came away clutching our precious purchases. Talk about the Last Chance Saloon…we felt it so strongly, the fact that this was to be our last chance of doing anything very much. Tomorrow will be, in the main, packing up day.

Oh God! This is awful! And I know I keep saying it but, I cannot help myself.

This is totally daft and you know it! Daft old woman! So, snap out of it and just get on with it. Besides, all is not lost…at least, not yet. I mean, who knows what kind of a miracle may happen between now and Saturday morning. Think positively, that's the thing. Not that I'm all that convinced of any such thing happening. However, you know the old saying…hope springs eternal…or some such thing. Ok, so I am grasping at straws but…well, you never know!

Having spent so much time in and out of the shops, our very precious, quickly running out time, seemed to pass at an even more alarming rate, not to mention the alarming rate at which my Jeffy considered that I had been spending money. Nevertheless, he was as pleased with our newly acquired treasures as I was…and you know full well that he didn't really mind. He would never refuse me anything!

And so, farewell to Westport. It really is a quite lovely town, the most vivid memory which I shall carry away with me being the flowers. Everywhere one looked, there were flowers, their bright and cheerful, showy brilliance of colour and the delightful perfumes which seemed to intermingle in the air, filled ones senses with such enormous pleasure. I don't think that I have ever seen a town which was so ablaze with such an abundance of magnificent, colourful blooms…great baskets of every summer flower you could think of, draped both sides of the many stone bridges which span the river. Lamp posts were also adorned with circlets of flowers and there were window boxes, flower beds…flowers were everywhere…and I wasn't joking when I remarked about the pretty little Police Station. It really does look like some small but, quite exquisite, Mediterranean villa, with geraniums, fuchsias, petunias, all crowding each other and trying to outdo each other with their brilliance.

We were still loathe to call it a day, I mean, the afternoon still had some way to go and there was still enough time available for us to be able to stretch it a wee bit. A few precious hours with which we could drag out every last second of this last full day and, by the time we got back to Tourmakeady, the late afternoon was still so beautifully mellow that we stopped off at Tourmakeady Woods.

It had been some hours since Misty had been able to let off any surplus steam…I mean, it was his birthday and so, being dragged around the shops is not exactly what he would have had in mind as a way of spending his precious time, time which could have been far better spent searching for rabbits or chasing wind-blown leaves…all good doggie pastimes, don't you know…and Bertra Strand was now just a canine dream which could have happened yesterday, as far as our dog was concerned. I firmly believe that all dogs live solely for the minute and what may have happened only an hour before is now of no consequence whatsoever and has been completely forgotten.

With his seemingly boundless energy, he was out of the car and heading down to the stream before we even had time to turn around…and it could not have been a more glorious scene which lay before us as we set off through this autumnal, woodland paradise, thrilling to the overwhelming vibrancy of all the beautiful October colours. As the sunlight came through the overhead canopy, the foliage of the trees was just one mass of amber and gold, copper and bronze and, as if to outshine everything else, the brazen, scarlet berries of the Rowan trees hung in glorious clusters, like rubies…and all of that was replicated, on the ground beneath, by the covering of glowing, burnished leaves which had succumbed to the breeze and were now decorating the winding pathway which would, in the fullness of time, lead us to the waterfall, that eternal source of the clear, fast flowing water which formed the stream at which Misty just had to go and quench his thirst. (By submerging his entire person into the water, of course…and making it all the easier for him to drink).

Not that it really mattered but, because of our unplanned visit to the Falls, we were later home than usual which resulted in a somewhat hasty, undignified push and shove to get to the bathroom in order to spruce ourselves up sufficiently to go out to dinner. Yes, we were dining out in great style this evening and would not have looked too impressive in our present slightly bedraggled condition. I mean, it had been a long time since hair had seen a brush, which is just one example and we had been blown by sea breezes, done the rounds of the town and then, lost ourselves in the deep, dark recesses of Tourmakeady Woods.

Suitably washed and changed, we set off, in great anticipation for The Lough Inn, in Partry. Partry was only five minutes, or so, up the road so it was convenient and meant that Jeff could have a drink with his meal and not have too far to drive home.

The menu was a glory of culinary delights and I won't go into my usual inability to make up my mind…I mean, you already know what I'm like. It is a well-known fact that, by the time that I have deliberated and then changed my mind, at least half a dozen times, the staff are just about ready to knock off, put their coats on and close the kitchen down for the night. Not tonight though! I would be suitably obliged if it could be noted that tonight I, personally, feel that I made my choice in quite remarkably record time. In fact, I think I even made my decision before Jeff had fully made up his mind. Now that really does have to be something of a record.

What a lovely treat though and what a perfect way with which to conclude this day of such mixed emotions. Pleasure and sadness…partners which always do seem to rub shoulders whenever we are faced with the prospect of leaving Ireland.

For now, we embraced the warm words of farewell and good will which were offered to us as we left The Lough Inn. Warm words from warm and honest hearts, which sent us back to our wee cottage feeling quite content, under the circumstances.

As soon as we got in, logs were introduced to a fire which soon added its own warmth and cheerfulness and the combination of the two filled the house with a special aura of peace and harmony, something which can only be achieved when the two people whose lives and hearts are combined, are as close as the two of us.

You, my friend, have been and gone…and I know that the feelings of sadness were mutual, as we acknowledged the unspoken truth that tomorrow will be our final night, our final meeting.

Sleep will be hard to find, tonight. I cannot seem to shut down, indeed, I don't particularly want to. I just want to go with the flow of my thoughts, just as we have, during this final week, this very special bonus week, gone with the flow of the stream which has carried us on our wee voyage of nostalgia.

Tonight, more than ever, I am so very aware of all that I have to thank God for. As I lie beside my husband and with Misty snoring for both Britain and Ireland, my thoughts are full of all the precious memories which have been made by us, in this wonderful country, over the past three weeks.

My darling Jeffy, we have shared so much and all of it will remain with us, living on, forever in our hearts to sustain us, in years to come, as we open up these indestructible mental images of joy and dreams and happiness…a special kind of happiness which can only be found in this wonderful land. Thank you, my love, for making it all happen.

God bless you, Jeff. My love for you is as eternal as the universe. Nothing could ever break that special bond which will forever bind the two of us together.

And as for you, my Misty. Wow! An Irish Setter in Ireland…and how you turn heads and endear yourself to all who come under your daft, comical Irish charm. How greatly do you belong to this country. Just like your mum, you come alive whenever you set a paw on Irish soil.

Sleep tight, funny face…my own, very special, four-footed Irishman. I love you, too.

And now, we must look toward to tomorrow…and for heaven's sake, get a grip, you daft woman. As a fully paid-up member of The Intrepid Trio, you have a certain reputation to live up to. It is not the done thing to let the side down now.

We can still give the day a good dose of indomitable Hall bravado. We do not let the small matter of having to leave Ireland get us down. Tomorrow, the whole of Ireland will still be out there and, as tomorrow's morn dawns, we will make sure that we make the most of it. Give it our best shot and make every second count.

With those words of rather false bravado I can, at last, say goodnight.

May God bless everybody…and, like I said, be ready to make tomorrow count!

◎◎◎◎◎◎◎◎◎◎◎◎

Sitting here now, in a cottage which has been de-personalized somehow, with all our own bits and pieces now packed away, I cannot help the feelings of sadness which are very close to being overwhelming, just at this moment.

It is hard for me to accept, as accept I must, that this is, as was, of course, inevitable, our last night. That inevitability making it nonetheless painful. But what a joy it has been when, each evening, two people of like minds…friends for always now, of that I am sure…have enjoyed the simple pleasures of conversation and reminiscence. You will never know what a privilege it has been to both Jeff and I, to enjoy your presence and welcome you into the warmth of our small, albeit temporary home.

Over a period spanning almost two years, our friendship has evolved and matured in the most unimaginable way…unimaginable, that is, at that moment in time when I first offered my tentative invitation to you to join our happy band in whatever adventures lay ahead of us, in this new and exciting life, a life which, from that moment on, would revolve around our young, wonderful and delightfully bonkers Irish Setter. Dear Misty, what a joy you have been!

You took up my invitation. You came with us on that first memorable journey into this land of Irish magic. And what a life-changing event that proved to be, especially for yours truly.

Anyway, let us now rejoice and celebrate our friendship. There will be no doom and gloom in this house, tonight. Come, take your usual place by the hearth. There may be a dampness lingering over the lake tonight but, any chill will remain out there. Within these stout walls, only the warmth and love of friends close together will prevail and that combination will fill up every corner of this house.

Friday
9th October 2009

It occurred to me this morning, as I looked out upon a wet and extremely dismal aspect, with the trees in Misty's meadow, dripping water, that we have had to resort to donning our rather stylish wet gear, just twice in the entire three weeks that we have been here in Ireland. I mean, this is The Emerald Isle and therefore, a certain amount of the wet stuff comes with the territory, so to speak and is only to be expected. We can only consider ourselves to be extremely fortunate…and many thanks are offered up to the particular angel, the chief assistant to the Main Man, who just happens to be in charge of the weather. I can only express our heartfelt gratitude. (Although I must admit that I always feel that we both cut quite a dash, in our Sunday-best wet gear. Especially my new nifty titfer.

I have to admit that breakfast was not the usual jolly, chatty, happy affair. Even Misty seemed to pick up on the general atmosphere of gloom which sort of hovered above our heads like halos of mourning. God love him, he just sat, still as a statue, by the bottom of the staircase, somehow intuiting that there was still some of our trappings remaining up there, in the bedroom, only awaiting someone to go up and bring them down. I'm sure he was feeling just the slightest twinge of anxiety that, just maybe, we might leave him behind. Oh, my darling, daft dog…as if we would.

That caretaker position at the foot of the stairs only changed when he thought that breakfast was about to be served and then he quietly took up his post by his feeding station. Low-lying cloud over the kitchen, or not, there were no circumstances under which he would run the risk of being deprived of his usual daily ration of sausage.

Jeff and I went about our wee chores which, over the last three weeks have become normal routine but, there was very little enthusiasm in evidence and we both respected each others privacy and special, personal thoughts…all the things which were uppermost in our minds and hearts, this Friday morning.

For all Jeff's laid-back nature, I know, purely because I know him so well, that he was feeling the understandable melancholy of the moment, just as much as I and yet, he was the one who eventually snapped us out of the doldrums and the clouds of misery were lifted and some semblance of enthusiasm emerged from the ashes of gloom and despondency. Once more, there was the sound of the usual morning banter around the table, followed by the sound of genuine laughter…something which is never too far away, in the home of the Hall family threesome. Thank God! Despite the natural feelings of regret, sanity, in the form of Jeffrey Hall, had restored the usual equilibrium of our daily routine.

There was no necessity for a meeting of the Board, this morning, indeed, the members of this particular Board, can now consider themselves out of a job. In all honesty, there seemed to be an unspoken accord with regard to how and where we would spend the precious hours of this morning, before having to return and begin the onerous task of packing up.

Cong!

There was no contest!

Apart from the fact that it wasn't too far away, it had, in its own right, captured our hearts with its simple charm…not to mention John Wayne.

Just to digress for a moment…and I'm wanting to access the thoughts of all you ladies out there…am I the only idiot? Or are we all the same?

OK, so, we have spent the last two weeks in this dear cottage…the two of us and one extra large canine with four equally large feet…and, as with the first cottage, in Donegal, or any other in which we have had the pleasure of residing, for whatever length of time, I always like to clean it, from top to bottom until, in my own mind, I am confident that I have left it as clean as it was when we first walked through the front door…if not cleaner.

It's the same when we are preparing to come away on holiday. I will be beavering away, with duster and vacuum, until our home is positively gleaming and Jeff will admonish me, in a nice sort of way, of course and say…'What on earth are you doing all that for, woman! We're going on holiday'. To which I will usually reply, in kind…'Well at least if we are burgled they will not have any cause to think it a dirty house'.

Daft, I know but, I suppose it is in our genes, or something. Anyway, apologies for the slight digression. I was simply curious. I mean, surely I cannot be the only complete nutter who just can't help reaching for a duster.

Gathering up all our accumulated enthusiasm and stowing it aboard our little boat, we followed suit and, setting out on what will be our very last voyage of nostalgia, we trimmed our sail and made course for Cong…a Cong which was so different today, with the dismal outlook and the wet and shiny pavements. Neither of which, in any way, spoilt the pleasure that we have always found in this special place. The contrast may have been quite marked but, it was still possible to see and feel its own special, roseate glow…despite the weather.

It really was a sort of pilgrimage of farewell, I suppose. The narrow streets were shiny wet and yet, they were as familiar and as much loved as they had ever been.

Having done the rounds of Cong, there was yet one place which we had to return to…yes! Ardnageeha Woods. Our special Leprechaun woods and, of course, the small, shingle shore upon which the beautiful Lough Corrib gently laps…only it wasn't gently lapping today. Wow! I could hardly believe the difference from only two days ago…and neither could Misty. Today, the usually gentle waters of this huge lake hurled itself onto the unsuspecting shingle beach with all the force of the Atlantic Ocean in a really pissed off mood. Poor Misty…without giving it any thought, he immediately set off in the direction of the lake, only to get the shock of his life as he placed his front paws into the water and got hit by a wave which just about drenched him. He shot up and back, as if he had just been electrocuted. I'm sorry but, it was impossible not to laugh. Cruel but, unavoidable. Poor old lad! He may be two years old now but, he still has a lot of learning to do.

I just would not have imagined that an inland lake, albeit a very large one, could possibly get itself worked up into such a frenzy and it may have scared my poor daft, pup but, these were just the ideal conditions to send Seasalt Vera into an ecstasy of joy, a joy which eventually manifested itself in a certain amount of jumping up and down in a most undignified fashion, much to my poor Jeffy's dismay…I mean, thank goodness there was not another soul about which thankfully, saved him from the usual acute embarrassment.

For once, Misty was quite easily separated from the water which he usually sets such store by and we headed off, for one last time, into the green and verdant undergrowth of the forest. The intrepid explorer soon forgot his trepidation caused by the suddenly unfriendly aspect of the lake and he was foraging ahead of us, sticking his nose into fern and bracken, on the scent of any rabbit who may be daft enough not to immediately scarper, as this huge, red, furry monster tracked them down. Not that they would be in any danger from this great, soft lump. He wouldn't harm a soul…or a rabbit.

Becoming, once again, under the mesmeric influence of these 'magic' woods, it suddenly came to us, just how rapidly the hours were passing and a momentary feeling of total panic set in.

Oh, I know that I have said it many times before, that one seems to enter a completely different time zone when one steps ashore onto Irish soil. That's when an hour becomes as inconsequential as a minute and a week can pass as quickly as a day. Well, as these, our final hours went by, I can only say that somehow, even 'Irish' time had actually seemed to speed up.

Having run everything down, with regard to the contents of our larder, we subsequently returned to Cong and took our pick of all the many pubs which blessed such a small area and finally entered the cosy atmosphere of The Bird's Nest.

Even before we were properly seated, we were immediately welcomed by the obvious proprietor and were made to feel at home, which did much to dispel the damp and chill of the streets of Cong and also the dismal thoughts which had, once again, started to poke a bony finger into the flimsy fabric of our fragile cheerfulness.

The food, as always, was excellent. Simple, wholesome Irish fare…and nothing could be better. As for this particular establishment, I can heartily recommend the wild mushroom soup. Served with warm, fresh Irish bread…nicely satisfying chunks of it…it was a feast worthy of a prince of the realm.

Whilst we had been talking to the landlord, I think that he had sensed our reluctance to leave his premises…and also the reason why…and so, he did his best to steer the conversation onto a more cheerful course, attempting, in his own generous way to lift the gloom which had, once again, descended upon we two hapless souls. Eventually, of course, we had to accept defeat. I mean, we just couldn't stretch it out any more and so, bidding farewell to our friendly landlord, we bade farewell, also, to Cong.

The drive back to the cottage was, for at least the first part of it, quite lacking in any conversation. Only dear Misty seemed to be completely oblivious of anything untoward. Oh, to be able to put myself into his dear, daft head, instead of my own.

Taking the route which would bring us into the glorious mountains, once more, we found a small place in which to pull in, way up in the heart of the mountains and just stopped and marvelled at the magnificence of the scene which was spread out before us. A vista of unimaginable colours and the awesome mantle of low cloud which draped itself around the towering shoulders of these eternal peaks.

A feeling of total devastation struck me like an icy-cold finger as I took it all in and I could not help but question my ability to leave all of this behind. No doubt, never to be seen again.

As if in an attempt at cheering, the sound of running, trickling, spurting water was everywhere. Torrents of it ran down the hillsides, finding any fissure that it could. Narrow waterfalls formed serpentine highways down the steep sides of the hills which, in turn engorged the fast-flowing rivers, way down in the deep, deep depths of the glens. Miniature cascades of water spurted from every small crevice and dripped from heather which was saturated with this precious moisture. It was a concerto of sound and it did, just for a moment lift my own personal misery. Not a lot! But just a wee bit.

Dragging ourselves away from the magnetic pull of Joyce's own mountains…I mean, we couldn't stay there forever…like the couple of daft numpties that we were, we finally arrived back at the cottage and went through the motions, like a pair of mindless zombies, of getting everything packed up and most of it in the car, leaving just the inevitable last minute bits and pieces which can only be left until the morning.

After this dismal chore had been completed to our satisfaction and the usual clean-up job had also been accomplished, Jeff took Misty for his walk up the lane. Not just for Misty's sake but to take in, for the last time, the peace and tranquillity of the lake. I paid my own homage, but in my own way. How lovely it was. Calm again now and mellow, with a rather watery evening sun lying over the water and lending that wee glimmer of cheer to everything.

This time tomorrow, we will be many hundreds of miles away and, therein lies an enormous sadness.

Oh, this is awful!…and I am completely aware that I am behaving like a spoilt brat, however, no matter how you may urge me to behave like an adult instead of a total idiot, the fact remains that this is even more difficult than it was the last time…which is saying a lot. I cannot help myself. The very thought of having to leave Ireland, early tomorrow morning, fills me with an enormous sadness and an equally enormous sense of loss.

Oh, if only!

How many times do we all say or think those two words during the course of a lifetime…If Only. Two very small words but, with a whole wealth of meaning.

My own, personal 'If Only' would have to be my desire to never leave Ireland. To never have to even think about leaving Ireland. A small cottage, just big enough for we three, with sea to the fore and mountains behind.

I could not wish for a more lovely and wonderful home than the one which my Jeffy has worked so hard to provide for us, not to mention the situation, high above the beautiful Cheshire plain, in the beauty spot which is

Delamere Forest. However, if we could only air-lift it, lock stock and barrel, across the Irish sea, that would do for me…and also for a certain large, furry personage.

Not that I ever hold out much hope. You see, my circumstances are so vastly different to Jeff's. I have absolutely nothing and nobody to tie me down and keep me in England. On the other hand, Jeff has everything. His whole life is in England.

I have no family, you see. My entire life is my Jeffy. He is my world and so, I could make a home and be blissfully happy anywhere…just as long as we were together. He is all I need…all that I will ever need.

It is, of course, understandable, that he could never sever the ties that bind. Not now. I mean, he has only just found his family again…a family which was lost to him for fifty years.

And so, my beautiful home will have to remain where it is, in Delamere and my daft dream will always remain just that…a daft dream. However, human nature being what it is, I expect that I shall always set some store by that dream. Silly old fool!

In the meantime, I shall continue to love the home which will always be special to both of us. It is our home, created by us, for us…and love has always been a vital part of the structure, indeed, it is and always will be, the very fabric of this home. It is the very cement which holds it all together.

Just to bring the dialogue back to a more cheerful tone, it has just come back to me that it is 'live' music night tonight, at Mare Luke's. What a joy it would have been to have been able to go along and enjoy the friendly warmth of the people of this dear Tourmakeady…as well as the music. However, there is daft and there is even more daft and so, with the prospect of a six o'clock start, tomorrow morning, we reluctantly gave it a miss. Pity, though. Again, those two words…if only.

Now, coming back to the moment, on this night of gentle reflection and the remembered happiness in all that the last three weeks has brought our way, I can only give praise and gratitude to the person to whom it rightly belongs.

Oh, my darling husband, you are the one who made it all possible. With love, you planned it all and with love you executed those plans, with one thought in mind. That of making everything special for me.

You are my life. You are my heart, my soul. Just as long as we have each other…and that big, daft, wonderful dog of ours, I will always be content. To be special to you is all that I could ever want because, to be special to you is to have treasure indeed.

I love you more than life itself. God bless you, always.

Sleep tight, my Misty.

Tomorrow will be a long day for a youngster like you so dream your own special, happy dreams, this night. In your own delightful way, you have given pleasure to so many people over the last three weeks. With your usual Irish charm, you have brought joy to all who have had the good fortune to be in your vicinity. Like a canine Errol Flynn, you have flashed those pearly whites in a roguish grin that would charm the birds out of the trees…and you have also given great joy to your mum and dad. Our very own, four-legged Errol Flynn.

God bless us all. God bless Ireland. May peace fill the heart of every Irishman and protect this blessed land from all harm.

See you tomorrow!

ⓔⓓⓔⓓⓔⓓⓔⓓⓔⓓⓔ

It has been a long day and a long journey…and I don't mean in mere road miles…although, as I talk to you now, it all seems, to me, to be a million of those road miles away.

Donegal. Tourmakeady. Connemara. Lettergesh and Bertra…Ireland! Was it merely a dream?

We have been back home, in England, for some hours now, with all the luggage unpacked and a washing in the machine…and that usual feeling of weird unreality, quite surreal, in fact, is much in evidence, as I potter around with no real idea of what I'm doing.

The house almost seemed to welcome us home, yet, I cannot seem to be capable of dispelling that sort of empty feeling…the enormous sense of loss…and so, I pretend. I pretend that we are still by the lake, with the moon casting its silver highway across the still waters, so that angels may walk across it without getting their feet wet.

In my mind, Jeff has just taken Misty, our boy, along by the lake-shore, where the peace of the evening is broken only by the gently lapping waters and the occasional sleepy call from one of the varied water fowl who have made Lough Mask their home…and I am waiting for you to arrive, just as you have done every evening.

It's silly, I expect but, it gives me some kind of closure…so, if it is OK with you, I shall make some small attempt at telling you of our day, of our journey, although, in all honesty, most of it went by in a kind of blur. However, this habit has become very hard to break and so, I shall endevour to do my best.

Strangely, you feel so very close as I settle myself down to begin!

Saturday
10th October 2009

There was little or no time for writing…or even for feeling sorry for myself, this morning. With a lunchtime sailing, from Dun Laoghaire, (1.30 to be exact) we left the cottage at 6 am…without the harsh cruelty of broad daylight to illuminate all that we were leaving behind. For which I was extremely grateful.

Without even a single glance back and under cover of the merciful mantle of darkness which still embraced the land, I just drove, with the only part of the passing scene which was visible, being the small section of the road illuminated by the car's headlights. And so, as the miles gradually piled up behind us, coming between us and all that we had grown to love and which had given us such joy, it just had to be the bleakest moment that either of us had shared. Even Jeff was not immune to it and, hard as it had been, that last time, when leaving County Kerry, this was, by far, the most difficult to come to terms with.

OK so, it may sound all very childish, very un-adult but, the feelings were real and, in their very depth, show some small part of the passion that, for me, is Ireland.

It was almost a physical effort to keep the car heading in the direction of Dublin when, given half a chance, I would, without the slightest hesitation, have turned around and headed back…back to the mountains, back to those laughing rivers and the lakes which shone like polished mirrors. Back to Lettergesh and Bertra Strand. Back to the Connemara and all that that very word evokes. Back to everything that had filled we two ordinary people with an extraordinary peace and joy.

It really is a different life here. Here in this blessed land, this Ireland.

Slowly, as the miles and time slipped by, dawn came up over the distant hills and a new day was beginning. Just as it was getting light, we pulled off the road and refreshed ourselves with a cup of coffee and gave our dear, good, seasoned traveller, a chance to unfurl his long legs and have a sniff around…as dogs do. I had no idea, at that precise moment, just where we were…and to be honest, I didn't particularly care. We were on the way to Dublin…when, all I really wanted was to be heading back the other way.

Apart from another couple of comfort stops, the remainder of the journey was uneventful, for which we should, of course, be grateful…no mishaps or anything and, with plenty of time ahead of us, we eventually arrived in Dun Laoghaire. Somehow, once here, in this attractive wee harbour, it always feels as though well, this is it. End of the line…and no going back! Want a bet? If I had even the most infinitesimal chance of legging it back to Tourmakeady, you would smell burning rubber a mile away.

Knowing there was absolutely no chance of that happening and with the knowledge that we had a quite comfortable time to wander around, before getting ourselves down to the ferry terminal, we took advantage of the pleasant late morning and walked around the yacht basin, where Saturday sailors were already applying canvas to sturdy masts and taking advantage of the prevailing conditions, which couldn't have been more perfect for filling sails with the joyful breeze and which sent them on their way with a quick flick of the stern.

What a pleasant atmosphere there is around a harbour such as this. I mean, the large part which deals with the big car ferries is only one feature. Everything connected with water can be experienced here, particularly at the weekend…with special training sessions for children and young people, in the arts and skills of sailing or canoeing. Both of which were being carried out, with an enormous amount of enthusiasm, I might add, by all concerned, accompanied by shrieks of wild elation and the spirit of the young.

Before we knew it, we almost had to sprint back to the car. Time, that relentless enemy of the whole of human kind, whose inexorable passage is the one thing over which we have absolutely no control, had crept up on us, as it does, in its usual stealthy, slippers on, kind of way and thus ensued a hasty, undignified scurry to get over to the check-in point and take up our place, in line, ready for embarkation.

All of which left us with no chance, whatsoever, with regard to doing a runner before the boat came in and legging it back to where we both longed to be…unless, of course, one could boast of having, as part of the car's spec, the ability to achieve vertical take-off. Regrettably, although the Toyota Prius is one of the most advanced technical miracles currently on the road, it cannot become airborne. Pity!

And then, dreams of doing an about turn were well and truly shattered…the boat was coming in.

All of a sudden, there she was, her vast presence looming above the high harbour wall, slowly drawing ever closer until she filled our vision with the sheer size of her…the good ship Stena Explorer…churning the sea into a maelstrom, as she turned herself in a huge circle, in order to negotiate the tricky manouvre of entering her berth and tying up.

With all my passion for anything associated with the sea, my heart leapt with the sheer thrill of watching this splendid vessel performing, what was, to her and her crew, just a normal, routine operation. She may have been there for the sole purpose of taking me and mine away from these hallowed shores but, that did nothing to detract from the excitement that this huge craft engendered within my daft Seasalt Vera persona.

And then, it all seemed to happen so quickly. The incoming traffic had come off and we were entering the cavernous interior of this colossus of the sea, where the vehicle decks look large enough to carry every car, lorry and bus in Ireland. Then we were parked up and heading up the nearest stairwell to the warm and quite luxurious passenger lounge…and, as always, I just cannot allow this moment to pass without mentioning the efficiency of the Stena Line staff. Both ship and shore, they really are quite exemplary. From the transition from dockside, to your seat in the well appointed passenger lounge, it is all executed speedily and efficiently and with every possible care of the welfare of the passengers, some of whom may be in need of a wee bit of TLC if they have boarded somewhat travel weary. So. Well done, once again, Stena. Of course, there are other shipping lines who do the Dublin or Dun Laoghaire crossing but, we have always sailed by Stena and shall, in all probability, continue to so do, on all our future trips to the Emerald Isle.

Once settled, the voyage passed so quickly. I mean, by the time that we had ordered our meal and eaten it and then, had a wee wander around the duty-free shop, as you do, we were nearing the port of Holyhead…and somehow, when we came out of the bowels of this large vessel, into the early evening sunlight of Anglesey, I had this weird feeling of total unreality. It was as if we had been living a dream, a dream from which we were only just becoming awake.

Life was just as we had left it, back in Ireland. The waterfall in Tourmakeady Woods, would still be falling in joyful torrents, into the still and quiet 'fairy' pool which lies at the base of the falls in eternal anticipation of the cataract's jubilant entry into its depths. If the conditions are the same as those which now lie over this small port, in North Wales, then the evening sun will be gilding the gentle waters of Lough Mask and the hills, those sublime and golden hills of Joyce's country, will be resplendent, dressed as they are, in their best autumnal colours…gowns of amber and bronze, slashed, here and there, with bands of heather purple. Not to mention the cheerful white polka dots which decorate the whole, as sheep continue to maintain their precarious foothold on the steeply sloping hillside.

Not exactly a brilliant idea to torture myself with, dwelling upon these images…images which were solid and real to us, only yesterday and now, are but golden memories. These precious, nostalgic mental photographs will be something which I can feed upon, like a starving man (or woman) with a voracious, desperate hunger, until such time as our feet touch the soil of Ireland, that magic and enchanting land of dreams come true, once again.

The journey up through Wales and back once more into Cheshire, was quiet and uneventful and, that same strange feeling of complete unreality, which had encompassed me as we left the boat, came over me again as we entered our own road which, in turn led to our own house.

As always, there was that quite nonsensical surprise that everything was still exactly the same, in every single detail, as it had been at the moment that you had left it. I mean…what on earth could one possibly imagine would have happened to make a difference. Possibly an invasion from outer space, maybe…or some cataclysmic force of nature which had actually rendered ones home into a heap of rubble.

In our case, it had been three weeks and, apart from the fact that the garden was looking a bit sorry for itself and the grass looked as though it could be concealing a tribe of never before discovered wild natives, everything else was ridiculously just the same. We had merely returned from a different way of life.

And so, the day which, for such a long time we had been dreading, has been dealt with, lived through. The trauma of this morning's departure was, thankfully, cushioned by the protective covering of darkness and now, here I am, pretending that all is as it should be and that you are with me, dear friend, as always…as I would wish, if only that wish were on offer.

Think about it…the silver lake, the velvet sky speckled with brilliant diamonds. The cosy room with the solid stone fire wall and the cheerful sounds of spluttering logs, as the fire blazes and provides the doorway into dreams and magic and castles in the flames.

Let us crack open a bottle of wine and, with all our love, Jeff and I toast the future and a hasty return to the land which we have come to love so much.

We also thank you for your faithful following of our simple pleasures. Pleasures which come from love and the joy of a life filled with love. You have walked in our footsteps. You have shared our joys. God bless you…and may the time be short until we are together once more.

Lying now, in our own bed, I find myself going over the day, minute by minute and, with some small amount of yearning, I am allowing myself to stray into the realms of nostalgia, picking out bits and pieces from the past three weeks…and driving myself bonkers as a result.

I wonder how many turned up for the live music night at Mare Luke's, last night? Oh, how I wish that we had been able to go. I don't think that I shall ever forget that wonderful night, at Pat's bar, in Dunkineely. For us, it was special. Very special.

So, my darling Jeffy. It is all over. When we first set out, three weeks seemed like a miracle, an eternity that would, surely, never come to an end.

But, as I said, that enemy, Time, just cannot be stopped. It will always win, in the end.

God bless you, my darling. We have shared so much but, we are home and, as always, wherever we two may happen to be, just as long as we are together, love is and always will be, all around us. That love will always be a safe harbour for the heart to find safe anchorage…two hearts, which will ever beat as one.

I love you, with body, heart and soul, my husband.

Dear Misty. You have been a star, this entire, long day…and you knew immediately, that you were home, just as soon as you set paw through the door. Yes, funny face, my own daft and wonderful dog, you are now home and beaches are now a long way away…still, you never know. We will just have to see what can be arranged for a special boy who, like his mum, loves the sand and the sea and the magical smells which, if only they could be bottled and saved, would be priceless. God love your open and faithful heart. We love you so much.

And so, goodnight and God bless. To everyone.

And a special goodnight to you, my Ireland. May God watch over you and yours. Always.

ⓔⓔⓔⓔⓔⓔⓔⓔⓔⓔⓔ

Conclusion

Today, I have just finished writing this, my second wee tale of we two ordinary people and our one, quite extraordinary, absolutely gorgeous, Irish Setter…and our latest adventures in the land we all love so much. Ireland. Of course, Misty is and always will be a vital part of my tales because, without him, there would be no story to tell but, because of him, we have experienced a quite unique happiness and enjoyed the innocent joy of simple pleasures. Dear Misty! What joy you have brought to our lives.

A humble cottage and The Intrepid Trio are, and always will be, from now on, the recipe for a very special kind of cake.

On this trip, we have covered a vastly more extensive area of Ireland and as the title indicates, the love which was born in 2007 has escalated and has now gone into orbit. Yes, the love affair will go on….and on….and on.

We have not finished yet and, what is more, Ireland has not yet finished with us. We will be back! Our love affair, with these wonderful Atlantic shores in particular, will go on, as there is still a section of it that we have still to explore…the area between Galway and Tralee. These Atlantic shores are where my heart truly lies…where the mighty Atlantic kisses the wild rocky shores and the white-sand beaches dazzle the eye in the sun. Images of which will haunt my dreams and fill my days with a deep longing, until we return. So yes, we will be back. It has, as I speak, been all arranged and so, for three more glorious weeks, from 14th May to 4th June 2011, The Intrepid Trio will be hitting the roads of this enchanting land once again. And for each member of The Intrepid Trio, it cannot come around quick enough.

There is still so much that is my beloved Ireland, to discover. There is a never ending wealth of beauty and splendour and adventure, that Ireland still, has to offer. Adventures which are just made for we three fully paid-up members of this intrepid gang.

So, Ireland beware. We will be back before you have even had chance to recover from the last time.

Misty is now three years old…or at least, he will be on Friday (which is tomorrow, for heavens sake) 8th October, which, as you will see, is exactly a year on from the time of the narrative. (How I shall always remember his last birthday, spent on Bertra Strand). How quickly that year has gone and what a joy it has been, writing this second book and hoping that, like the first, it will open up a new and wonderful world for you, as you follow in the footsteps, once again, of the Hall family…Jeff, Veronica and last but, my no means least, Misty. The real star of the writings of Veronica Hall.

May I thank everyone. All of you who bought and read my first book…My Love Affair with Ireland…and all who have given me such genuine encouragement. I hope that you will enjoy this, the sequel and derive pleasure and entertainment from our simple exploits. Go to Ireland! Live Ireland. Love Ireland. Breathe Ireland. You will never regret it. Follow the rainbow and, who knows. Even if you don't find the crock of gold, you will find a different treasure. You will find Ireland!

In parting, I just want to offer my own continuing love to the land that I have made mine own. God bless you, Ireland and God bless these warm and gentle people who are the beating heart of this wonderful country.

Until we meet again, I will leave you with this, my own favourite Irish Blessing….

MAY LOVE AND LAUGHTER LIGHT YOUR DAYS AND
WARM YOUR HEART AND HOME,
MAY GOOD AND FAITHFUL FRIENDS BE YOURS
WHEREVER YOU MAY ROAM,
MAY PEACE AND PLENTY BLESS YOUR WORLD
WITH JOY THAT LONG ENDURES,
MAY ALL LIFE'S PASSING SEASONS
BRING THE BEST TO YOU AND YOURS.

Veronica Hall
Thursday 7th October 2010

Part of UKUnpublished.co.uk

UKBookland gives you the opportunity to purchase all of the books published by UKUnpublished.

Do you want to find out a bit more about your favourite UKUnpublished Author?

Find other books they have written?

PLUS – UKBookland offers all the books at Excellent Discounts to the Recommended Retail Price!

You can find UKBookland at www.ukbookland.co.uk

Find out more about **Veronica Hall** and her books.

Are you an Author?

Do you want to see your book in print?

Please look at the UKUnpublished website:
www.ukunpublished.co.uk

Let the World Share Your Imagination

Lightning Source UK Ltd.
Milton Keynes UK
06 February 2011

167041UK00001B/24/P

9 781849 440905